Medieval Psychology

Recent Titles in
Contributions in Psychology

Personality, Power, and Authority: A View from the Behavioral Sciences
Leonard W. Doob

Interactive Counseling
B. Mark Schoenberg and Charles F. Preston, editors

Assessing Sex Bias in Testing: A Review of the Issues and Evaluations of 74
Psychological and Educational Tests
Paula Selkow

Position and the Nature of Personhood: An Approach to the Understanding
of Persons
Larry Cochran

Ecological Beliefs and Behaviors: Assessment and Change
David B. Gray in collaboration with Richard J. Borden and Russell H. Weigel

Sexuality: New Perspectives
Zira DeFries, Richard C. Friedman, and Ruth Corn, editors

Portrait and Story: Dramaturgical Approaches to the Study of Persons
Larry Cochran

The Meaning of Grief: A Dramaturgical Approach to Understanding Emotion
Larry Cochran and Emily Claspell

New Ideas in Therapy: Introduction to an Interdisciplinary Approach
Douglas H. Ruben and Dennis J. Delprato, editors

Human Consciousness and Its Evolution: A Multidimensional View
Richard W. Coan

From AI to Zeitgeist: A Philosophical Guide for the Skeptical Psychologist
N.H. Pronko

Inevitability: Determinism, Fatalism, and Destiny
Leonard W. Doob

The Psychology of Writing: The Affective Experience
Alice Glarden Brand

Medieval Psychology

Simon Kemp

Contributions in Psychology, Number 14

GREENWOOD PRESS

New York • Westport, Connecticut • London

Library of Congress Cataloging-in-Publication Data

Kemp, Simon.
   Medieval psychology / Simon Kemp.
      p. cm. — (Contributions in psychology, ISSN 0736–2714 ; no.
14)
   Includes bibliographical references.
   ISBN 0–313–26734–0 (lib. bdg. : alk. paper)
   1. Psychology—Europe—History. I. Title. II. Series.
BF93.K46   1990
150′.9′0902—dc20   89–29782

British Library Cataloguing in Publication Data is available.

Library of Congress Catalog Card Number: 89–29782
ISBN: 0–313–26734–0
ISSN: 0736–2714

First published in 1990

Greenwood Press, Inc.
88 Post Road West, Westport, Connecticut 06881

Printed in the United States of America

The paper used in this book complies with the
Permanent Paper Standard issued by the National
Information Standards Organization (Z39.48-1984).

10 9 8 7 6 5 4 3 2 1

Copyright Acknowledgments

The author and publisher gratefully acknowledge the following sources for granting
permission to reprint:

The Oxford University Press for excerpts from *De Anima*, by Aristotle, translated by J. A.
Smith, in W. D. Ross, ed., *The Works of Aristotle*. (Clarendon: Oxford, U. K., 1931).

Macmillan Publishing Company for excerpts from *The Opus Majus* by Roger Bacon,
translated by Robert B. Burke. (Russell and Russell: N. Y., 1962).

Contents

Illustrations

Preface

A book that attempts to depict the state of medieval psychology should ideally be written by someone who commands the skills and knowledge of a psychologist, a philosopher, an historian, a classicist, and a theologian. I am not that person. My background is in academic psychology, and I make no claim to anything remotely approaching the skills of, say, the professional historian or philosopher. I wish I had their abilities and apologize for the liberties I have taken with their subjects. I comfort myself a little by reflecting, first, that the ideal writer of this book probably does not exist and, second, that the approach of a present-day psychologist may perhaps have its own strengths as well as limitations.

I am grateful to a number of people, particularly Garth Fletcher, Oyvind Norderval, Evan Rogerson, and Colleen Ward for stimulating discussions on aspects of medieval psychology. I am particularly thankful to Martine Eller, Ken Strongman, and Leonard Zusne, each of whom read at least one draft of the entire book and provided me with numerous helpful suggestions for its improvement. I am also grateful to Martine and Ken for their encouragement and interest throughout the entire project. My thanks are due to Robin Phillips for preparing the figures and to Lynley Clarke, Lynette Stewart, and Vivienne Silcock for their expert typing.

Finally, I should like to thank my wife, Cora, and daughter, Alice, for their continuing support and enthusiasm for the project.

Medieval Psychology

1

Historical Background

The Middle Ages are generally reckoned to run from the fourth or fifth century A.D. to somewhere near the end of the fifteenth century. Two frequently used events to mark their commencement are the adoption of Christianity as the state religion of the Roman Empire by Constantine at the beginning of the fourth century and the end of the Roman Empire in the west with the deposition of Romulus Augustulus in 476. Similarly the end may be marked by the fall of Constantinople and the end of the Byzantine Empire in 1453 or the discovery of America in 1492.[1]

The fact that the Middle Ages lasted for a thousand years suggests that great changes, in the intellectual as well as the political sphere, might have occurred during the period, and what might be true of psychological thinking in the fifth century might not hold in the fifteenth. In fact, medieval thinking about psychological issues did show considerable change and development in the period, and later chapters investigate those changes. As, however, many of these changes relate to historical change, generally, and, in particular, to other intellectual changes, it is worthwhile to consider briefly the social and political nature of the Middle Ages and the intellectual life of the period.

SOCIETY AND POLITICS OF MEDIEVAL EUROPE

The end of the Roman Empire in Western Europe signaled the begin-

ning of the Dark Ages. This period was marked by invasion and reset-
tlement of the provinces of the empire from without: for example, France
and western Germany were invaded by the Franks; Spain by the Goths
and, later, the Saracens; and England by the Saxons. Italy suffered a
long struggle for control between the Ostrogoths and the Byzantine
Empire. Although Charlemagne, at the end of the eighth century, managed to unite a large part of the old empire and be crowned emperor
by the pope, this unification proved transitory, as did the brief cultural
"renaissance" that appears to have accompanied it. The ninth and tenth
centuries, indeed, saw more invasions, of Western Europe by the Vi-
kings and of Central Europe by the Magyars.

By the end of the tenth century, society in Western and Central Europe
was generally feudal and rural, characterized by a subsistence economy
and containing few towns or cities of any consequence. In most areas,
society was divided into three classes: the knights, who fought; the
clergy, who prayed; and the peasants, much the largest class, who
worked. The feudal society persisted to the end of the Middle Ages—
indeed, in some places, well into the modern era. From the end of the
tenth century, however, there was a slow increase in trade, a slow return
to a cash economy, and an increase in the number of urban inhabitants—
members of the bourgeoisie or the urban proletariat. In the eleventh
century, also, there was expansion of a political kind. The first crusade,
promulgated by Pope Urban II in 1095, succeeded in occupying most of
Palestine and captured Jerusalem in 1099. The reconquest of Spain from
the Moors began in the eleventh century, although it was not completed
until 1492.

The political and economic recovery of Latin Christendom after the
eleventh century did not undo the process of fragmentation that marked
the end of the Roman Empire in the west. Instead, nation states such
as France, England, and Aragon began to emerge, along with lesser or
more ephemeral political units such as the duchy of Burgundy or the
kingdom of Jerusalem. Probably the major unifying force in this period
was the Papacy, which often wielded international secular as well as
religious authority. That it was able to do so was a consequence of the
near universal Christianity of the Europeans of the time.

MEDIEVAL LEARNING

Medieval learning, indeed medieval culture as a whole, was dominated by two great influences: Christianity and the writings left by classic
authors. The central theme of medieval scholasticism, which had important implications for psychology, was the attempt to synthesize and
reconcile the teachings of Christianity—the Bible and the writings of the
Church Fathers—with the more secular knowledge that was believed

to be contained in the classic writings. The task, demanding enough in itself, was complicated by the fact that the classic writings, particularly those originally written in Greek, were often known only by reputation. One of the important intellectual activities of the Middle Ages was the gradual discovery and translation into Latin of many of the classic works.

The decline and fall of the Latin-speaking Roman Empire of the west brought with it the loss or inaccessibility of most classic learning. The works of the more important early Christian writers, Augustine, for example, and the Bible itself were preserved, particularly when these were originally written in Latin or had been early translated into it. Some of the works of secular classic authors were preserved intact, too, but much of this secular writing was preserved only in summarized form: Isidore of Seville (ca. 560–636 A.D.) *On Medicine,* for example, summarized classic medicine in under 5,000 words.[2] Generally, too, the preservation or summary was done by churchmen who gave priority to Christian writers rather than their pagan predecessors.

It is important also to realize that in the Dark Ages the existence of a manuscript in a monastery or the occasional translation of a Greek or Arabic work into Latin, was no guarantee that the work would be read or understood. There were no universities at this time, although there were some cathedral and monastic schools. Some indication of the general lack of literacy at even the highest levels of society is given by the fact that Charlemagne, who made a real effort to encourage learning and education in his empire, was himself effectively unable to read or write.

Although intellectual activity was at a low level before the eleventh century in Western Europe, it was pursued more vigorously in the Byzantine Empire in Eastern Europe and in the Islamic countries that bordered on medieval Christendom. Arabic scholars in particular not only preserved and read many of the classic texts but also produced genuine philosophical and scientific innovations. When the revival in learning came in Western Europe, it was influenced by Arabic scholarship as well as by the works of the earlier Greek and Roman thinkers. The philosophical writing of Averroes, the optical theory of Alhazen, and the medical writings of Avicenna were widely read along with Aristotle and Augustine in the Christian universities of the later Middle Ages.

The political and social revival that commenced in the eleventh century was accompanied by a revival in learning as well. The revival was remarked by contemporaries as well as present-day historians. Abbot Guibert of Nogent, writing in the early twelfth century, remarked that when he was young there were few teachers and those who did teach had less learning than the wandering scholars of his adult years.[3]

A cause, perhaps an effect as well, of this revival in learning was an increase in the tempo of translating works from Greek and Arabic into Latin. In the late eleventh century Constantinus Africanus (ca. 1015–

1087) translated a number of Greek and Arabic texts into Latin, as well as adding his own commentaries on many of them.[4] Translation of ancient and Arabic medical texts continued throughout the Middle Ages, and often the translation of an incomplete or corrupt text was succeeded by a more authentic version. Galen's text on the parts of the body (*De usu partium*), for example, originally written in the second century A.D., was partially translated from an Arabic abridgement in the late twelfth century, but a translation from the original Greek text was not completed until the early fourteenth century.[5]

A similar pattern characterizes the translation of writings in other areas. The most important medieval text on psychology, Aristotle's *De Anima* (*On the Soul*), seems to have been first translated directly from the Greek in about 1150. Aristotle's other psychological writings (mainly the *Parva Naturalia*) were probably translated at about the same time. The most important ancient astrological text, Claudius Ptolemy's *Tetrabiblos*, was translated into Latin in 1138 by Plato of Tivoli.

The fact that inaccurate translation or faulty copying might distort the original content was widely known in the Middle Ages, and the importance of accuracy was recognized. Awareness of the possibility of inaccuracy or of a corrupt text seems to have encouraged many medieval scholars to synthesize or to reconcile opposing theoretical viewpoints. Faced, say, with a disagreement between two earlier writers or an inconsistency between the statements of a single writer, medieval scholars often tended to ascribe the difference to an error in translation or transcription and not to a real difference of opinion.

The appearance of new translations of ancient or Arabic texts often had a relatively rapid impact. Marsilio Ficino's fifteenth-century translations of Plato, Plotinus, and various hermetic writings, for example, appear to have heavily influenced his own and subsequent thinking on astrology and astrological psychology.[6] The translation of Aristotle's works seems to have led to their widespread use. Aristotle's natural philosophy was condemned by the bishop of Paris in 1210, but was prescribed reading for courses in liberal arts at the University of Paris from at least 1252. This status as a prescribed text seems to have been retained at Paris and other universities throughout the Middle Ages.[7] Aristotle's *De Anima* had then a double impact on medieval thinking about psychology. First, it was a great influence on "original" medieval philosophy, and the psychological thinking of writers such as Thomas Aquinas was heavily based on it. Second, it had what might be termed a direct influence on generations of medieval students who read it. In considering what the educated medieval community thought about psychology, Aristotle's *De Anima* may itself have been more important than the new writing on psychological theory that took place in the Middle

Ages. Similar considerations apply to other ancient writers, for example, to the influence of Galen on medieval medicine.

Another feature of the revival in learning, necessary to disseminate as well as to inspire both new translations of ancient writings and original work, was the establishment and growth of the universities. The School of Salerno, where Constantinus Africanus was frequently based, was already a kind of university in the eleventh century, as was the Law School at Bologna. The University of Paris evolved, rather than was founded, during the twelfth century. At first it appears to have functioned as a meeting place for scholars, but gradually acquired official recognition, and promulgated rules and regulations. The first college at Paris was founded in 1180, for example, while in 1215 a cardinal legate named Robert laid down rules for the academic and social life of the university.[8] In the thirteenth century, the University of Paris attracted students from outside of France and there were, for example, lecturers who taught in Flemish and English. At the same time, however, universities were founded at a number of other centers. A university evolved at Oxford in the twelfth century, and others were founded in the thirteenth century at a number of French, Italian, English, Spanish, and Portuguese locations. In the fourteenth century, further universities were established in the Holy Roman Empire (present-day Germany, Austria, and Czechoslovakia) and Poland.

At the University of Paris, which served as a model for others in Northern Europe, students were usually churchmen in minor clerical orders. There were faculties of Arts (much the biggest), Canon Law, Medicine, and Theology. The Italian universities had a much greater proportion of lay students and seem to have placed relatively more importance on the more applied disciplines of Law (Civil and Canon) and Medicine.[9]

The discipline that we now call psychology was unknown as such during the Middle Ages, although the first use of the word (by Marko Marulic, 1450–1524) may have come late in the period.[10] Various aspects of the discipline, however, seem to have been studied in the different faculties. Study of the nature of the soul—primarily through readings of, or commentaries on, Aristotle's De Anima and the Parva Naturalia— was a required part of the Parisian Bachelor of Arts degree from at least 1255. Curiously, the uncertain or dual status of the discipline as an art or a science in present-day universities finds a medieval echo in the fact that De Anima was occasionally read with the books on nature and occasionally with the logic texts.[11] Abnormal and physiological psychology were studied as part of a medical course, as was astrology. Questions about the nature of man were also important to theologians: a part of Thomas Aquinas' Summa Theologiae, for example, is concerned

with them.[12] Finally, even medieval law was at least peripherally concerned with mental disorder, as, for example, a defense plea.

Although aspects of psychology were taught in different faculties, it
would be a mistake to assume that the different approaches were independent of each other. On the contrary, many writers seem to have
had a detailed knowledge of the different approaches, and, in particular,
those from a liberal arts or theological background often seem to have
had a good grasp of contemporary medical thinking. In fact, as will
become clear in subsequent chapters, medieval thinking about psychology, as about knowledge in general, attempted to synthesize the
different aspects and approaches.

A striking example of the general value of medieval education is given
by the career of Peter Juliani (ca. 1215–1277), who taught in the medical
faculty of the University of Siena, and wrote extensively on medical,
philosophical and even psychological topics. He was appointed personal
physician to Pope Gregory X and later became archbishop and cardinal.
Finally he was elected pope under the name John XXI in 1276.

One final aspect of medieval learning should be emphasized: it was
restricted to a rather narrow segment of society. Although literacy spread
in the later Middle Ages, particularly among the nobility and the
bourgeoisie, universities, particularly in northern and western Europe,
were attended primarily by the clergy. In consequence, many of the
most important medieval scholars of psychology were clergymen.

THE MEDIEVAL CHURCH

The Church was the most important and powerful institution of the
Middle Ages, and its influence covered almost every aspect of medieval
life. Not only did it have universally acknowledged religious authority
but it was also capable of exerting enormous secular power. It is worth
remembering in this context that the most successful of all medieval
military expeditions, the first crusade, was proclaimed and launched by
Pope Urban II and partly led by his legate. Thus in comparison with its
Roman Catholic successor of today, the medieval Church possessed both
more power and more secular and administrative responsibility.

It is perhaps difficult for a twentieth-century observer, whose examples of powerful institutions are almost completely secular, to evaluate
accurately the Church's role and influence when it was a powerful institution. Certainly, the Church's attitude to the revival of learning and
the development of new ideas in the Middle Ages is widely misper-
ceived. The popular view today is that the Church had a stifling influence
on the acquisition of knowledge and, in particular, on the development
of science. For example, Edwin Boring, probably the most influential
historian of psychology, wrote,

In the thirteenth century Western science began to reappear; nevertheless the medieval milieu (ca. 1200–1500) was not favorable to scientific progress. In these centuries the revival of learning was centered almost entirely in theology, and the resultant frame of mind was unfavorable to science.[13]

Gregory Zilboorg, writing of the medical psychology of the twelfth century, stated, "The medical man dared not look independently [i.e., of the Church] into normal or abnormal psychology. Those suffering from psychological difficulties were treated as heretics, but the few who were fortunate enough to be considered 'naturally' ill were for centuries treated with exorcisms."[14]

This popular view of the Church is not altogether a myth. The near-universal belief in Christian doctrine certainly affected people's views on other subjects. Moreover the Church was always concerned to ensure that religious views were kept within what were perceived as reasonable bounds. Even in the first centuries of its existence, the Church was involved with combating heresy—religious views that resembled but differed from orthodox beliefs—and writers such as Athanasius and Augustine devoted much time to combating beliefs they saw as heretical and in the process defining or redefining orthodoxy. In the Dark Ages, heresy seems to have been a rather unimportant issue; perhaps the times did not permit such intellectual luxuries as arguing over the merits of rather similar dogmas. With the revival of learning, however, came a renewal of the opportunity for heresy. The Catharan heresy became particularly strong in the south of France at the end of the twelfth century; Pope Innocent III reacted by launching the Albigensian Crusade that restored orthodoxy to the accompaniment of massacre and general brutality.

The Office of the Inquisition was established in 1233 by Pope Gregory IX. Originally it was set up in southern France to repress the remaining Cathars, but it quickly spread to most of the rest of Latin Christendom. Friars, either Dominican or Franciscan, served as inquisitors and were charged with the chief responsibility for detecting heresy and punishing it. The chief feature of the Inquisition was that the process did not require prosecution by an accuser in a normal court procedure. In addition, the proceedings were normally conducted secretly and often used torture to extract confessions. Punishments ranged from enforced pilgrimage to death at the stake, which was reserved for relapsed heretics. Toward the end of the Middle Ages, the Inquisition was also used to investigate witchcraft.[15]

It is clear that in the Inquisition the Church possessed a potentially powerful instrument for suppressing scientific enquiry. Its use for this purpose, however, seems to have been infrequent. For example, despite the Church's opposition to astrology, particularly in its more deterministic form, only one astrologer, Cecco d'Ascoli in 1327, seems to have been condemned to death for his views, although in fact astrology was quite widely practiced throughout the late Middle Ages.[16] In general, the Church seems to have used rather milder means to deal with intellectual doctrines that were regarded unfavorably. For example, the penalty of excommunication (which seems to have been rather ineffective) and orders that books be expurgated were occasionally used by the authorities at Paris to prevent unorthodoxy.[17]

It should be remembered that in the Middle Ages orthodoxy was less well defined by the Church than it became after the Reformation. In fact, disagreement on not only secular but also theological issues was quite common between leading scholastic clergymen, and intellectual debate rather than repression was used to attempt to resolve the issues.

Furthermore, if the Church occasionally acted repressively to prevent the spread of certain ideas, in other ways it did much to encourage them. Nor was the church exclusively interested in the teaching of theology. Augustine provided an excellent authority for the notion that Christians should be generally knowledgeable; he maintained that it was disgraceful for Christians to talk nonsense about secular matters to educated infidels, as "if they find a Christian mistaken in a field they themselves know well . . . how are they going to believe [Christian writings] in matters concerning the resurrection of the dead?"[18] The university system itself was largely staffed by clergymen and, particularly in France and England, can be thought of as a part of the wider institution of the Church. The universities were extensively used by the Church, in part to obtain literate priests and monks who were capable of understanding and promulgating Christian doctrine and in part also to define the doctrine itself. The University of Paris, in particular, attained a special status toward the end of the Middle Ages as the leading arbiter of theological questions.

The complexity of the relationship between the medieval Church and intellectuals can be illustrated by briefly considering three of the monastic orders founded in the Middle Ages.

The eleventh-century revival in politics and learning had its counterpart in the Church where the period saw both an increase in piety and a number of institutional reforms, initiated in particular by Pope Gregory VII (r. 1073–1085). There also seems to have been renewed interest in the monastic life. In the early twelfth century, Stephen Harding (d. 1134) provided a new constitution for what was later known as the Cistercian Order. The new order, which stressed the value of contemplation and austerity, spread rapidly throughout Europe. Although not primarily a scholastic order, many of its members, especially St. Bernard of Clairvaux (1090–1153), wrote extensively; moreover, the order initiated many technological improvements, particularly in agriculture.

The medieval order with the most strongly intellectual tradition was that of the Dominican friars, founded by St. Dominic (ca. 1170–1221), partly in response to the Catharan heresy. St. Dominic believed the heresy could only be countered by friars who displayed poverty and austerity and actively preached the orthodox faith to the heretics. There was a very strong emphasis on learning, particularly theology, and the two principal houses of the order were located near the universities of Paris and Bologna. Albertus Magnus (1193–1280) and his one-time disciple Thomas Aquinas (ca. 1225–1274) were prominent Dominicans who were also interested in psychological questions.

The Franciscan friars, named after St. Francis of Assisi (ca. 1181–1226), also emphasized poverty and austerity and were strongly evangelical. They, too, quickly developed an intellectual tradition, particularly in England. Franciscans who considered psychological issues included Roger Bacon (1214–1292), Bonaventure (ca. 1217–1274), Duns Scotus (1260–1308), and William of Ockham (ca. 1285–1349).

The Dominicans and Franciscans, then, were in the forefront of the new interest in learning and, while they were greatly and often primarily interested in theological questions, they were also interested in psychological and other issues and inquired freely into them. Thus these two religious orders were both primarily responsible for staffing the Inquisition and for the advancement of medieval learning. Such a state of affairs may seem paradoxical but it is simply explained: who but a trained intellectual could determine whether a given belief might or might not be heretical?

Overall, the attitude of the medieval Church toward learning and the spread of new ideas tended to be liberal, and there is little evidence of repression of scientific thinking. Indeed, many of the leading theologians, such as Thomas Aquinas, whose thought is considered in more detail in subsequent chapters, seem to have maintained an open-minded approach to scientific issues, for which they suffered little, if at all, from higher ecclesiastical authorities.

NOTES

1. For general reading on the Middle Ages see Charles H. Haskins, *The Twelfth Century Renaissance* (Cambridge, Mass.: Harvard University Press, 1927); Maurice Keen, *The Pelican History of Medieval Europe* (Harmondsworth, UK: Penguin, 1971); and C. W. Previte-Orton, *The Shorter Cambridge Medieval History* (Cambridge, UK: Cambridge University Press, 1952).

2. W. D. Sharpe, "Isidore of Seville: The Medical Writings." *Transactions of the American Philosophical Society* 54 (1964): 3–75.

3. See Lynn Thorndike, *A History of Magic and Experimental Science during the First Thirteen Centuries of Our Era*, Vol. 1 (London: Macmillan, 1923), 742–759;

and M. Bassan, "Chaucer's Cursed Monk, Constantinus Africanus." *Medieval Studies* 24 (1962): 127–140.

4. Guibert of Nogent, *Self and Society in Medieval France: The Memoirs of Abbot Guibert of Nogent*, ed. John F. Benton (New York: Harper & Row, 1970), 45.

5. Galen, *On the Usefulness of the Parts of the Body*, trans. Margaret T. May. (Ithaca, N.Y.: Cornell University Press, 1968), 6.

6. Paul O. Kristeller, *The Philosophy of Marsilio Ficino*, trans. V. Conant (Gloucester, Mass.: Peter Smith, 1964); and Thomas Moore, *The Planets Within— Marsilio Ficino's Astrological Psychology* (London and Toronto: Associated University Presses, 1982).

7. Lynn Thorndike, *University Records and Life in the Middle Ages* (New York: Columbia University Press, 1944), 26, 52, 64ff.

8. Ibid., 21, 27–30.

9. Previte-Orton, *The Shorter Cambridge Medieval History*, 621–627.

10. Francois H. Lapointe, "Who Originated the Term 'Psychology'?" *Journal of the History of the Behavioral Sciences* 8 (1972): 328–335.

11. Thorndike, *University Records*, 65.

12. Thomas Aquinas, *Summa Theologiae* (London: Blackfriars, 1964). Note that this work is also known by the name *Summa Theologica*.

13. Edwin G. Boring, *A History of Experimental Psychology*. (New York: Appleton, Century, Crofts, 1929), 18.

14. Gregory Zilboorg, *A History of Medical Psychology*. (New York: Norton, 1941), 130.

15. See Norman Cohn, *Europe's Inner Demons* (London: Chatto/Heinemann, 1975).

16. Theodore Wedel, *The Medieval Attitude toward Astrology, Particularly in England* (Hamden, Conn.: Archon, 1968).

17. Thorndike, *University Records*, 26, 39–40, 48–50.

18. Augustine, *The Literal Meaning of Genesis*, trans. John H. Taylor (New York: Newman, 1982), 1.19.39.

2

The Medieval Soul

This chapter considers medieval accounts of soul, the usual English translation of the Latin word *Anima*. To the twentieth-century reader, the word *soul* has religious rather than psychological significance, but in ancient and medieval writing the word *Anima* denoted the principle, substance, or entity that animated the body of living things.

Soul was possessed not only by humans but also by the most primitive of plants, although the soul of the latter was capable of only basic functions such as nutrition, growth, and propagation. Thus an ancient or medieval discussion of the soul of man treated what a present-day reader would consider as psychological and even biological questions as well as religious and philosophical ones. As a rule, psychological issues predominated, and it is with them, rather than the philosophical or religious issues, that we shall be concerned. The remainder of this chapter covers important general features of soul as perceived by different writers.

Of the various accounts of the soul discussed by ancient writers, two were particularly influential in the Middle Ages. These were the accounts given by Aristotle (ca. 384–322 B.C.) and that given by Plato, (ca. 427–347 B.C.) as modified by Neoplatonic Christian writers. Even though Aristotle's account succeeded that of Plato and was, moreover, virtually unknown in the early Middle Ages, it is considered here first. This is because the early Christian accounts, although basically Platonic, incorporated some of Aristotle's thinking and, in particular, his system of approach to the soul.

ARISTOTLE'S PSYCHOLOGY

Aristotle's psychological thinking is contained principally in his work *De Anima* (*On the Soul*), although some specific aspects of psychology, relating to sensation (*De Sensu et Sensibili*), memory (*De Memoria et Reminiscentia*), and sleeping and dreaming (*De Sommo, De Somniis*) are contained in the *Parva Naturalia*. These works and particularly *De Anima* were very widely read and commented on in the later Middle Ages. Even before the translation of the works in the twelfth century, however, some of Aristotle's approach had been incorporated into early Christian thinking. This incorporation occurred because early Christian writers such as Augustine and Nemesius were influenced by the Neoplatonists, one of whose aims was the reconciliation of the views of Plato and Aristotle.[1]

Aristotle's *De Anima* is divided into three books. Broadly, the first book considers various previous accounts of the soul, while the second and third books outline Aristotle's account. In the first book, Aristotle rejects a number of definitions of soul: for example, that it is that which originates movement (sensation is a counterexample here) or that it is whatever knows or perceives, as Plato defined it.[2] Nor can it simply be defined as a form of harmony. Aristotle maintains that the soul is not composed of elements and does not possess a spatial magnitude.

The fact "that plants and certain insects go on living when divided into segments . . . means that each of the segments has a soul in it identical in species." Thus "in each of the bodily parts there are present all parts of soul [and] the several parts of the soul are indisseverable from one another, although the whole soul is divisible."[3] Hence, although the soul has distinct powers, for example, those of sensing and initiating movement, these powers are not located in separate places.

Much of the first book is concerned with the analysis of movement and in what sense the soul can be regarded as moving or being moved. A consequence of this discussion is the rejection of the idea of the soul as a sort of homunculus that inhabits the body. Thus, for example, "to say that it is the soul which is angry is as inexact as it would be to say that it is the soul that weaves webs or builds houses."[4] Movement, Aristotle went on to say, is sometimes initiated by the soul (as in reminiscence) and sometimes ends in the soul (as occurs in sensation).

The mind, by which Aristotle and other ancient writers meant rational or intellectual capability, "seems to be an independent substance implanted within the soul and to be incapable of being destroyed." That the mental processes of, for example, the elderly sometimes seem to be impaired is due to deterioration not

of the soul but of its vehicle. . . . Thus it is that in old age the activity of mind or intellectual apprehension declines only through the decay of some other inward part; mind itself is impassible. Thinking, loving, and hating are affections not of mind, but of that which has mind. . . . That is why, when this vehicle decays, memory and love cease; they were activities not of mind but of the composite which has perished.[5]

In the second book, Aristotle finally presented his formal definition of the soul "as the first grade of actuality of a natural organised body."[6] This means that the soul is defined in terms of the function or potential function of the body. Aristotle gave a clear analogy that illustrates the definition:

Suppose that the eye were an animal—sight would have been its soul, for sight is the substance or essence of the eye, . . . the eye being merely the matter of seeing [i.e., the bodily organ responsible for sight]; when seeing is removed the eye is no longer an eye, except in name. . . . As the pupil plus the power of sight constitutes the eye, so the soul plus the body constitutes the animal.[7]

The "*first* grade of actuality" indicates that even when a particular faculty of the soul is not being used, it still exists potentially. For example, the power of sight is not lost if one closes one's eyes, although the *second* grade of actuality, that of actually seeing, is not present.

The powers of the soul, in ascending order, are those of nutrition, appetite, sensation, locomotion, and thought. Plants possess only the power of nutrition (which is believed inseparable from that of reproduction), while animals necessarily possess appetite and frequently sensation and locomotion as well. Finally, only man possesses the power of thought. Aristotle goes on to consider the different powers of the soul individually. Nutrition, which is of little psychological interest, is discussed briefly, then sensation is considered both generally and sense by sense.

Accounts of sensation, including that of Aristotle, are discussed in more detail in the next chapter. In brief outline, for Aristotle, sensation requires an outside stimulus or some property of the stimulus to act on the perceiver. Each sense has a special object, for example color is the special object of sight and sound the special object of hearing, for which no error is possible. In addition, however, there are "common sensibles," such as movement, rest, number, figure, and magnitude, which are not restricted to one sense but common to two or more senses. These common sensibles are "perceived directly."[8] A common sense is also necessary to discriminate between qualities of, for example, whiteness and sweetness, which are perceived through different senses.[9]

Thinking is distinguished from perception and "held to be in part imagination, in part judgment."[10] Imagination, that is the ability to form mental images, is distinct from sensation although "imaginations remain in the organs of sense and resemble sensations."[11] The power of imagination is found in animals as well as man. Mind, "that whereby the soul thinks and judges,"[12] is restricted to man and is conceived as an active process operating on images; thus "the soul never thinks without an image."[13] Aristotle's general description of mind is, however, both condensed and difficult, and later Arabic and European commentators interpreted his description is rather different ways. The most important issue for these commentators, which is considered in more detail in Chapter 4, concerned the question of how the mind comes to know anything. In most of *De Anima*, Aristotle appears to adopt the empirical position that knowledge is obtained by abstraction from what is perceived. In places, however, he apparently tends toward Plato's view that knowledge is of forms and ideals that are innately present in the mind. The following passage illustrates the latter tendency:

Actual knowledge is identical with its object: in the individual, potential knowledge is in time prior to actual knowledge, but in the universe as a whole it is not prior even in time, mind is not at one time knowing and another not. When mind is set free from its present conditions it appears as just what it is and nothing more: this alone is immortal and eternal, . . . and without it nothing thinks.[14]

The processes of sensation and thought are seen as complementary, the former operating on physical objects in the external world and the latter on forms or objects capable of being thought. Both processes require the soul to reproduce the forms of things—the mind becomes "the form of forms and sense the form of sensible things."[15] The similarity of the two processes enhances the role of the image in thought and also underlines Aristotle's basically empirical approach to knowledge—"no one can learn or understand anything in the absence of sense."[16]

The faculty of appetite, which includes both desire or motivation and emotion, is responsible for originating motion, both in animals and man. The faculty of appetite itself is set in motion, although, as Aristotle is careful to point out, it is a different kind of motion, by the imagination or the mind. Thus a human or animal desire might arise from seeing or remembering an external object. For an animal the combination of imagination and appetite invariably results in movement, but for human beings, who also possess mental powers of calculation or deliberative imagination, conflicting desires may be set up. This happens because humans have the ability to wish, an appetite that is itself a part of the mind. Ideally in man wish should prevail over the animal appetite but where there is moral weakness this does not always happen.[17]

In his discussion of appetite, as throughout his account of the soul, Aristotle is concerned with how the powers of the soul interact with each other in order to produce the resulting behavior. Movement is originated by appetite but this in turn requires imagination and hence past or present perception to be aroused. The human power of thought is dependent on images for its functioning, but in turn can originate movement by wishing. An important feature of Aristotle's account is that the soul is always seen as a single entity in which the various powers are integrated, not as a collection of different faculties.

THE NEOPLATONIC SOUL

The Neoplatonic account of the soul derives from the works of Plato and, in particular, from *Timaeus*. Basically the view presented in *Timaeus*, which is central to the Neoplatonic account, is that the body exists to serve the soul: "God created the soul before the body and gave it precedence both in time and value, and made it the dominating and controlling partner."[18] Souls are created from the same substance as the stars—there is a very pronounced astrological element in *Timaeus*—and then incarnated:

After this necessary incarnation . . . anyone who lived well for his appointed time would return home to his native star and live an appropriately happy life; but anyone who failed to do so would be changed into a woman at his second birth. And if he still did not refrain from wrong, he would be changed into some animal.[19]

The parts of the body and their uses are briefly described as are the operations of the senses. The human soul is held to comprise an immortal rational element, located in the head, and two mortal elements, located in the trunk:

The part of the soul which is the seat of courage, passion, and ambition [is] located nearer the head between midriff and neck; there it would be well-placed to listen to the commands of reason and combine with it in forcibly restraining the appetites. These are located lower still in the body, secured . . . there like a wild beast.[20]

This tripartite form of the human soul is not found in all living things: plants, for example, have appetites but are entirely passive and incapable of self-awareness.[21]

Although Plato's account stresses the primacy of the soul, the soul is by no means independent of the body. The soul is dependent on the body for sensing the outside world; diseases of the soul can be brought on by bodily pain or infirmity; and the mind (i.e., the rational part of the soul) and the body should be in correct proportion. Hence the soul should ensure that the body is maintained in good order.

At least the first part of the *Timaeus* was itself available in Latin translation throughout the Middle Ages,[22] but, in the main, Plato's influence on the Middle Ages was exerted in a much more indirect way. This influence was mediated in the first place by Neoplatonist thinkers, in particular by Plotinus (205–270 A.D.) whose *Enneads* provide a systematic account of Neoplatonist philosophy. Plotinus' philosophy is mystical in orientation and a recurrent theme is that we should strive to attain the perfect life that transcends material considerations such as the body and is concerned only with the intelligible world of ideas. The soul should "ascend to intellect and there will know the Forms, all beautiful, and will affirm that these, the Ideas, are beauty. But these are as a screen before God."[23] In addition to mysticism, however, Plotinus also discusses a number of psychological questions, the nature of visual perception, for example, and how memory might work.[24] On memory, he remarks that men "think about perception and memory as they do about letters written on tablets or pages," but this is an incorrect view because with mental exercise we can improve our ability to assimilate new knowledge. If the tablet theory were correct, exercise should make our memory less rather than more effective.[25]

Plotinus' works were themselves almost unknown in the Middle Ages—the first complete translation of his works into Latin was made by Marsilio Ficino at the end of the fifteenth century—but during the early centuries of Christianity Neoplatonic ideas were widespread and profoundly influenced the early Christian writers, and it was their thought rather than that of Plato or Plotinus that was primarily important in the Middle Ages. Two such writers were Augustine of Hippo (354–430 A.D.) and Nemesius of Emesa (ca. 400 A.D.). In the works of both Augustine and Nemesius, a clear Platonic influence is apparent, particularly in the way the soul is regarded as inhabiting the body. On the other hand, Plato's belief in astrology and reincarnation has been replaced by Christian theology, and there is also considerable influence from other pagan writers. For example, Nemesius refers frequently to Galen, although his writings in turn, especially his work *De Placitis Hippocratis et Platonis* (*On the Doctrines of Hippocrates and Plato*), reveal a considerable debt to Plato.[26] Also evident in Nemesius' account is an Aristotelian influence, particularly in the way the account is set out.

Augustine's voluminous writings were mainly devoted to theological rather than psychological issues, and, in consequence, his thinking on psychology is often contained in a religious context or even used as a metaphor to illuminate a religious problem, as it is in his work *De Trinitate* (*On the Trinity*). Not only do his psychological writings appear as parts of different works but also they were written at different times, giving occasionally the impression of changes of opinion, if not inconsistency.

Possibly Augustine's most complete account of the soul is contained in *De Quantitate Animae* (*The Greatness of the Soul*). The work virtually assumes a Platonic model of the soul at the outset: the questions to be answered include "Why was [the soul] united with the body? What results from its union with the body?"[27] It is then established that the soul is created by God, lacks bodily dimensions or, indeed, fixed location, and is defined as "a special substance, endowed with reason, adapted to rule the body."[28] The operations of vision are described in some detail as an example of sensation, and a distinction drawn between sensation, shared by both animals and man, and knowledge, which arises from reason and is possessed by man alone. The soul is indivisible—the argument is actually constructed from the fact, also reported by Aristotle,[29] that segments of a vivisected worm can each behave as apparently entire worms—but is conceived as having seven levels. The first level, that of vitalization, which is common to all living things, is the organism's ability to nourish, grow, and reproduce itself. The second level (sensation) is common to animals and man, and the third level (art) is common to all men. The remaining four levels, virtue, tranquility, initiation, and contemplation, appear to represent ideals for human behavior rather than characteristics of human psychology. The most interesting feature of the levels of the soul is their number, which, like the divisions of soul in *Timaeus*, equals the number of planets known to the ancient and medieval world.[30]

In his later work *On the Trinity*, Augustine reiterates his view that the soul is an incorporated substance lacking bodily dimensions. There is also, however, greater investigation of the mind, that is, the rational part of the soul, and the identification of its powers of understanding, memory, and will.[31] Augustine goes on to consider how the act of sensation leads to the formation of an image in the mind, a question examined in more detail in the next chapter.

For Augustine, as for Plato, sensation is not the source of all knowledge because certain forms or ideals are innately present in memory, and the role of sensation is rather to "remind" one of what is already known. For Augustine, and indeed for many later theologians, the epitome of such innate knowledge was that of God himself, but more secular knowledge, for example, that concerning numbers and the laws of mathematics, was also present in this way.[32]

A more coherent account of the soul, in a single work, is presented by Nemesius' *A Treatise on the Nature of Man*.[33] Nemesius carefully considers all the ancient accounts of the nature of the soul, and rejects the view that the soul is itself a body. Nor is it harmony, temperament or any other quality. Rather it is incorporeal being that is immortal, but usually united with the body.[34] That this union is somewhat tenuous is reflected in Nemesius' account of sleep, during which the soul actually separates from the body, retaining just sufficient connection to maintain vital functions such as breathing so that the body does not die. Although the physical state of the body resembles death, the soul is actively involved in dreaming, and even in foretelling the future.[35]

Nemesius considers the soul to consist of a rational and irrational part. The faculties of the rational soul are imagination, intellect, and memory.[36] Each of these faculties is associated with a cell of the brain: imagination with the front, intellect with the middle, and memory with the rear cell of the brain. The nerves of the sense organs are held to connect to the foremost cell: hence, sensation and perception are closely related to imagination. Although the account given has clearly a strong basis in physiology—particularly the physiology of Galen—it is important to note that the soul uses the organs of the body. For example, the faculty of sense perception is held to belong to the soul while parts of the body serve as its instruments.[37] The theory of perception advocated by both Nemesius and Augustine is in fact an active one in which the soul directs the activities of the sense organs.

The irrational part of the soul is itself partly subject to rational control and partly not.[38] Subject to reason are concupiscence and anger. Concupiscence, which includes desire, pleasures, grief, and fear, involves reaction to something perceived or imagined, and is essentially passive. Anger, on the other hand, involves a more energetic and active response. In contrast, other faculties, for example the operation of the digestive process, are not under the control of reason.

In the last part of the book, Nemesius discusses the will. Like most other Christian writers Nemesius was concerned to retain an important place for free will in his psychology and to deny deterministic accounts of behavior, for example, that given by astrology.[39] Thus the faculties of the soul are subject to the will, which is responsible for the production of movement of different kinds. The physical locus of the origin of willed movement, according to Nemesius, is in the brain and the spinal column. Nerves carry the impulses to move to the ligaments and muscles.[40]

THE MEDIEVAL DEBATE

With the revival of learning and the establishment of universities from the twelfth century onward came a renewed intellectual interest in the nature of the soul. Probably the dominant intellectual influence at first was that of Augustine, but the discovery of the works of Aristotle and the Arabic commentators on him, in particular Avicenna (980–1037) and

Averroes (1126–1198) introduced a new perspective on the soul that conflicted in a number of ways with the accounts given by Augustine and Nemesius. The consequence was a large number of works on the soul written by medieval writers, usually churchmen, a principal object of which was either to defend one or another view or to reconcile them. Such writers include, to mention only some of the more important, Alexander of Hales (ca. 1180–1245), William of Auvergne (ca. 1190–1249), Roger Bacon, Bonaventure, Albertus Magnus, Thomas Aquinas, Duns Scotus, and even one pope, John XXI. Frequently their works were also titled *De Anima* or written as commentaries on Aristotle's *De Anima*.

Naturally the debate concentrated on the apparent and real differences between the two viewpoints, but it is important to realize that there were also similarities that were not subject to great debate, and, in consequence, formed a common basis for medieval psychology. In the first place, soul was discussed as a psychological or biological concept, rather than a religious one, although the religious implications of the discussion were never forgotten and often occupied chief place. Second, it was commonly believed that there were different kinds of soul. Plants were clearly different from animals, which in turn were distinguished from human beings by their lack of a rational soul or mind. This unquestioned assumption had definite consequences for the medieval account of cognition, which is considered in Chapter 4. It is also, of course, an assumption that is not generally held by present-day psychology. Third, there was agreement that the soul possessed different powers or faculties and reasonable agreement as to what those powers were. Fourth, the soul was held to be incorporeal. Although it combined with the body, it was itself immaterial and did not consist of any of the four material elements or a combination of them, or of some fifth element or *quintessence*.[41] Finally, at least some part of the human soul was immortal.

In addition to this common ground as to what the soul was, there was also in practice a common method of inquiry into its nature. The inquiry proceeded using reasoned deduction from commonly observed or believed facts. Such a procedure was broadly similar to that used by the ancient and early Christian writers. Much of the medieval writing, however, followed the highly structured scholastic method in which propositions were debated singly, arguments for and against the proposition presented, and finally a conclusion reached and objections countered.

Usually the reasoning process included references to previous writers. It would be a mistake to assume that such appeals to authority were accepted uncritically; indeed as a rule a reference would be produced, if possible, for both the proposition and its antithesis. On the other hand, references to empirical observations or questions of observable fact rather than theoretical issues seem to have been rarely challenged.

Indeed a key difference between the approach of a present-day psychologist and that of the medieval schoolman was that the latter did not perform experiments or other research to test the validity of reported facts. Numerous examples can be found of the reliance of medieval scholars on unfounded facts. One of the best-known of these concerns the *rete mirabile*, a system of interwoven blood vessels found in the brain of many animals.[42] The existence of the rete system was first reported by Galen, who believed that it was responsible for the refinement of vital spirits used in perceptual and cognitive processes in animals and man.[43] It was not, however, until 1543 that Andreas Vesalius revealed that, while the rete system exists in many mammals, it does not exist in man. This fact, had it been known in the Middle Ages, would have necessitated revision of much of the accepted physiology of the human brain.

If the medieval approach to psychology differed from the modern one in its failure to use the experimental method and attempt systematic replication of reported observation, it resembled it in its general scepticism as to the value of introspection. Augustine acknowledged the limits of introspection when in his discussion of memory in the *Confessions*, he stated, "I do not myself grasp all that I am."[44] A more profound scepticism was voiced by Aquinas, who held that our knowledge of our "habitual dispositions" arises from our observation of our own acts rather than by direct knowledge.[45] Furthermore, while we are conscious of images produced when we are thinking or of the fact that we are thinking, we are not conscious of the thoughts themselves.[46]

Although there were unifying ideas in medieval psychology, there were also important differences between the Augustinian and Neoplatonic account of the soul and the Aristotelian one. Perhaps the most striking difference is in the basic definition of the soul. In Aristotle's account the soul is the "completion" of the body, while in the Neoplatonic account the soul inhabits and makes use of the body. This rather philosophical distinction has important psychological implications. Aristotle's view is most compatible with a passive, intromissionist account of sensation while the Neoplatonic view blends naturally with an active, extramission theory. This subject is considered in more detail in the next chapter.

Also different are the rival accounts of sleep. According to Nemesius, as we have seen, sleep is the temporary desertion of the body by the soul. During sleep the soul is actively thinking and dreaming, and even engaged in prophecy. The idea that at least some dreams had especial visionary or prophetic significance was common in the Middle Ages, and much effort was expended on dream interpretation. The belief even gave rise to a particular literary form, that of dream poetry.[47] The Aristotelian approach to sleep and dreaming was quite different. Although he did not definitely exclude the possibility of prophetic or clairvoyant dreams, Aristotle was quite clear that most incidents claimed to be prophetic were actually coincidences.[48] His basic view of sleep was that it is primarily a paralysis of the organs of sense perception, caused by heat produced in the digestive process rising to the brain.[49] Dreams then arise from residual movements of the blood in the sensory organs.[50]

The aspect of soul most frequently debated by medieval philosophers seems to have been: How does the soul acquire knowledge? The motivation for this debate was largely theological: How do we come to know God? The processes suggested, however, also applied to knowledge in general, although the acquisition of such knowledge was of rather less concern to the writers themselves. Medieval theories of cognition are considered in Chapter 4; however, some of the issues are briefly considered here, because they relate to the wider issue of the nature of the soul.

Augustine's position, like that of Plato, was that certain ideas, like that of God, are innate, although they may need to be drawn out by teaching or sensory input. In contrast, Aristotle's position was that knowledge is abstracted from sensory information, but his description of the abstracting process, which involves both an "impassible" potential intellect, capable of receiving knowledge, and an active or agent intellect, is both condensed and rather unclear.[51] In consequence, it was subject to a number of different interpretations and gave rise to considerable debate especially concerning the nature and role of the "agent intellect."

A particularly provocative view of the agent intellect was that held by Averroes.[52] Averroes followed Aristotle in holding a rather materialist view of man; to this material man, however, was added an agent intellect capable of divining and understanding universals, that is, general truths rather than specific sensory information. This agent intellect was essentially divine in nature and existed apart from the human soul with which it conjoined. Not only did Averroes' account effectively place human understanding and intelligence outside of the individual but also the account effectively denied the immortality of the individual soul. In Aristotle's account the intellect was the only immortal part;[53] its removal from the human soul left the remnant as mortal as the body. Not surprisingly Averroes' doctrine was vigorously attacked by the Church for its theologically unacceptable consequences. For example, among the errors condemned by the bishop of Paris in 1270, was Averroes' view "that the intellect of all men is one and the same in number."[54] Also, because of the increasing popularity of Aristotle's account of mundane phenomena, there was increasing pressure to produce an account of the soul that reconciled an Aristotelian view of the world with Christianity.

Overall, between say the beginning of the twelfth century and the end of the thirteenth, there was a discernible shift in the psychological

accounts from an Augustinian or Platonic view of the soul to an Aristotelian point of view. Thus, for example, there was a gradual tendency
to discount the importance of innate ideas and a greater emphasis on
the empirical nature of knowledge.[55] In this context many of the later
medieval scholars, led by William of Ockham (ca. 1285–1349) actually
went beyond Aristotle's thinking to cast doubt on the reality of abstracted
forms themselves.[56] To give some idea of these medieval accounts, the
next section considers in detail probably the most influential of them—
that given by Thomas Aquinas in the *Summa Theologiae*.

THOMAS AQUINAS' ACCOUNT OF SOUL

Aquinas' voluminous writings are largely concerned with the theological issues. However, and particularly in the *Summa Theologiae*, these
writings also contain a coherent account of psychology. This section is
concerned with giving an outline of Aquinas' account of the soul and
his solution to some of the problems involved in trying to reconcile the
empirical and materialist approach of Aristotle with Christian thinking.

Although Aquinas' doctrines were influential at the time, they were
by no means universally accepted, either by his fellow scholastics—
Aquinas spent most of his adult life teaching in the faculty of theology
at the University of Paris—or by the hierarchy of the Church. In the
centuries since his death, however, much of his thinking has gradually
been accepted by the Catholic Church. Hence Aquinas' psychological
ideas are of contemporary as well as historical importance, because they
form an important part of the view of the nature of man held by an institution that exerts considerable influence in the twentieth century.

Aquinas' basic approach to the soul is Aristotelian, and throughout
his writing he speaks frequently of the human being as made up of a
soul-body compound. Although the soul is the root principle of life,
man is not merely the soul alone.[57] Although the soul is a unity—
Aquinas expressly rejects the possibility of a person being "inhabited"
by more than one soul[58]—it contains a number of different powers,
divided into Aristotle's five classes: vegetative, sensitive, appetitive, lo-
comotive, and intellective.[59] The first four of these powers are shared
with animals, the last is possessed by humans alone of terrestrial crea-
tures, although angels, whose nature Aquinas spends much effort in
attempting to elucidate, also possess intellectual souls.[60]

Aquinas' discussion of the vegetative powers is limited simply to defining them as those of nutrition, growth, and reproduction.[61] Under
sensitive powers he defines five external senses, sight, hearing, touch,
taste, and smell, and also four inner senses.[62] The inner senses are held
responsible for a number of what are generally referred to today as
cognitive abilities, and include the ability to form and retain mental

images of objects seen or imagined, as well as instincts and memory. Belief in the existence of these inner senses and their localization in the ventricles of the brain was near-universal in the Middle Ages, as was their classification as part of the sensitive power, and the nature and implications of this belief are considered in Chapter 4.

The appetitive powers divide into the will and the sense appetite, which in turn can be broadly divided into an affective and a spirited appetite. Aquinas' account of these is considered in detail in Chapter 5; here it suffices that the sense appetite broadly consists of drives and emotions.[63] In animals, the sense appetite alone supplies the impetus to action; in humans, however, which possess an intellectual appetite or will, the sense appetite is not the immediate cause of behavior.

The intellectual powers that distinguish man from animals consist for Aquinas of the understanding or reasoning power and the will.[64] Memory, the third of the triumvirate suggested by Augustine to comprise the mind, is subsumed by understanding.[65] The intellectual powers, for Aquinas as for other medieval thinkers, are clearly thought of as the ruling or controlling parts of the soul. Although the sense appetite might indicate a course of action, the resultant behavior is the consequence of an act of will. Like other Christian writers, Aquinas ensures a prominent place for free will in human action and rejects deterministic accounts of human behavior.[66]

Reason and will also differ from the other powers in not requiring a bodily organ for their function (as, for example, sight requires an eye); it is in fact this feature of the intellectual soul (that is, a soul possessing intellectual powers) that suggests that it is immortal.[67] However, in the living person, the intellectual powers are dependent on the other powers for information for their proper operation. The human soul "needs a body for the sake of sensation."[68] Moreover, Aquinas follows Aristotle in believing that thinking is impossible without an image of some kind, and the production of these images is the province of the inner senses.[69] The intellect acquires understanding by abstraction from these sensations and images; hence knowledge is acquired empirically rather than innately as suggested by Plato.[70] The acquisition of knowledge thus depends on the body as well as the soul, and Aquinas is prepared to concede that one person may have a better understanding than another because of bodily advantages, for example, because of a superior memory or superior ability to form the required mental images.[71]

Aquinas' reasoning with respect to the intellect rouses a problem frequently encountered by medieval philosophy: how to reconcile the idea of an immortal soul that functions after death with the Aristotelian psychology in which the functions of the soul depend on the existence of the body. In Aquinas' account, how can the soul sense or even think without access to sensations or images? As we have seen, Averroes attempted to solve this problem by positing that only the intellect, which is not unique to any individual person, survives death. For Plato, on the other hand, the nature of the soul is, to use Aquinas' term, "angelic" and hence not dependent on the body at all. Aquinas faces up to the issue, and concedes, for example, that the soul has a natural tendency to embodiment, and that sensory powers do not survive death.[72] Basically, however, his answer is that the soul when separated from the body acquires a new mode of understanding, similar, although rather inferior to, that used by angels.[73]

Overall Aquinas' psychology is empirical rather than mystical in nature, and one in which human interactions with the environment rather than inner contemplation are stressed. In some respects Aquinas' account is actually more empirical than than of Aristotle—the obscurities associated with the status of the agent intellect do not cloud Aquinas' psychology. Although his empirical approach to understanding was rather extreme at the time he wrote, his thinking generally is illustrative of the way medieval scholars tried to integrate different disciplines. In this case Aquinas' aim was to produce an account of the nature of man that would be both psychologically and theologically acceptable.

Some of Aquinas' writings on specific psychological functions are interesting in themselves and are considered in more detail in later chapters. There are however some further general features of his acccount that call for comment here.

In the first place, and here Aquinas is typical of medieval scholastics, his account makes frequent reference to the physiological beliefs of the time. Such reference occurs because all of the powers of the soul except the intellective one are held to depend on the working of the soul and body together. Thus, in his account of emotion, Aquinas stated that it invariably involves some kind of physiological change,[74] and in his discussion of particular emotions he indicated what kind of change is involved.

Second, while Aquinas' approach to psychology is in no way experimental, it is often empirical, and he made frequent reference to observed behavior. It is also clear from several passages that Aquinas was quite prepared to consider psychological findings that are true on average rather than invariably true. For example, when discussing why memory is important for prudence, he remarked:

Prudence . . . is engaged with contingent human doings. Here a person cannot be guided only by norms which are simply and of necessity true, he must also appreciate what happens in the majority of cases. . . . Now to know what is true in the majority of cases we must be empirical. . . . Consequently recalling many facts is required for prudence.[75]

Thus it is clear that Aquinas had some understanding of the statistical issues underlying present-day experimental psychology, although on the whole his own approach is logical and deductive rather than empirical.

SPIRIT

The present-day connotations of the word *soul* are, as we have seen, rather different to those accompanying the word in the Middle Ages. The word *spirit* (Latin: *spiritus*) presents a similar problem to the modern reader. In this case the problem is exacerbated by the fact that the same word actually had a number of rather different meanings in ancient and medieval psychology. Moreover, these different meanings are not always clearly distinguishable from each other.

The first and most fundamental meaning of spirit was simply the breath. Thus Aristotle's *De Spiritu* is concerned largely with the functions and mechanisms of respiration.[76] However even by Aristotle's time there was a long tradition in which the breath (Greek: *pneuma*) was in some way connected or even identified with the soul.[77] This tradition, which was represented particularly in stoic philosophy, ensured that spirit in the Middle Ages had not only a physical meaning as air exhaled or inhaled but also other, less physical and perhaps metaphorically derived, meanings.

A rather different use of the term *spirit* that originated historically from the discussion of the breath but then acquired an almost independent but still physiologically based meaning of its own is found in ancient medical writings, most significantly those of Galen.[78] The Galenic account of spirit was adopted, with occasional minor modifications, as a standard medical and physiological model throughout the Middle Ages, and almost every writer from about 400 . . who was concerned with physiology and psychology seems to have employed it. The following brief summary of the model is based on that given by Bartholomaeus Anglicus in his popular medieval encyclopedia *De Proprietatibus Rerum* (*On the Properties of Things*), written about 1230, and translated into English by John Trevisa around 1399.[79]

Spirit, according to this account, is a "subtil, aiery substaunce" that can be obtained by distillation. *Natural spirit* is obtained from the liver by a process of "strong boilinge and sethinge."[80] This spirit is mixed with the blood and goes to all the limbs; some is also conveyed to the heart where it is further refined to produce *vital spirit*, which is spread throughout the body. The most refined spirit of all is called *animal spirit* and is produced in the forebrain, according to Galen actually in the rete system,[81] and fills the ventricles of the brain and the nerves. Animal spirit also issues from the eyes in the process of vision.[82] Thus animal spirit was a necessary component for all psychological processes in animals and many of those in humans.

A third medieval meaning of spirit is as a sort of intermediary between body and soul. Such an interpretation is, in a sense, an extension of the physiological account of spirit just examined. In the extension, however, spirit was not conceived as an ordinary physical substance composed of the four known elements, but as a fifth element or *quintessence*. In Stoic philosophy this had often been taken as the substance of the soul itself; more usual in medieval thinking however was to assign it an intermediate status: the most ethereal of physical substances and, at the same time, the grossest substance capable of interaction with the soul.

The notion of spirit as an intermediary was by no means universally accepted. Aristotle did not use the notion, and indeed, with his concept of the soul there was no need of an intermediary. Aquinas scorned the notion on logical grounds.[83] From a philosophical point of view, an intermediate spirit seems to have been suggested by scholars working in the Platonic tradition where there was more of a problem in explaining how the body and soul were to interact.[84] A popular aspect of the belief is found in *The Book of Quinte Essence*, a manuscript dating from about 1460 . .[85] In this work the quintessence is conceived as an incorruptible substance that may be obtained by distilling wine, blood, or some other organic substances. The author seems to have regarded it as an almost magical cure-all, effective in counteracting the effects of old age and many physical illnesses. It was also recommended for driving out devils and curing mental disorder: "it cures also mad men and lunatic men and it restores again wit and discretion."[86]

Finally, spirit could be used to describe something completely incorporeal such as the soul. This meaning, which was already old by the Middle Ages, is seen, for example, in Bartholomaeus Anglicus' reference to devils as evil spirits (*De spiritibus malignis*).[87]

Other definitions of spirit can also be found, particularly at the time of the Roman Empire. Augustine, for example, who was aware that the word was being used in different ways, defined it as a power of the soul inferior to the mind that was responsible for producing images.[88] By the later Middle Ages, however, the word was used by philosophers and physicians mainly in its Galenic sense, as a physical substance refined in the human body, and spirit will be generally given this meaning in the remainder of this book. It is perhaps ironic that, of all the different meanings, this relatively exact physiological use of the word is probably the most obscure to the modern reader, who is most likely to encounter it in a bar or a church.

CONCLUSIONS

The medieval enquiry into the nature of the soul was centrally concerned with psychological issues and should not be seen as exclusively, or even primarily, concerned with religious issues. The nature of the enquiry was clearly different to that of present-day psychology; in particular there was much less emphasis on experimentation and rather more on deduction and inference from a few known facts and examples. In consequence, the medieval enquiry did not discover many new empirical phenomena. On the other hand, medieval enquiry should not be simply dismissed as sterile: medieval scholars were prepared to consider new psychological ideas and, in the thirteenth century, replaced an essentially Platonic paradigm of psychology with an Aristotelian one. Moreover, the "Aristotelian" psychology that was produced, for example by Aquinas, differed in a number of features from that originally proposed by Aristotle.

A feature of medieval psychology was the very clear emphasis on the unity of the human being and the interrelatedness of the various human functions or powers of the soul. Often this unity of human function was held in microcosm to reflect the unity of creation or the unity of a kingdom. The following passage, from the *De Anima* of William of Auvergne, is a typical example of this medieval view of psychology.

The human soul has a certain likeness to a well ordered kingdom or to a well planned city; for in it the will is like a king or emperor, and the intellectual faculty, or power of reason, like his councillor. The inferior powers, namely the irascible and concupiscible, and the powers of movement . . . are like ministers whose office is to execute the commands of the sovereign will; all the senses, in turn, are ministers and inspectors travelling hither and thither across country, and reporting whatever outside events they have apprehended.[89]

By contrast no such clear view of what constitutes human nature and how different psychological functions relate to each other is commonly held by modern psychologists. Typically modern psychologists are chiefly concerned with a rather narrow area of human functioning. They are expert, for example, in the study of perception or of learning or of clinical psychology. It is true that some modern psychologists have attempted to extend their theories beyond the confines of one of these areas; Sigmund Freud and B. F. Skinner are well-known examples of psychologists who have attempted to give such broad accounts. Moreover humanist psychologists have stressed the importance of a unitary approach.[90] These broader accounts, however, differ from that of medieval psychology in that they are not commonly believed. Few modern psychologists, for example, subscribe to the overall view of either Freud or Skinner, although many would concede that they have provided interesting insights into human behavior. If, in fact, any unifying principle exists at all in modern psychology, it is to be found not in a commonly held view of human nature but in the commonly held belief that the scientific method of empirical research is the means necessary to reveal it.[91]

NOTES

1. See H. J. Blumenthal, "Neoplatonic Elements in the *De Anima* Commentaries." *Phronesis* 21 (1976): 64–87.

2. Aristotle, *De Anima*, trans. J. A. Smith. In W. D. Ross, ed., *The Works of Aristotle*, Vol. 3 (Oxford, UK: Clarendon, 1931), 1.2.404a–404b.

3. Ibid., 1.5.411b.

4. Ibid., 1.4.408b.

5. Ibid., 1.4.408b.

6. Ibid., 2.1.412b.

7. Ibid., 2.1.412b–413a.

8. Ibid., 3.1.425a.

9. Ibid., 3.2.426b.

10. Ibid., 3.3.427b.

11. Ibid., 3.3.429a.

12. Ibid., 3.4.429a.

13. Ibid., 3.7.431a.

14. Ibid., 3.5.430a.

15. Ibid., 3.8.432a.

16. Ibid., 3.8.432a.

17. Ibid., 3.9–11.432a–434a.

18. Plato, *Timaeus*, trans. H.D.P. Lee (Harmondsworth, UK: Penguin, 1965), 46.

19. Ibid., 57–58.

20. Ibid., 96.

21. Ibid., 103.

22. Ibid., 23.

23. Plotinus, *Enneads*, trans. A. H. Armstrong (London: Heinemann, 1966–1984), 1.6.9.

24. Ibid., 2.8; 4.3–6.

25. Ibid., 4.6.3.

26. Galen, *On the Doctrines of Hippocrates and Plato*, trans. P. De Lacy (Berlin: Akademie-Verlag, 1980).

27. Augustine, *The Greatness of the Soul*, trans. Joseph M. Colleran (Westminster, Md.: Newman, 1964), 13.

28. Ibid., 40.

29. Aristotle, *De Anima*, 1.5.411b.

30. Augustine, *The Greatness of the Soul*, 98–109.

31. Augustine, *On the Trinity*, trans. A. W. Hadden. In P. Schaff, ed., *A Select Library of the Nicene and Post-Nicene Fathers of the Christian Church*, Ser. I, Vol. 3 (Grand Rapids, Mich.: Eerdmans, 1956), 10.

32. Augustine, *Confessions*. In A. C. Outler, ed., *The Library of Christian Classics*, Vol. 7, *Augustine: Confessions and Enchiridion* (London: SCM Press, 1955), 10.10–12.

33. Nemesius, *A Treatise on the Nature of Man*. In W. Telfer, ed., *The Library of Christian Classics*, Vol. 4, *Cyril of Jerusalem and Nemesius of Emesa* (London: SCM Press, 1955).

34. Ibid., 292.

35. Ibid., 297.

36. Nemesius regarded imagination as being sometimes a faculty of the rational and sometimes of the irrational soul. See Ibid., 320–323, 347.

37. Ibid., 322–323.

38. Ibid., 348.

39. For example, Ibid., 397–403.

40. Ibid., 371–372.

41. The view that the soul was composed of some material essence was quite common in ancient philosophies, especially that of the stoics.

42. A modern account of the rete system and a brief history of its discovery may be found in M. A. Baker, "A Brain-Cooling System in Mammals." *Scientific American* 240 (1979): 114.

43. Galen, *On the Usefulness of the Parts of the Body,* Book 9; Galen, *On the Doctrines of Hippocrates and Plato,* 3.8.31.

44. Augustine, *Confessions,* 10.8.

45. Aquinas, *Summa Theologiae,* 1.87.3.

46. Thomas Aquinas, *Commentaria in Libros Aristotelis De Anima,* trans. Alois Mager (Vienna: Jakob Hegner, 1937), 3.8.718. Also 3.9.724–725.

47. See A. C. Spearing, *Medieval Dream-Poetry* (Cambridge, UK: Cambridge University Press, 1976). Examples of medieval dream-poems include the anonymous "Pearl," Chaucer's "The Parliament of Fowls," and Langland's "Piers Plowman."

48. Aristotle, *De Divinatione per Somnium,* trans. J. I. Beare. In W. D. Ross, *The Works of Aristotle,* Vol. 3 (Oxford, UK: Clarendon, 1931).

49. Aristotle, *De Somno et Vigilia,* trans. J. I. Beare. In W. D. Ross, ed., *The Works of Aristotle,* Vol. 3 (Oxford, UK: Clarendon, 1931).

50. Aristotle, *De Somniis,* trans. J. I. Beare. In W. D. Ross, ed., *The Works of Aristotle,* Vol. 3 (Oxford, UK: Clarendon, 1931).

51. Aristotle, *De Anima,* 3.4–5.429a–430a.

52. For example, Averroes, *The Epistle on the Possibility of Conjunction with the Active Intellect,* trans. K. P. Bland (New York: Jewish Theological Seminary of America, 1982).

53. Aristotle, *De Anima,* 3.5.430a.

54. Thorndike, *University Records,* 80.

55. See L. J. Bowman, "The Development of the Doctrine of the Agent Intellect in the Franciscan School of the Thirteenth Century." *Modern Schoolman* 50 (1973): 251–279.

56. See Gordon Leff, *William of Ockham: The Metamorphoses of Scholastic Discourse* (Manchester, UK: Manchester University Press, 1975).

57. Thomas Aquinas, *Summa Theologiae,* 1.75.1; 1.75.4.

58. For example, Ibid., 1.76.3.

59. Ibid., 1.78.1.

60. For example, Ibid., 1.50–64.

61. Ibid., 1.78.2.

62. Ibid., 1.78.3–4.

63. Ibid., 1.80–82.

64. Ibid., 1.81.3.

65. Ibid., 1.79.7.

66. For example, Ibid., 1.2.10.3.

67. Ibid., 1.75.2.

68. Ibid., 1.76.5ad. 2.

69. For example, Ibid., 1.75.6; 1.76.2.

70. Ibid., 1.79.3–4.

71. Ibid., 1.85.7.

72. Ibid., 1.75.7ad.3; 1.76.1ad.6; 1.77.8.

73. Ibid., 1.89.1.

74. Ibid., 1.2.22.3.

75. Ibid., 2.2.49.1.

76. Aristotle, *De Spiritu*, trans. J. F. Dobson. In W. D. Ross, ed., *Works of Aristotle*, Vol. 3. (Oxford, UK: Clarendon, 1931).

77. A discussion of the development of the idea may be found in Mark D. Altschule, "The Pneuma Concept of the Soul." *Journal of the History of the Behavioral Sciences* 1 (1965): 314–320.

78. Galen, *On the Usefulness of the Parts of the Body*, esp. Books 8 and 9; Galen, *On the Doctrines of Hippocrates and Plato*, Book 7.

79. Bartholomaeus Anglicus, *On the Properties of Things*, trans. John Trevisa (1398–1399), ed. M. C. Seymour (Oxford, UK: Clarendon, 1975).

80. Ibid., 121–122.

81. For example, Galen, *On the Usefulness of the Parts of the Body*, 430–431.

82. Bartholomaeus Anglicus, *On the Properties of Things*, 182–183.

83. Aquinas, *Summa Theologiae*, 1.76.7.

84. For example, Ernest A. Moody, *Studies in Medieval Philosophy, Science, and Logic* (Berkeley, Cal.: University of California Press, 1975), 41–42.

85. Frederick J. Furnivall, ed., *The Book of Quinte Essence or the Fifth Being* (London: Early English Text Society, Old Series No. 16, 1866).

86. Ibid., 22.

87. Bartholomaeus Anglicus, *On the Properties of Things*, 84.

88. Augustine, *The Literal Meaning of Genesis*, 7.21.30, 12.9.18–20.

89. Moody, *Studies in Medieval Philosophy*, 40.

90. See Frank T. Severin, *Discovering Man in Psychology: A Humanist Approach* (New York: McGraw-Hill, 1973).

91. The extent of the belief is most readily grasped from the frequency with which it is mentioned in the opening chapters of almost any introductory text in psychology.

3

Sensation and Perception

The question of how an immaterial entity such as the human soul could interact with a material world was an important and difficult one for both ancient philosophers and medieval scholars. Psychologically there are two aspects to the question. First, one can ask how the soul can initiate action or produce change in the outside world. Second, there is the question of how the soul can sense and acquire knowledge about the outside world. Medieval scholars did not produce much psychological theory related to the first question, but they did consider seriously the second question, and, like their Greek predecessors, produced accounts of the processes involved in sensation and perception.

Both in modern and medieval psychology, accounts of perception place heavy stress on physical and physiological processes, and issues include, for example, what the eye is composed of, how it functions when light enters it, what messages the eye transmits to the brain, and how they are processed there. Up to the twentieth century and throughout the ancient and medieval period the main focus of attention was on the functioning of the receptors, particularly the eye. In recent times most attention, at least in vision, has been directed to the study of the neural processes that occur after the physical energy in the outside world has been transduced into nervous impulses. In both periods, however, the fundamental rather mechanical approach of explaining sensation by reference to physiological processes that can be measured in much the same way as physical processes in the outside world is the same.

Medieval psychology included under the heading of sensation and perception the workings of the inner senses and psychological functions of imagination, memory, and other mental processes. These are discussed in the next chapter under the heading of cognition, in accordance with the modern division of psychological functions. In medieval, as in modern, psychology, perception was not simply explained by a mechanical, physiological reaction to energy impinging from the external world. The cognitive processes of the inner senses and of the mind itself were also held to be important.

The preceding chapter considered differing approaches taken in the Middle Ages to the basic idea of what the human soul was. These different accounts of the soul had implications for perceptual theory and particularly for theories of vision. In general, those who held an Aristotelian view of the soul, in which the soul is basically the functioning of the body, tended to hold an intromission account of vision; that is, an account that tried to explain vision by what enters the eye. On the other hand, those who held the Platonic or Augustinian view, in which the soul makes active use of the body, tended to concur with the extramission account of vision, in which spirit actually flows out from the eye into the outside world. Thus the Aristotelian account tended to favor a passive and the Platonic an active theory of perception.[1]

The debate and implications concerning the different accounts of perception will be taken up shortly. In the meantime, a few common features of medieval perceptual accounts will be considered, and some frequently encountered terms explained.

Things exist in the physical world. These things possess different qualities that may be, for example, seen or touched. Qualities that can be sensed are often called *sensibles*. Thus, for example, temperature and color are sensibles but the magnetic field of an object is not. When something is perceived, it causes some alteration in, or impression on, the sense organ of the perceiver. The impression is called the *sensible species*. Clearly this species conveys information about only some of the qualities of the thing perceived, depending on the sensibles to which the sense organ is sensitive and, for example, on the angle of the view: a friend's face viewed from the front does not produce the same species as the same face seen in profile. Species enable the determination of the *form* of the thing perceived. Precisely what the real form of a thing is was a tricky philosophical question that is of little immediate relevance. In visual perception, form more readily corresponds to the identity of an object than its outline.[2]

It should be noted that this general account is not a naive theory of perception. In particular, the necessity of the species, although generally accepted from the time of Plato to that of William of Ockham, is not intuitively obvious. St. Augustine provided a clear statement both of the problem and of its solution:

We do not distinguish, through the same sense, the form of the body which we see, from the form which is produced by it in the sense of him who sees. . . . And hence it is very difficult to persuade men of duller mind that an image of the visible thing is formed in our sense, when we see it. . . . [But] when we have looked for some little time at a light, and then shut our eyes, there seem to play before our eyes certain bright colors variously changing themselves, and shining less and less until they wholly cease; and these we must understand to be the remains of that form which was wrought in the sense, while the shining body was seen.[3]

Although Augustine's own account of visual perception was not popular in the later Middle Ages, the theoretical argument for the existence of species was practically unquestioned before William of Ockham.

As with other aspects of medieval psychology, much of the perceptual theorizing derived from Aristotle and it is to his description that we now turn.

ARISTOTLE'S SENSATION AND PERCEPTION

Aristotle's account of sensation and perception is contained principally in De Anima and De Sensu et Sensibili (On Sense and Sensing), which formed part of the Parva Naturalia and, like De Anima, was widely available and read in later medieval Europe.[4]

Perceptible sensory qualities, according to Aristotle, fall into two kinds. There are special "objects of sense," which are perceptible only to a single sense; for example, color is the special object of sight, sound of hearing, flavor of taste, and odor of smell. More than one quality is determined only by touch. There are also "common sensibles" such as movement, number, or magnitude, which are perceptible by more than one sense.[5] Sensory error is possible with common sensibles but not with special objects of sense. Each of the five senses—Aristotle maintained there are only five senses[6]—in addition to possessing at least one special sensible or object of sense possesses a sense organ and requires a medium between the organ and its object.

To see an object it is necessary that the object possess color and also that there be a transparent medium containing light between the object and the eye. Thus light is not itself the special object of sight but rather a necessary feature of the medium for sight to take place. The necessity of the medium is suggested by the fact that, if a colored object "is placed in immediate contact with the eye, it cannot be seen."[7] In De Sensu, Aristotle rejects the idea that rays of light issue from the eye. Instead the eye is translucent and filled with water to admit light. Aristotle does not specify where the actual sensing or seeing takes place but suggests it is the brain, because "soldiers wounded in battle by a sword slash on the temple so inflicted as to sever the passages of the eye, feel a sudden onset of darkness, as if a lamp had gone out."[8]

Sound occurs when two bodies impact on one another and is transmitted through air or water. The organ of hearing works because it is itself filled with air and so can resonate or echo to incoming sound.[9] Hearing, Aristotle remarks, is the sense most used "for developing intelligence."[10] This is, of course, because we use sound principally to communicate ideas when we speak.

Aristotle's description of smell begins with the observation that "men have a poor sense of smell . . . inferior to that of many species of animals."[11] Smelling takes place through the medium of either air or water. Man only smells when he inhales, but other animals that do not breathe have a sense of smell, as do animals that live in water. Odors divide into two classes: those that run parallel to tastes and produce the same sensations (for example, of sweetness or astringency) and those, like the odors of flowers, that produce pleasure. The latter are only perceptible by humans.[12]

Odors and flavors differ in their moistness: "Smells come from what is dry as flavours from what is moist."[13]

Water is needed for taste although water itself is tasteless. Aristotle distinguishes seven flavors—analogous to seven colors—that vary on a dimension from sweet to bitter. The flavors harsh, pungent, astringent, acid, and saline fall between these extremes.[14]

Touch and taste are alike in that the medium for each is a part of the human body: flesh for touch and the tongue for taste.[15] Aristotle leaves unanswered the question that arises here: If the flesh and the tongue are media, what are the organs of sense for these modalities? Nor is there a solution to the problem of how many sensibles or special objects of sense are tangible. Aristotle's final comments on touch indicate two ways in which touch differs from the other sensations. First, it involves perception by immediate contact. Second, "without touch there can be no other sense, and [its loss] must bring about the death of an animal." This is because excess of light, say, merely blinds an animal, while excess of heat or hardness destroys it. Hence for survival, all animals must possess a sense of touch.[16]

Aristotle's account of perception is amplified by some observations on special objects of sense and common sensibles. Special objects of sense, e.g., temperature and flavor, are generally organized on dimensions with "contraries"—what a modern psychologist might call bipolar dimensions. For example, hot is contrary to cold; and sweet, to bitter. While the underlying dimension is infinitely divisible, the subjective dimension is not. A sufficient difference between two stimuli is required for their discrimination and when the difference is too small, for example, when the frequency of two sounds differs by a quarter tone, the stimuli are not discriminable.[17] Aristotle's discussion of this point is surprisingly modern in character and in fact in general agreement with present-day accounts of psychophysics. Also in good agreement is his recognition of the possibilities that take place when two or more sensory stimuli are presented together. Sometimes "the greater stimulus tends to expel the less";[18] that is, in modern terminology, one stimulus masks the other and renders it imperceptible. Sometimes, "if the two stimuli are equal but heterogeneous, no perception of either will ensue; they will alike efface one another's characteristics" and give rise to a new perception (as, for example, occurs when colors are mixed).[19] Finally it is possible to perceive two stimuli at once; as when two sufficiently different notes of music are presented.[20]

Common sensibles, like number or movement, are scaled on dimensions that do not have contraries. They differ from the special objects of sense also in not being perceived through a particular sense organ; instead they are perceived by some general sensibility. Furthermore, while sensation cannot err in the perception of special objects of sense, illusion and error are possible with common sensibles. A feature of perception remarked by Aristotle is that there must be a common sense that enables the discrimination of sensory qualities from each other, for example, the discrimination of white from sweet.[21]

Aristotle's account of perception is enlarged on a little in other places. In *De Somniis*, for example, aftereffects and adaptation are described. Aristotle believes that both result from the continuation of sensation in the absence of its object, so that when we look at a color and then away from it the color remains in our gaze. Similarly when we look at objects in motion, like fast-flowing rivers, and then at things that are really at rest, they appear to be in motion. Aristotle's account of these phenomena is interesting because it is, unusually for him, empirically incorrect. In fact, as the reader can easily verify, the aftereffect in these cases is opposite to, and not in the same direction as, the original perception. For example, the prolonged viewing of green results in a white object taking on a reddish hue not a green one as Aristotle states.[22]

Aristotle's account of sensation and perception was held in great esteem in the Middle Ages, and his systematic approach and many of his specific doctrines were widely copied. To take a rather minor example, his point about the special status of touch being a necessary sense, because its destruction involves the destruction of the animal, appears in, for example, Nemesius' *Treatise on the Nature of Man*, Avicenna's *Psychology*, Bartholomaeus Anglicus' *On the Properties of Things*, Aquinas' *Summa Theologiae*, and the writings of Albertus Magnus.[23] More importantly, his belief that sensation requires a medium was frequently re-iterated. Aquinas, for example, stated that a medium was necessary for smell because otherwise it was impossible to explain how a vulture could detect carrion at distances of several hundred miles. No vapor or other material substance could possibly travel so far.[24] Similarly, although different theories of vision were available, Aristotle's retained its popularity throughout the medieval period.

On the other hand, it would be a mistake to describe medieval accounts of perception as dogmatically Aristotelian or to consider Aristotle's influence as inhibiting inquiry into perceptual problems. There seem to have been two main factors encouraging further inquiry. In the first place, opposed to Aristotle's theory of vision was another well-elaborated rival account of vision as a process involving the extramission of rays of light or spirit. In the second place, Aristotle's account was brief and clearly incomplete. In particular, physiological processes, and in some cases the identity of the sense organs themselves, were left unspecified. Thus it was possible for subsequent writers to attempt to fill in the important gaps left in Aristotle's account.

One of the bigger gaps was in describing the physiological process of representation of sensory information in the brain. This gap was filled by joining together Galen's medical description of animal spirits with Aristotle's account of perception. How this theoretical conjunction took place or who was responsible for it is unclear. It appears, however, almost in its final form in Nemesius' *Treatise on the Nature of Man* in the fourth century A.D..

Animal spirit, in this account, fills all of the sensory nerves that connect the sense organs to the front ventricles of the brain. The animal spirit serves to convey sensory information; it also fills the ventricles of the brain.[25] In Avicenna's and most subsequent accounts of perception, common sense—responsible for perceiving Aristotle's common sensibles and discriminating, for example, white from sweet—is located in the front ventricles, as is the faculty of representation, which preserves the content of the common sense even when the objects sensed are absent.[26] In the extramission account of vision to which we now turn, the animal spirit performed a further function: vision resulted from the emission of this spirit from the eyes.

THE EXTRAMISSION-INTROMISSION DEBATE

To the modern reader, the extramission theory of vision, in which animal spirit or rays of light are supposed to be physically emitted by the eyes, may appear naive and ridiculous. The modern intromissive account of vision, however, which stresses the importance of the retinal image, has had the benefit of centuries of theory and research that have largely removed the problems raised by the theory. To the medieval scholar the choice between the rival theories was much less clear.[27]

Before examining the history of the extramission theory and the debate between its adherents and those of intromission, it would perhaps be useful to state a few of the general factors that made an extramission theory appealing. In the first place, although none of the human sensory capabilities use an extramissive process, there is no general reason why they should not. In fact, although this was not known in the Middle Ages, bats make extensive use of extramission. They navigate at night by emitting high frequency calls whose echoes are used to perceive obstacles or prey. This system works very successfully, so successfully in fact that the general principle has also been employed by humans in the design of underwater sonar detection instruments. A variant of the principle, using electromagnetic radiation rather than sound, is used in radar detection. Perhaps more surprisingly, not only can blind people be trained to use a fitted sonar system as a sensory aid, but they also often use echoes, from a tapping cane or from footsteps, for example, to perceive obstacles in front of them. It is true that in these examples different organs or equipment are used for the emission of sound than for its reception, while in the visual extramission theory one organ, the eye, was generally held to perform both tasks. Common, however, to the examples and the medieval theory is emission of some physical quality. Extramission sensory processes then are viable as a way of perceiving the outside world, and, while it may be incorrect, it was by no means ridiculous to suppose vision could work in this way.[28]

Second, extramission accounts much more naturally than intromission for attention processes in vision. It is obvious that people do direct their gaze so as to focus on something glimpsed out of the corner of the eye. It is also true that people sometimes do not see an object that is actually in their field of vision. These phenomena were remarked in the Middle Ages by those attempting perceptual theorizing. For example, Nemesius reported;

It often happens that, gazing at the ground, we fail to see the coin lying there that we are straining our eyes to the full to see, until rays from both eyes light upon that portion of ground where the coin is lying. Then we suddenly see it, as though at that moment we had just begun to take notice.[29]

Nemesius, incidentally, also remarked on how difficult it is to perceive number spontaneously: "As for the number of objects seen, when it exceeds three or four, it is not taken in a single glance.... One cannot count five, six, seven, or more objects without calling in memory for help."[30]

The validity of this observation has been investigated and confirmed for a number of sensory dimensions in the twentieth century, although the upper limit of sensory recognition is generally placed at six or seven rather than three or four.[31]

That visual perception is an active process in which the soul directs the activity of the sense organs is a frequent and important theme in extramission theory. "Sensation," as Augustine put it, "belongs not to the body but to the soul acting through the body."[32] Hipparchus (ca. 146–126 B.C.) even believed "that rays that extend from the eyes lay hold with their ends upon external bodies, as though grasping them with hands, and render them perceptible by the sense of sight."[33] In an early work, Augustine stated that "sight extends itself outward and through the eyes darts forth far in every possible direction to light up what we see. Hence it happens that it sees rather in the place where the object seen is present, not in the place from which it goes out to see."[34] It is interesting to note that Augustine's view of vision here, radical even for an advocate of extramission, is only possible because in his psychology the soul is not tied to the body but can extend beyond it.

In general, extramission seems to have been more popular than intromission as an optical theory in the ancient and early medieval period. Advocates of an extramission theory included Plato, Euclid, Nemesius, Augustine, and Galen. It should not be thought, however, that all extramission theorists were in complete agreement on the mechanisms involved in vision. In Plato's version, for example, the eyes emitted a kind of fire or light, whereas in the Galenic version, which was the most frequently used medieval account, the eyes emitted animal spirits that had descended via the optic nerves from the ventricles.[35] Still, the spirit itself was believed by Galen to contain light and, according to him, at night, when lions and leopards turn their pupil toward their nose, a small circle of light can be seen on the side of the nose.[36] Augustine and Hipparchus, at least in the passages cited above, held that perception actually took place out in the world. In Galen's version, on the other hand, the emission of animal spirit renders the air itself perceptive so that it becomes similar to a nerve in the body. The air in turn acts on the crystalline lens in the eye, which thus serves simultaneously both to exude spirit and to sense.[37] Finally, we should note the geometrical optics used by Euclid and Ptolemy, who pointed out that many aspects of vision could be explained by rays issuing from the eye and continuing indefinitely in straight lines until meeting with some object. This mathematical theory ignored physiological (and many psychological) issues, but was successful at explaining visual perspective; that is, why things look different seen from different points of view.[38]

There was also more than one version of the intromission theory of vision. Apart from that given by Aristotle, there was that of the atomists, in which, as Epicurus (ca. 340–270 B.C.) put it, particles are continually streaming off from the surface of bodies. . . . And those given off for a long time retain the position and arrangement which their atoms had when they formed part of the solid bodies, although occasionally they are thrown into confusion. . . . We must also consider that it is by the entrance [i.e., into the eye] of something coming from external objects that we see their shapes and think of them.[39]

Thus objects emit coherent patterns or forms that are composed of small packets of atoms.

The rival merits of the different extramission and intromission theories of vision were keenly debated by the Islamic philosophers of the early Middle Ages.[40] The account finding least favor, ironic in that it is that closest to the modern one, was the theory of the atomists. One difficulty, perceived by Al-Kindi (d. ca. 866 A.D.), is that if the form of an object is conveyed by small packets of atoms, akin to small mobile pictures, then the appearance of an object should remain unchanged as perspective changes. This is because the form of the object, supposed to be preserved by the order of the atoms, remains unchanged. A further difficulty with intromission theories, stated by Hunain ibn Ishaq (d. 877 A.D.), is that it is difficult to conceive how a form can become small enough to enter the eye. Moreover, if there are a large number of observers, the forms would have to enter into the eyes of all of them. Al-Kindi, whose optical writings were widely read by Christian scholars, ended up favoring an extramission theory that combined elements of Euclid's and Galen's thinking.

Avicenna (980–1037 A.D.), perhaps the most influential of all the Arabic thinkers, favored the intromission theory of Aristotle, and gave a number of arguments against the various extramission accounts. The Euclidean theory is weak because if the rays do not return to the observer's eye, there can clearly be no perception. If, however, they do return, how are we to explain rays that can travel in all directions as far as the stars and then return? Either the rays must separate and thus give a spotted impression of distant objects, which clearly they do not, or they must fill the whole of space, at least as far as the stars. This is obviously impossible. To the Galenic theory, Avicenna objects that sight should be affected when the wind is blowing and that, if the emission of spirit makes the medium perceptive, weak-sighted people should be helped when normally sighted people stand beside them to view an object. Clearly neither of these phenomena takes place.

Although Avicenna provided a devastating critique of extramission theories, he did little to advance intromission theory. This was left to Alhazen (ca. 965–1039 A.D.), who managed to produce a basically intromissive account of vision that also accounted for the geometrical optics of Euclid and the physiology of the eye, as revealed by Galen and other anatomists.[41] In Western Europe, Alhazen's optical theory was taken up and popularized in Latin Europe in the thirteenth century, first by Roger Bacon (ca. 1214–1292) and later by John Pecham (1230–1292), and the theory, modified somewhat by Bacon, is considered in detail in the next section. In brief, Alhazen's account rests on two major features. First, he held that objects radiate light in all directions and it is the impact of this light on the eye that is responsible for the sensation of vision. Second, he held that visual perception is not purely a matter of optics but involves processes of discrimination, recognition, and memory. The importance of such processes provided Alhazen with yet another and perhaps most convincing argument against extramission:

Because the visible object is perceived in its own place, the upholders of the doctrine of the ray came to believe that vision occurs by means of a ray issuing from the eye and ending at the object, and that vision is achieved by the end points of the ray. They argued against natural scientists, saying: if vision takes place by a form that comes from the object to the eye, and if the form exists inside the eye, then why is the object perceived in its own place outside the eye while its form exists in the eye? But these people forgot that vision is not accomplished by pure sensation alone, but is rather accomplished by means of discernment and prior recognition, and that without these no vision can be effected by sight, nor would sight perceive what the visible object is at the moment of seeing it.[42]

ROGER BACON'S ACCOUNT OF VISION

Although a number of earlier Christian writers, notably Robert Grosseteste (ca. 1169–1253) and Albertus Magnus, concerned themselves with optical and visual perception, Bacon seems to have been the first medieval scholar with both an abiding interest in vision and a knowledge of Alhazen as well as the earlier writers. Bacon was a Franciscan monk who worked in Oxford and Paris. He seems to have repeatedly fallen foul of his superiors, but the cause or causes of these difficulties is not accurately known.

Bacon's chief writings on vision are contained in the fifth part of his *Opus Majus*.[43] The work begins with a brief acknowledgement of some of his important predecessors in optics, notably Aristotle, Al-Kindi, and Alhazen, [44] and then proceeds to Bacon's version of the doctrine of the inner senses. In the brain are three cells or ventricles, the first of which (i.e., that one nearest the forehead) contains the two faculties of common sense (which perform the functions specified by Aristotle) and imagination (the faculty which forms and retains an image). These two inner senses judge the special and common sensibles, a total of twenty-nine different qualities. Other, more "cognitive" qualities, for example, whether something perceived is useful or harmful, are assessed by the faculties of estimation, memory, and cogitation located in the two posterior cells of the brain.[45] All that Bacon describes here was common knowledge in the Middle Ages, although with some variation as to detail. Bacon, as he acknowledges, actually follows Avicenna's account quite closely.[46]

The optic nerves descend from the right and left of the front cell of the brain, meet at the optic chiasma, and then diverge again to the left and right eyes. The anatomical detail and presumed operation of the eye are described at length. Briefly summarized, however,

the crystalline humor is called the pupil, and in it is the visual power, just as in a subject that at first is changed, although not radically, since the common nerve [i.e., optic chiasma where the nerves to left and right eyes meet] is the radical organ, and there vision is completed, as far as the visual power can.[47]

Bacon's optics are principally those of Alhazen. Objects radiate light in all directions from every point on their surfaces. The light travels in straight lines through the medium until it reaches the crystalline lens of the eye. The lens has the property that light rays that fall *perpendicular* to its surface are passed through undiminshed in strength, while those that fall at an *oblique* angle to the surface are refracted and diminished in strength. The perpendicular rays then effectively mask the weaker oblique rays, in the same way as the light of the sun hides the light of the stars in daytime.[48] The theorized operation of the lens enables the solution of an obvious problem with the account which is, as both Alhazen and Bacon clearly saw, that all points on the visible object radiate light to all points of the lens. As is indicated in Figure 1, however, the rays of light that fall perpendicular to the surface of the lens create a two-dimensional image of the object on the surface. It should be noted, moreover, that, although the theory is basically wrong, and the crystalline lens does not operate in the way suggested by Alhazen and Bacon, it produced exactly the same answers for the purposes of optics and visual perception as the correct one. The lower panel of Figure 1 shows for purposes of comparison how the image is produced on the retina in the modern account (first enunciated by Johannes Kepler in 1604). In particular, both Bacon's account and the modern one successfully incorporate the geometrical optics of Euclid's version of the extramission theory, because it is important in both that light rays travel in straight lines.

In the modern account, the visual power is completed, to use Bacon's

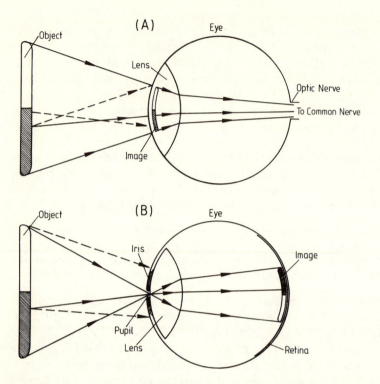

Figure 1. Medieval and modern optics. This figure shows simplified versions of Alhazen's and Bacon's account of the optical processes of the eye (A) and the modern optical account (B). Although there are no essential anatomical differences between the two accounts, different anatomical features are shown in the two diagrams—the optic nerve in the medieval and the pupil and retina in the modern—because different features are stressed by the two accounts. In both diagrams, solid rays are transmitted to the ultimate source of perception, the common nerve in the medieval and the retina in the modern accounts. Dashed rays are not transmitted, in the medieval account because they do not fall perpendicular to the surface of the lens, and in the modern because they do not enter the pupil, which alone permits the passage of light. Note that the retinal image in B is inverted while that on the lens in A is not.

term, on the retina, where the light energy is converted at the photoreceptors to neural impulses. In Bacon's account, forms are extracted where the species from both eyes mingle in the common nerve or optic chiasma. In order for the species to arrive at the common nerve, however, refraction of the rays that have passed through the crystalline lens takes place in the vitreous humor, which fills the eye and the optic nerves. This refraction is necessary because otherwise the image of the object will be formed in the eye itself and not, as Bacon wished, in the

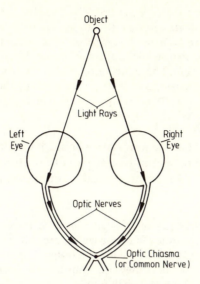

Figure 2. A problem for medieval optics. The light rays, according to Bacon, travel in straight lines, but if they do this they cannot meet in the optic chiasma (Bacon's common nerve) where perception takes place. Therefore, they must somehow bend in the optic nerve. (Modern studies have shown that the optic nerve is not on the line of sight but about 16° to the nasal or inner side of it.)

more distant optic chiasma. The lengthening of the visual axis due to this refraction is shown in Figure 1. Even with this refraction, however, there is a difficulty, which Bacon acknowledges, in that the optic chiasma is not in a straight line with the object seen, so that the visual rays must travel "along a tortuous line" (Figure 2). Bacon has no optical explanation for how they do this. Instead, "owing to the necessity and nobility of the processes of the soul, species in an animated medium keeps to the path of the medium and disregards the common laws of natural multiplications, rejoicing in the special privilege of the soul."[49]

Bacon spends some time resolving optical problems with the account, for example, the question of why the species that are transmitted through the medium do not mix there but instead remain separate.[50] To enable the transmission of these species, the medium must be enabled, and this, according to Bacon, is performed by the issue of animal spirit from the eyes. Thus having adopted Alhazen's intromission theory, which is perfectly capable of explaining all the optical phenomena discussed, Bacon refuses to reject extramission completely. His stated reason for retaining some element of extramission is as follows:

Vision must perform the act of seeing by its own force. But the act of seeing is the perception of a visible object at a distance, and therefore vision perceives what is visible by its own force multiplied to the object. Moreover, the species of the things of the world are not fitted by nature to effect the complete act of vision at once because of its nobleness. Hence these must be aided and excited by the species of the eye, which travels in the locality of the visual pyramid, and changes the medium and ennobles it, and renders it analogous to vision, and so prepares the passage of the species itself of the visible object, and, moreover, ennobles it, so that it is quite similar and analogous to the nobility of the animate body, which is the eye.[51]

Perhaps to this reason, however, should be added the outlook of a medieval scholar whose first instinct was to try to reconcile apparently opposed accounts. Early in his optical account Bacon states that he will confine his

description of the structure of the eye mainly to three authorities [Alhazen, Constantinus, and Avicenna]; for these writers are sufficient and they treat more definitely the matters in which we are interested. I cannot, however, give the exact words of each, because they are sometimes at variance owing to faulty translation, but from them all I shall form a single statement of the truth.[52]

The accounts of Greek or Arabic experts, for Bacon as for many of his contemporaries, might differ from each other because of textual or translation difficulties, not because they were really in disagreement.

Although much of the remainder of Bacon's account of optical science deals with physical optics and is of little psychological interest, there are also interesting discussions of aspects of visual perception in the second part of the *Opus Majus*, which is concerned with direct vision. Bacon considers the circumstances in which objects will be seen as single or double and even suggests that the reader construct a board and place small objects in different places on it to demonstrate the phenomenon for himself. Bacon's treatment of the issue throughout is both accurate and experimental.[53]

Perhaps most interesting from a psychological point of view is his discussion of size constancy and illusion. Following Alhazen, Bacon is at pains to point out that perception cannot be wholly explained by sensory processes, and that knowledge and reasoning are also involved. Provided the distance of an object is moderate, it is judged by virtue of the presence of a continuous series of sensible objects lying between the eye and the remote object.[54] Knowledge is necessary here because the eye must have viewed the objects and "made certain of their measurements."[55] At extreme distances, distance judgment can break down. "Therefore both sun and moon appear to be plane surfaces although they are spheres";[56] the nearer point of the moon, for example, does not appear nearer than the apparent circumference.

The estimation of size is also the result of a reasoning process. Bacon correctly points out that the size of the angle made by the object at the eye does not determine the perceived size of the object. It is also necessary to know the distance of the object, which is, as we have just seen, determined by the size and number of known intermediate objects. When the angle and distance of the object are known, its size can be calculated on geometrical principles.[57]

This analysis of the estimation of distance and size can be used to explain the moon illusion in which the moon—Bacon actually spoke of the stars—appears larger near the horizon than when it is directly overhead.

It can be explained owing to the fact that the vision judges the sky as though it were a plane figure extended above the head to the east and to the west, when the eye looks toward either of these. But what is seen near the head seems nearer, and therefore a star when it is at the meridian seems to be nearer, and therefore when on the horizon it seems to be more distant. But what seems to be more distant seems to be larger, since it is seen under the same angle, just as a matter of fact what is more distant is larger since it is seen under the same angle with a smaller object.[58]

It is worth remarking that this explanation of the moon illusion is often quoted today, and, in fact, Bacon's whole approach to distance and size estimation is surprisingly modern in conception.

Bacon's account of vision contains little that was really new. In particular, as he acknowledges, there is a huge debt to Alhazen. On the other hand, the account is a clear advance over that offered by Aristotle, in complexity, in the range of phenomena addressed, and in physiological detail. This advance illustrates the fact that, while Aristotle was greatly respected in the Middle Ages, his authority was frequently questioned and alternatives preferred where they appeared to offer greater explanatory power.

SENSES OTHER THAN VISION

The progress made in understanding visual phenomena in the Middle Ages was not matched by a similar progress in understanding other sensory modalities. In fact, throughout the Middle Ages there was a tendency to ignore the other senses and concentrate on vision, while expressing the conviction that the general principles applying to vision should also hold true for the other senses. Augustine supplied both an example and a model for this practice:

It is both a good deal of trouble, and is not necessary, that we should enquire of all these five senses about that which we seek. For that which one of them declares to us, holds also good in the rest. Let us use, then, principally the testimony of the eyes.[59]

Probably the main advance over Aristotle that occurred in the subsequent theorizing about the minor senses was in the elaboration of sensory physiology. Perhaps the discussion of the sense of smell provides the clearest example. It seems to have been recognized quite early on that this sense has a rather different neural arrangement than the other senses. Nemesius stated that the sense of smell differed from the other senses in not possessing a sensory nerve at all. Instead he believed that the surface of the brain perceived the vapors directly via small holes in the nasal cavity.[60] Nemesius' view is not in fact correct, but it is true that the neural connections between the nose and the cortex are more direct than for any other sense.

Avicenna described the faculty of smell as "located in the two protuberances of the front part of the brain which resemble the two nipples of the breasts."[61] This description, which clearly refers to the olfactory bulbs, is echoed in subsequent medieval accounts. Bacon, for example, also refers to the olfactory process as extending "between the two nipples near the brain."[62]

The description of the olfactory nerves is an example of the influence of Galen's anatomical writings on medieval perceptual accounts. Galen's extensive discussions of the sensory nerves, their anatomy, and presumed functions filled an obvious gap in Aristotle's discussion of sensory processes and in consequence were widely used in the Middle Ages.[63] Galenic influence in this respect occurred even in the early part of the period: both Augustine and Nemesius discuss the sensory nerves of the minor senses.[64]

The network of sensory nerves serving the senses of touch and taste as described by Galen were known in the Middle Ages.[65] Avicenna also clearly enunciated a view often expressed since: that the sense of touch could be regarded as a number of quite separate faculties: "Probably [touch] is not one species but a genus including four faculties which are all distributed throughout the skin. . . . But their coexistence in the same organ [i.e., the skin] gives the false impression that they are essentially one."[66] Avicenna's four faculties sensed temperature, moistness, hardness or softness, and surface roughness or smoothness.

It is unsurprising that little attention in the Middle Ages was paid to the chemical senses or touch because these senses are today referred to as the minor senses, and, as Aristotle and his medieval commentators remarked, they are less important for human perception than vision and hearing. Indeed, modern research into perception reflects this ancient and medieval bias. The minor senses are still much less well understood

than vision or hearing, and perceptual textbooks, like the medieval scholars, devote relatively little space to their description.

In contrast, however, modern researchers have not ignored the investigation of hearing, while the medieval accounts of hearing are often
even briefer than those given of smell or taste. In view of the obvious
importance of the sense for communication, the lack of interest, or at
any rate of detailed description, is hard to explain. Possibly the relative
inaccessibility of the cochlea, the organ of hearing, which is both delicate
and almost completely encased in bone, made its study diffcult. Whatever the reason both the psychology of hearing and the psychology of
speech and language received little medieval attention.

CONCLUSIONS

Although medieval accounts of perception were heavily influenced by
Aristotle, his theory was by no means slavishly followed. Bacon's account of vision, although agreeing with Aristotle in regarding vision as
fundamentally due to intromission, owed much less to him than to
Alhazen or even Avicenna. Even in the minor senses, where much less
substantial progress is evident than in vision, Aristotle's account was
often enriched by Galen's physiology.

Some of the issues raised by the ancient and medieval debate over
the nature of visual perception correspond to issues raised in the present-
day study of perception. In modern terms, the intromission-extramission
question can be partially viewed as a debate over whether vision is
primarily a passive or an active process. Extramission, in which visual
rays or spirit are directed by the perceiver, is clearly an active process,
whereas intromission in which the eyes receive input from the outside
world, is a more passive description. Note, however, that even within
the intromission models some scope was allowed for active processing
of the incoming stimulus. In Aristotle's intromission scheme, for example, the potential of the sense organ is brought into action by the
stimulus object.[67] In Bacon's account of visual perception, the application
of reasoning and knowledge, as well as the simple sensing of the object,
is necessary for the estimation of size of the object.

In twentieth-century perception, the role of active processes has also
been debated, although not, of course, within the context of an extramission model of visual perception. In the approach of J. J. Gibson and
other proponents of "direct perception," the role of the perceiver in
actively searching out and constantly interacting with the environment
is emphasized.[68] Such an approach seems to have been particularly pro-
ductive in describing a perceiver who is moving through the environment. At the other extreme are some of the physiologically based
accounts of vision in which the visual process is characterized by a set

of fixed processes through which the representation of the stimulus is successively passed. Frequently such accounts are passive, in the sense that little allowance is made for higher-order processes to modify the operation of the lower ones so as, for example, actively to select out important stimuli or important aspects of the stimulus.[69]

Another issue in modern psychology that parallels one raised in medieval perception concerns the extent to which perception is direct. In Bacon's account, as we have seen, the distance of an external object can only be determined after a process involving memory and reasoning. Moreover, calculation is required to deduce the object's size from the sensed visual angle of the image and the inferred distance away of the object. In such an account, which is quite close to that given by many present-day perceptual theorists, the perception of the size and distance of the object is indirect, as it is mediated by cognitive processes. An alternative modern approach, again suggested by Gibson, is that perception is direct and does not require mediating processes, and in particular does not require knowledge of the object. In this approach the distance, for example, of objects is specified directly by a variety of stimulus cues available in the real world, such as the object's height in the visual field or its textural detail, and does not depend on memory or cognitive processing.[70]

Again Gibson's approach seems to have been anticipated. Some of the earlier extramission accounts in which the soul was held to extend beyond the body clearly implied a form of direct perception. A direct account seems also to have been held by William of Ockham, who criticized the way in which representations of the stimulus were generated by different internal processes in the conventional medieval account of perception. He, in fact, denied the existence of these representations or species, holding instead that perception is an intuitive rather than an abstractive process. As such, the senses and intellect apprehend the external objects directly.[71]

One final aspect of medieval perception, which does not appear to have a parallel in modern psychology, needs to be mentioned. The idea that the sensed species of an object acts as a kind of sign from which the nature or form of the real object could be inferred was itself seen as a metaphor by which objects themselves could act as signs denoting a higher theological reality.[72] Augustine himself was an influential advocate of this view. In his work, *On the Trinity*, he finds a kind of trinity in the perceptual process itself, in which the physical object, the vision or image of the object, and the attention of the mind are united. This process then is a metaphor, although not in Augustine's view a particularly good one, by which the Trinity of Father, Son, and Holy Ghost can be partially understood.[73] A less obscure and more common aspect of the medieval belief may be found in the statement of Bonaventure

(1221–1274) "that the invisible things of God are clearly seen, from the creation of the world, being understood by the things that are made."[74] The world, according to this view, was created to indicate higher spiritual realities and has no other purpose beyond that. Indeed, as Augustine argued, it is spiritually harmful to make use of perception merely to become "a connoisseur of sauces . . . or to date a wine by its vintage."[75] This kind of reasoning was quite common—although not universal—in the Middle Ages, and it is possible that some of the interest shown in visual perception was because its study suggested ways in which spiritual realities might be understood when the "sign" of the external world was correctly deciphered.

NOTES

1. Although some caution is needed here. In particular, Aristotle's account of sensation and perception is by no means purely a passive one.

2. For some general accounts of medieval perception, see Peter K. Machammer and Robert G. Turnbull, eds., *Studies in Perception* (Columbus: Ohio State University Press, 1978); G. A. Kmiek, M. L. LaDriere, and R. T. Zegers, "The Role of the Sensible Species in St. Thomas' Epistemology: A Comparison with Contemporary Perception Theory," *International Philosophical Quarterly* 14 (1974): 455–474; and David C. Lindberg, *Theories of Vision from Al-Kindi to Kepler* (London: University of Chicago Press, 1976).

3. Augustine, *On the Trinity*, 11.2.3–4.

4. Aristotle, *De Sensu et Sensibili*, trans. J. I. Beare. In W. D. Ross, ed., *The Works of Aristotle*, Vol. 3 (Oxford, UK: Clarendon, 1931).

5. Aristotle, *De Anima*, 2.6.418a.

6. Ibid., 3.1.425b. Incidentally, some indication of the authority of Aristotle is given by the prevalence of this belief today, although the senses of balance and kinesthetic feedback conform to all the usual definitions of a sense.

7. Ibid., 2.7.419a.

8. Aristotle, *De Sensu*, 2.438b.

9. Aristotle, *De Anima*, 2.8.419b–420a.

10. Aristotle, *De Sensu*, 1.437a.

11. Aristotle, *De Anima*, 2.9.421a.

12. Aristotle, *De Sensu*, 5.443b–444b.

13. Aristotle, *De Anima*, 2.9.422a.

14. Aristotle, *De Sensu,*, 4.441a–442b.

15. Aristotle, *De Anima*, 2.11.422b–424a.

16. Ibid., 3.13.435b.

17. Aristotle, *De Sensu*, 6.

18. Ibid., 7.447a.

19. Ibid. The example is mine.

20. Ibid., 7.447b.

21. Aristotle, *De Anima*, 3.1–3.

22. Aristotle, *De Somniis*, 2.459a–459b.

23. Nemesius, *A Treatise on the Nature of Man*, 332; Avicenna, *Avicenna's*

Psychology: An English Translation of Kitab Al-Najat, Bk. II, Ch. VI with Historico-Philosophical Notes and Textual Improvements on the Cairo Edition, trans. F. Rahman (London: Oxford University Press, 1952), 31; Bartholomaeus Anglicus, *On the Properties of Things*, 120; Aquinas, *Summa Theologiae*, 1.78.3; Nicholas H. Steneck, "Albert on the Psychology of Sense Perception." In James A. Weisheipl, ed., *Albertus Magnus and the Sciences: Commemorative Essays, 1980* (Toronto: Pontifical Institute of Medieval Studies, 1980).

24. Aquinas, *Commentaria*, 2.20.494.

25. For example, Nemesius, *A Treatise on the Nature of Man*, 320–328.

26. Avicenna, *Avicenna's Psychology*, 31.

27. A recent account of medieval optics with a good coverage of the optical and physiological aspects of the extramission-intromission debate is given by Lindberg, *Theories of Vision*.

28. See D. R. Griffin, *Echoes of Bats and Men* (New York: Doubleday, 1959); and W. N. Kellogg, "Sonar System of the Blind." *Science* 137 (1962): 399–404.

29. Nemesius, *A Treatise on the Nature of Man*, 325.

30. Ibid., 328.

31. E.g., George A. Miller, "The Magical Number Seven; Plus or Minus Two: Some Limits on Our Capacity for Processing Information." *Psychological Review* 63 (1956): 81–97.

32. Augustine, *The Literal Meaning of Genesis*, 3.5.7.

33. Nemesius, *A Treatise on the Nature of Man*, 324.

34. Augustine, *The Greatness of the Soul*, 66. It should be noted that this account does not quite square with that given in *On the Trinity* Bk. 11 or *The Literal Meaning of Genesis*.

35. Plato, *Timaeus*, 61–62; and Galen, *On the Doctrines of Hippocrates and Plato*, 7.4.4–11. A good summary of Galen's theory of vision is given by Rudolph E. Siegel, *Galen on Sense Perception; His Doctrines, Observations and Experiments on Vision, Hearing, Smell, Taste, Touch, and Pain, and Their Historical Sources* (Basel, Switzerland: Karger, 1970).

36. Galen, *On the Doctrines of Hippocrates and Plato*, 7.4.18.

37. Ibid., 7.5.5ff.

38. Lindberg, *Theories of Vision*, 11–17.

39. Ibid., 2.

40. Ibid., 18–85, on which the following summary is based. See also David C. Lindberg, "The Intromission-Extramission Controversy in Islamic Visual Theory: Alkindi Versus Avicenna." In Peter K. Machammer and Robert G. Turnbull, eds., *Studies in Perception* (Columbus, Ohio State University Press, 1978), 137–159.

41. Summaries of Alhazen's theory are given by Lindberg, *Theories of Vision*, 58–86, and A. I. Sabra, "Sensation and Inference in Alhazen's Theory of Visual Perception." In Peter K. Machammer and Robert G. Turnbull, *Studies in Perception* (Columbus: Ohio State University Press, 1978), 160–185.

42. Sabra, "Sensation and Inference," 179.

43. Roger Bacon, *Opus Majus*, trans. Robert B. Burke (New York: Russell & Russell, 1962).

44. Ibid., 420.

45. Ibid., 421–427.

46. Avicenna, *Avicenna's Psychology*, 30–31.
47. Bacon, *Opus Majus*, 435.
48. Ibid., 457.
49. Ibid., 467–468.
50. Ibid., 458–465.
51. Ibid., 471.
52. Ibid., 430.
53. Ibid., 510–516.
54. Ibid., 523.
55. Ibid., 524.
56. Ibid., 525.
57. Ibid., 530–531.
58. Ibid., 532–533.
59. Augustine, *On the Trinity*, 11.1.1.
60. Nemesius, *A Treatise on the Nature of Man*, 337.
61. Avicenna, *Avicenna's Psychology*, 26.
62. Bacon, *Opus Majus*, 452.
63. See Galen, *On the Doctrines of Hippocrates and Plato*, Bks. 6 and 7; Galen, *On the Usefulness of the Parts of the Body*, Bks. 8–10; and Siegel, *Galen on Sense Perception*, 127–193.
64. Augustine, *The Literal Meaning of Genesis*, 7.13.20–23; Nemesius, *A Treatise on the Nature of Man*, 331–337.
65. For example, John XXI (Pedro Hispano), *Scientia Libri de Anima*, ed. P. Manuel Alonso (Madrid: Bolanos and Aguilar, 1941), 6.10–11.
66. Avicenna, *Avicenna's Psychology*, 27.
67. Aristotle, *De Anima*, 2.5.
68. E.g., J. J. Gibson, *The Ecological Approach to Visual Perception* (Boston: Houghton-Mifflin, 1979); and C. F. Michaels and C. Carello, *Direct Perception* (Englewood Cliffs, N.J.: Prentice-Hall, 1981).
69. For example, David Marr, *Vision* (San Francisco: Freeman, 1982).
70. J. J. Gibson, *The Perception of the Visual World* (Cambridge, Mass.: Riverside, 1950). See also the references in note 68.
71. See Leff, *William of Ockham*, 2–55; and Lindberg, *Theories of Vision*, 140–142.
72. Umberto Eco's novel *The Name of the Rose*, trans. W. Weaver (London: Seeker and Warburg, 1983) takes this belief as one of its themes.
73. Augustine, *On the Trinity*, 11.
74. Bonaventure, *The Mind's Road to God*, trans. G. Boas (Indianapolis, Ind.: Bobbs-Merrill, 1953), 21.
75. Augustine, *The Greatness of the Soul*, 53.

4

Medieval Cognition and Memory

The distinction between perception and cognition is not always clear in present-day psychology. It is even less clear in medieval psychology and indeed no particular effort was expended by medieval scholars on trying to distinguish them. Thus the division of material between this chapter and the preceding one follows a modern rather than a medieval dichotomy. Some indication of the essentially arbitrary nature of the division imposed is that the doctrine of cognitive processing that we consider next was generally described in the Middle Ages as an account of the inner senses.

THE INNER SENSES

The inner senses or inward wits were psychological faculties that, throughout the Middle Ages, were assumed to be located in the ventricles of the brain.[1] These ventricles were supposed to be sense organs performing functions such as remembering or imagining in the same way that the eye was responsible for seeing or the ear for hearing. The theory was created by assigning the various perceptual and cognitive facilities identified by Aristotle in his *De Anima* to the spirit-filled cerebral ventricles described by Galen in his discussion of the anatomy of the brain.[2] However, neither of these writers attempted the combination of these two different elements. Aristotle seems to have held that the sensory center and the cognitive faculties were housed in the region of the heart and not in the brain at all.[3] Galen firmly rejected Aristotle's location of the faculties in the heart and placed them in the brain, but in the body of the brain itself and not in the ventricles. Galen, in fact, seems to have employed vivisection in coming to the conclusion that the soul is located in the actual brain matter, and that the spirit that fills the ventricles and the nerves acts as its instrument.[4]

Precisely who was responsible for formulating the theory is unclear but the basic idea of ascribing different faculties to the ventricles is contained in the writings of both Augustine and Nemesius. In Augustine's account, the front ventricle serves as the sensory center, the middle as the seat of memory, and the rear as the initiator of motion.[5] This version of the theory, however, was without subsequent influence. In Nemesius' version, the front ventricle contains the faculty of imagination, the middle that of intellect, and the rear that of memory.[6] In the Middle Ages, belief in something like Nemesius' version of the theory was practically universal among both scholars and physicians, although there was some debate about the details.

Although Galen had given a fairly accurate decription of the placement of the ventricles in the brain, their complex anatomy tended to be simplified in medieval accounts into a linear arrangement. Lanfranc in his *Science of Cirurgie*, written about 1295 A.D., states that the front ventricle is the largest and feeds into the middle ventricle, which is the smallest of the three, broader at the front than the back and operating like a worm. The smaller end of the middle ventricle enters the rear ventricle, which is also broader in front and sharper to the rear.[7] Figure 3 illustrates this simplifed medieval arrangement and, by way of contrast, the actual anatomy. Although the medieval arrangement is clearly grossly inaccurate, it is important to note that it makes good psychological, if not physiological, sense. The medieval arrangement preserves the order in which the incoming information—in medieval terminology the species—was believed to be processed. Species were transmitted to the front ventricle by the sensory nerves, were processed there, and were passed on to the middle ventricle, and thence to the rear ventricle.

In Nemesius' account of the inner senses, only three faculties, those of imagination, intellect, and memory, were proposed. The faculty of imagination handed on sensory and perceptual information to the faculty of intellect and then the faculty of intellect made judgments on the basis of the information received and passed these on to the faculty of memory.[8] Nemesius' system of faculties and his apportionment of them to the ventricles was used subsequently—very similar systems were suggested by Albertus Magnus for human cognition and by medical writers such as Bartholomaeus Anglicus and Lanfranc.[9] Also common, however, was a more complex and detailed system suggested by Avicenna.[10] This

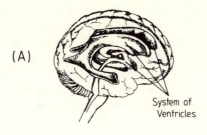

(A)

System of
Ventricles

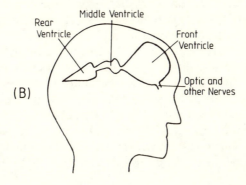

Middle Ventricle

Rear
Ventricle

Front
Ventricle

Optic and
other Nerves

(B)

Figure 3. Actual and medieval versions of the anatomy of the cerebral ventricles. A shows the actual placement of the system of cerebral ventricles in the human brain; B shows the medieval idea of their placement in the head. (The medieval version is based on the description in Lanfranc's *Science of Cirurgie*, but I have also taken into consideration an actual medieval drawing reproduced as the frontispiece to E. Ruth Harvey's, *The Inward Wits*.)

system, with minor variations, appeared in, for example, the *De Anima* of Pope John XXI, Albertus Magnus' account of animal cognition, and Bacon's *Opus Majus*.[11] In this system there are five faculties, two apportioned to each of the first two ventricles, and one to the last. The first faculty, that of the common sense (*sensus communis*), is housed in the front of the front ventricle and performs the perceptual function identified by Aristotle and discussed in the preceding chapter. The common sense acts quickly and does not retain the sensation inspired by a stimulus if the stimulus is removed. A longer lasting record is supplied by the faculty of imagination (*imaginatio*),[12] which is located at the rear of the front ventricle and which can retain images because it is drier and less slippery than the front of the ventricle. A frequently used medieval analogy to illustrate the difference between the common sense and the imagination was to consider the different impressions made by a seal or some other solid object on water and on wax. In water the impression is instant, but it vanishes when the object is removed. The impression in wax, on the other hand, is retained.[13] The faculty of imagination thus provides a storehouse of sensible forms. The faculties of imagination and common sense together perform the functions now described as visual imagery. If I wish to recall, say, the color of a bee's head, to use one of Stephen Kosslyn's recent examples, the sensible form of the previously seen bee is transmitted back to the common sense, where it is visualized.[14]

The medieval account of imagination actually bears a marked resemblance to Kosslyn's account of visual imagery. In the modern account, stored representations of a previously seen stimulus are projected on to a surface, analogous to the operation of a cathode ray tube. This representation is then viewed by a "mind's eye interpretive function."[15] A similar account of visual imagery is given by Augustine who describes the copying in the mind's eye of a previously perceived and retained form or species. This process, for both Kosslyn and Augustine, resembles the process of perception itself. "In place of that vision which was outward when the sense was informed through the sensible body, there comes a similar vision within, while the eye of the mind is informed from that which the memory retains, and the corporeal things that are thought of are absent."[16]

The nature of visual imagery is currently a hotly debated issue, particularly as to whether the process is entirely an abstract one in which images are remembered as propositions or whether some picturelike representation is used.[17] Clearly the medieval answer was that the representation is picturelike, and the propositional possibility was rarely considered at all. Avicenna, however, did consider alternative possibilities, at least to the extent of giving some reason why a physical, internal representation of the image on a bodily substrate should be preferred.

The imagined form as we imagine it, e.g. the form of man, is sometimes big and sometimes small. Now when these big and small forms are imprinted, they must be imprinted on one and the same thing not on a number of similar things, for if they were imprinted on the latter then their difference in size [could not] be attributed to their essential nature. . . .

Moreover, we cannot imagine black and white together in the same imagined figure, although we can imagine them in two different parts of it. Now if these two parts were not distinct in position but both imagined forms were imprinted on one single indivisible thing as independent units as it were, not as parts of the same thing, we should not be able to distinguish between the impossible and the possible of the two cases. The two parts are therefore distinct in position.[18]

A feature of the medieval account of imagination was the general recognition, again following Aristotle's lead, that dreaming reflected the activity of the common sense and the imagination.[19] In Augustine's view, for example, dreams, whether they had visionary significance or not, were basically similar to visual images experienced when awake.[20] A good summary of the medieval belief is provided by Averroes:

[During sleep], after the imaginative faculty has formed an image of the object, which it has received either externally or from the memorative faculty, it, in turn, will move the common sense and the common sense, in turn, will move its faculties. . . . Sometimes, a similar condition will occur during waking to one who is frightened or sick, and this as a result of the excessive activity of the imaginative faculty on such occasions. . . . Indeed the movement of the imaginative faculty will be excessive during sleep because it is released from the bond of the cogitative faculty and is no longer subject to its control.[21]

Curiously the probable connection between processes involved in dreaming and those involved in wakeful cognition has been rather neglected by modern psychology. This neglect probably results from the fact that much twentieth-century research on dreaming has been inspired by Sigmund Freud's views on the subject and he was relatively uninterested in this aspect of dreaming.[22] There has, however, been at least one recent attempt to relate dream phenomena to the findings of modern cognitive psychology.[23]

The retained forms present in the imagination are passed on to the middle ventricle. In the front of this ventricle is located the cogitative faculty (*imaginativa* or *cogitativa*), which has the power to create new visual images from the forms contained in the imagination. Thus, for example, a flying horse or a golden mountain can be visualized even though they have never been seen in the external world. Their images are constructed from components retained in the imagination, for example, the known appearance of gold and the shape of a previously seen mountain. Bacon described the cogitative faculty in lyrical terms as

the mistress of the sensitive faculties and . . . is the ultimate perfection of brutes just as reason is in man, and because the rational soul in man is united directly with it. By this faculty the spider weaves its geometrical web, and the bee makes its hexagonal house, choosing one of the figures that fill out space, and the swallow its nest. . . . Man by means of this faculty sees wonderful things in dreams, and all the faculties both posterior and anterior . . . obey it. . . . In man there is an addition . . . the rational soul, which is united with the cogitative faculty primarily and immediately, and uses this faculty chiefly as its own special instrument. Species [intelligible, not sensible] are formed in the rational soul by this faculty.[24]

Bacon's designation of the cogitative power as the mistress of the faculties was not followed by all medieval scholars. Indeed, Thomas Aquinas believed that there were only four inner senses and discarded the cogitative power completely on the grounds that the power to combine images was unnecessary for animals, and performed by the imagination alone in humans.[25]

In the rear of the central ventricle is the estimative faculty or instinct (*aestimativa*) "which perceives the non-sensible intentions [*intentiones*] that exist in the individual sensible objects, like the faculty which judges that the wolf is to be avoided."[26] The faculty assesses imagined or perceived forms for whether they indicate a threat or an aid to the self-preservation of the organism. In humans such a function is provided in part by the rational soul, but in animals this function is provided wholly by the faculty of instinct. It is interesting to note that in postulating the existence of this faculty, medieval writers clearly recognized that the potential for harm or good was not explicit in the perception itself. Instead the perception had to be interpreted in terms of previously experienced or innate knowledge.

Finally, the rear ventricle contains the memory, which acts as a storehouse for the cogitative and estimative faculties, just as imagination does for the common sense. For animals the contents of this memory consist mainly of intentions—for example, a dog might run away from a stick because it has previously been beaten by one and retains a memory of the experience. For humans, however, the content was more debatable because the rational soul itself was often held to contain a memory.[27]

While the doctrine of the inner senses was known in outline form to the Christian medieval scholars, most of the accounts given describe it in little more detail than has been given here. Many important issues— at least to a present-day psychologist—such as how the cogitative faculty could retrieve particular forms from the countless numbers that must be contained in the imagination, seem not to have been considered at all. Where attempts were made to explain the system at work, the results were often crude. Costa ben Luca (864–923 A.D.) gave the following explanation of how memory, housed in the rear ventricle, might be made available to the faculty of cogitation: "He who wishes to remember something tilts his head steeply, or turns about tilting it backwards, and gazes upwards with unmoving eyes, for this position and stance is of assistance to him in opening that little aperture [between the middle and the rear ventricles]."[28] His explanation, however, seems to have found little favor with succeeding writers.

Perhaps the most puzzling thing to the modern reader about the medieval doctrine of the inner senses is why it was accepted at all. Not only is the doctrine completely false in its physiological aspects—the ventricles of the brain fulfill no psychological functions at all—but also the adoption of the doctrine meant that the rational soul had many of its psychological functions stripped from it. This was awkward from a theological point of view. How would the immortal and incorporeal soul be able to remember anything or form visual images when deprived of its inner senses? This issue was particularly important for philosophers such as Nemesius and Avicenna who held the Neoplatonic view that the soul acted through the body, and after a certain stage of development no longer needed its external or internal senses. Hence one might inquire as to what theoretical advantages were obtained from the doctrine of the inner senses that rendered it attractive to medieval thinkers. The answer seems to be that the doctrine produced an explanation for two facts that were otherwise difficult to explain: that human psychological disorders often follow head injury and that the behavior of animals suggests some sort of information processing capacity on their part.

That disordered thinking often results from head injury seems to have been well known to the ancient physicians, and some of Galen's case studies were discussed by medieval scholars. An indication of the sort of thinking that took place is given by Nemesius:

The most convincing proof [of the doctrine of the inner senses] is that derived from studying the activities of the various parts of the brain. If the front ventricles have suffered any kind of lesion, the senses are impaired but the faculty of intellect continues as before. It is when the middle of the brain is affected that the mind is deranged, but then the senses are left in possession of their natural faculties. . . . Galen describes such a case of a man suffering from inflammation of the brain who was in a room, with a weaver working there. This man started up and took hold of some glass vessels, and running to a window he demanded of the passers-by whether they would like him to throw down such and such a glass vessel, naming each correctly. When some stopped and said that they would, he first threw the vessels down, one by one, and then asked those who were there whether they would like the weaver thrown down. Some of them, taking the whole thing for a joke, said, Yes. The man thereupon took and pushed the weaver out, and down he went![29]

As Nemesius points out this is not a case of a sensory problem, because the man could name the glass vessels correctly and discriminate them from the weaver. Therefore some other, higher cognitive faculty must have been impaired, and, because the man's brain was inflamed, it follows logically that at least some cognitive functioning must be mediated by parts of the brain.

The doctrine was also suggested by the behavior of animals. It was universally accepted in the Middle Ages that animals did not possess rational souls as humans did. Yet they exhibited "intelligent" behavior by, for example, building webs or hives or by showing evidence of learning, like the dog cringing from the stick it had been beaten with. Clearly they must possess some kind of information processing capacity, and, equally, as this capacity could not be provided by an incorporeal, immortal soul, the capacity must have physiological, material organs. That such reasoning was important in the Middle Ages is indicated by the fact that most of the examples of the faculties of the inner senses in action referred to animal rather than human behavior.

The fact that humans show psychological disorders after brain damage, coupled with Galen's failure to report differences in structure between animal and human brains, suggested that the inner senses should be the same for humans and animals. Hence Aquinas, for example, disbelieved in the existence of a separate cogitative faculty in the middle ventricle because animals did not need to combine portions of images.[30] This view, however, was not universally accepted: Albertus Magnus held that the faculties, and their places in the ventricles, were different in animals and man.[31]

Although modern psychology has undertaken extensive research into correlating brain structure and processes with psychological processes, no modern theory undertakes such an ambitious union of the two as did the medieval doctrine of the inner senses. In fact, modern theories of, for example, visual imagery typically ignore the question of physiological representation altogether. Despite this difference, however, the medieval theory has much in common with the kind of theories that have dominated cognitive psychology in the last twenty years but were relatively uninfluential before, say, 1960. Like these theories, the medieval account is basically an information-processing model: incoming sensory information is transformed or processed in stages, and the output of each stage or level of processing becomes the input for the next stage. Normally in modern accounts the stages are given functional rather than anatomical or physical labels. For example, a common present-day model of how a list of words may be remembered is that the words pass through a short-term store, which holds "images" of the words in acoustic form, following which the "images" are passed to a longer-term store in which the words are represented by their meaning rather than their sound.[32] In the modern and medieval accounts different processing stages or different cerebral ventricles are responsible for the production of different representations or species of the external information.

Despite the lack of detail in the medieval doctrine it proved useful in helping to explain a range of psychological phenomena, some of which remain to be examined in later chapters of this book. Moreover some aspects of it, especially the account given of visual imagery and the way in which animal behavior was explained, seem ingenious. It is perhaps ironic that part of the success of this physiologically based doctrine should derive precisely from the fact that the physiology was quite wrong. The erroneous linear placement of the ventricles enabled the development of an information processing model. It is difficult to see how any such model could have been constructed from their actual anatomical arrangement.

Despite the range of mental processes that were wholly or partly explained by the doctrine, it was never supposed to be a complete account of these processes in animals. Humans, who possessed a rational soul as well as inner senses, had cognitive capabilities that extended well beyond those attributed to the ventricles of the brain. These higher capabilities made use of the information provided by the inner senses, sometimes called the intelligible species, in the same way as the person as a whole made use of the sensible species, the information available from the external world. The next section considers the medieval accounts of the contribution of the rational soul to cognition.

COGNITION AND THEORIES OF KNOWLEDGE IN MEDIEVAL PHILOSOPHY

The medieval accounts of sensation and perception and the doctrine of the inner senses that have been considered so far have been largely concerned with the specification of the physiological mechanisms responsible for the psychological processing of incoming information. Still remaining however is the problem of how the rational soul comes to know anything about reality. In effect the adoption of the doctrine of the inner senses delayed the problem—instead of considering how reality is inferred from information presented to the senses, i.e., the sensible species, the problem is now one of how reality is inferred from information present in the ventricles. The essence of the problem, however, is unchanged: how does one get from a material representation to a mental representation, that is, a representation in the incorporeal soul?

To a modern reader, both problem and solution may seem to be a part of philosophy rather than psychology, and the issues involved are today generally studied by philosophers rather than psychologists. As, however, the problem has psychological as well as philosophical relevance, and, moreover, as the fields were hardly differentiated at all in the Middle Ages, it is worthwhile to examine the issues briefly here.

According to the Platonic theory of knowledge there is a qualitative difference between matter and form. External objects have a form that is immaterial and can be extracted from its matter somewhere in the perceptual process. Another way of putting this is to say that a universal, ideal form can be intimated from a particular image of an object or a universal truth from particular examples. Human beings are composed of material bodies and immaterial souls. Material objects in the outside world are sensed by the (also material) external and internal senses. The forms that are implicit in the material world, however, are perceived not by the senses but by the rational soul. Thus the dichotomy of matter and form in the external world corresponds to a dichotomy in the perceiver: matter is sensed by the body, form by the soul. In Aristotle's succinct summary the soul is "the place of forms."[33]

Now this basic dichotomy of matter and form, which also relates to distinctions between particulars and universals, was commonly recognized by philosophers in the Middle Ages, particularly because the distinction was also adhered to by Aristotle.[34] The obvious problem raised by this distinction was a critical issue in the Middle Ages: How are the forms obtained or abstracted from the external world or from sensory information? At first sight, the species available to the mind in the inner senses seem to provide the answer. As Avicenna pointed out, these faculties do provide some degree of abstraction "for, even after the absence or corruption of matter, the form remains in the representative faculty." But "even here it is not divested of its material accidents,"[35] because not only is sensory information retained but also the faculties themselves require bodily organs for their functioning, as is shown by the way that visual imagery works.[36]

The Neoplatonic answer to the problem of how the mind abstracts forms and universals from species is simple, if surprising. It doesn't. Instead these concepts are innately present in the mind already. Augustine, in his *Confessions*, gave a good summary of this idea:

Whence and how did these things enter into my memory? I do not know. For when I first learned them, it was not that I believed them on the credit of another man's mind, but I recognized them in my own; and I saw them as true, took them into my mind and laid them up, so to say, where I could get at them again whenever I willed. There they were, then, even before I learned them, but they were not in my memory. Where were they, then? How does it come about that when they were spoken of, I could acknowledge them and say, "So it is, it is true," unless they were already in the memory, though far back and hidden, as it were, in the more secret caves.[37]

A philosophical difficulty raised by this belief is the question of what benefit there is to the mind in receiving sensory information about the outside world at all. The usual answer to this, given by Augustine himself, is that some contact with the external world is necessary to "remind" the mind of what it already contains. This purpose served, further interest in the sensory world, as would be entailed by becoming a connoisseur of wines, for example, is not only unnecessary but also spiritually damaging. Augustine's basic reasoning, which was quite common in the Middle Ages although never universally accepted,[38] was elaborated by various subsequent scholars, most notably Bonaventure, who, as we have seen, held that the world was especially created redolent with symbols to serve just this purpose.[39] Curiously enough, even Avicenna, whose philosophy begins as a commentary on Aristotle, arrived at a rather similar conclusion: "When the soul becomes perfect and strong, it isolates itself absolutely in its actions, and the faculties of sensation and imagination and all the other bodily faculties divert it from its activities."[40] A man, he goes on to say, may use a horse to travel to a place, but once arrived has no further use for it. For Avicenna, as for Augustine, Bonaventure, and the Christian mystics, the mind, having acquired or reminded itself of the principles of reality, should engage in contemplation.

Now as a theory of cognition, or of how one acquires or uses knowledge, all this may appear bizarre. It becomes less so, however, when the presumed nature of the innate universals or forms is considered.[41] What Augustine thought of as innate knowledge was, in the first place, mathematical principles such as $2 + 2 = 4$. To acquire these principles when one is learning arithmetic it is helpful perhaps to be able to see different numbers of objects, and, for example, to count two groups of two apples each. However the mathematical truth itself is universal and exists independently of the particular objects (and also independently of the mode in which the truth is expressed, for example verbally or in writing). Indeed the truth can be deduced independently of the objects, just as mathematical theorems can be deduced independently of real world examples. In fact, mathematicians often do reason at an abstract level.[42] In short, when applied to mathematical knowledge, the Neoplatonic theory of cognition gives at least a reasonable description of what seems to happen.

Although medieval scholars showed interest in mathematical and logical truth, the main intellectual interest of many of them, it is worth remembering, was the nature and purposes of God. For these scholars, as for Augustine, the real application of the theory of cognition was to the question: How do we know about God?[43] Here again the Neoplatonic theory was useful: while it may be questioned whether the idea of God is innate, even to medieval eyes his existence was not generally obvious in the external world.

Clearly not all knowledge is of mathematical and theological principles, and not all kinds of cognitive processing or even of abstraction were believed to result from universals present in the mind. Consider, for example, the question of the recognition of George who comes to work one day wearing a new yellow pullover, which I have not seen him wear before. How do I recognize that it is George? The answer would seem to be that I have in my imagination stored images of George without a yellow pullover. I also have an image of a yellow pullover (or I can easily construct one from an image of a pullover and an image of yellow). By subtracting the pullover from the present image of George, which I can do using the cogitative faculty in my middle ventricle, I arrive at an easily recognized previous representation of him. Thus a simple recognition task of this kind can be understood in terms of the operation of the inner senses and need not involve the cognitive abilities of the mind at all.[44]

In between this apparently simple recognition task and thinking about mathematics, however, lie a great number of mental activities whose use of universal principles and particular sensory information was not clearly defined by medieval scholars. Thus the relative contributions of the two kinds of processes—those involving the cognition of the mind and those making use only of the inner senses—were not mapped out in detail for many kinds of mental processes. One aspect of this issue is considered in more detail in the next section where memory, which was generally placed both in the mind and in the rear ventricle, is discussed.

The Neoplatonic theory of knowledge did not go unchallenged in the Middle Ages and, indeed, by its close had been largely eclipsed. The challenge to it was inspired by Aristotle's account of the mind, which he claimed to consist of two kinds of intellect, one passive and one active. The passive or potential intellect consists of a capacity to receive form, and can be compared to a writing tablet on which something might or might not be written. The potential intellect has no bodily organ; one proof of this is that while sense organs invariably adapt to stimuli and become less receptive to them, the potential intellect does not. The active or agent intellect, on the other hand, is essentially active, acting on the potential intellect in the same way a light acts to reveal the actual (as opposed to the potential) color of an object.[45]

Aristotle's description of the mind, and the potential and actual intellects therein, is brief, lacking in detail, and not particularly clear. In consequence, later philosophers working within the Aristotelian framework were able to produce rather different accounts of mind, so that the debate over the nature of the mind was not solely between the Augustinean and the Aristotelian accounts but over the nature of the Aristotelian account itself.

One well-articulated version of Aristotle's theory was put forward by Avicenna. This version, quite influential in the Christian West, in effect produced a Neoplatonic version of Aristotle's theory. Avicenna effectively interpreted Aristotle's active intellect to be, like Augustine's memory, a storehouse of innately acquired ideal forms and principles.[46] Moreover, as we have seen, Avicenna held that after a certain state of knowledge is attained, sensation has little further use. Far more controversial than Avicenna's version of Aristotle's theory, however, was that put forward by Averroes.[47] In essence, Averroes retained Aristotle's physiological bias and equated the imagination with Aristotle's potential intellect. The only wholly incorporeal power of the soul now remaining, the active intellect, was removed from the individual mind, and placed outside the individual, with whom nevertheless it interacted. Averroes' doctrine, like Avicenna's, had considerable influence on medieval scholastic thinking. Unlike Avicenna's, however, it was frequently proscribed by the Church because one of its consequences were denial of an individual immortal soul. The only immortal component in Averroes' soul (as indeed it is in Aristotle's) was the active intellect, but for Averroes the active intellect exists outside the individual. Moreover, in Averroes' psychology there is only one active intellect that is shared or conjoined with all human beings.[48]

Understandably, Averroes' psychology was attacked on various grounds by Christian philosophers. Aquinas gives a number of objections to it, pointing out, for example, that Averroes had misinterpreted Aristotle, particularly in equating the potential intellect with the imagination, and that in Averroes' system people would not think but rather be thought by the active intellect. On a more flippant level, he remarks that, if individual people did not think, then no one could hold Averroes' view, and so we would not have to listen to it.[49] Averroes, however, could not be countered solely by objections; in consequence a number of scholars attempted to construct theories of knowledge that reconciled Christian doctrine with Aristotle.

One fairly common Christian approach to the active intellect was to equate it with a divine light either emanating from, or an actual property of God. This idea of illumination seems to have been held, for example, by William of Auvergne, Alexander of Hales, and, in his later philosophy, by Roger Bacon.[50] Although similar to Averroes' thinking in placing the active intellect outside rather than within the human soul, it was not so theologically problematic because the adherents of the idea combined it with individual, immortal human souls. On the other hand this notion of the active intellect came under fire because it placed much of human reasoning ability outside the human soul itself.

Perhaps the most influential attempt at producing a version of Aristotle's theory of cognition that was both theologically acceptable and distinguishable from the Neoplatonic account was that made by Aquinas.[51] Like Avicenna and Averroes, Aquinas accepted the existence of potential and active intellects,[52] but firmly rejected Averroes' notion that the active intellect is singular.[53] The soul knows material things through the intellect but not through naturally innate species or subsistent material forms.[54] Aquinas' intellect is, in fact, closely tied to the operations of the body and in particular to those of the inner senses. Thought is impossible without an image, and the operation of the imagination and the other inner senses are essential for the intellect to understand anything, both in regard to new knowledge and in the application of existing knowledge.[55] This is clear, first, because head injury or a coma impairs understanding and, second, because we are aware of ourselves forming images to understand things. Understanding in fact comes about by abstracting species from sense images by a process of combining and separating.[56] Thus for Aquinas understanding involves learning new things empirically, and not by in some way reminding ourselves of what is already present in our minds.

There are some awkward consequences of Aquinas' theory of understanding that he bravely faces. For example, abstract ideas, which do not have images, are understood by analogy to physical objects of which we do have images.[57] Mathematical concepts can only be understood if some physical substance is imagined as representing the underlying quantity, although the choice of substance is not restricted to any particular one.[58] Most awkward of all perhaps are the theological corollaries that are implied. Immaterial substances cannot be understood in themselves and only imperfectly by way of the knowledge of material substances. Moreover, God himself can only be known imperfectly and is not the first thing known by the human mind.[59]

Aquinas' doctrines have probably had more influence than those of any other theologian on the present doctrines of the Roman Catholic church. However neither his theological doctrine nor his psychological thinking were immediately accepted in the Middle Ages. Some of his doctrines, along with those of Averroes, were condemned in 1277 although the condemnation was later rescinded.[60]

Aquinas' account of cognition was by no means the last medieval word on the subject. Duns Scotus, for example, considered in rather more detail than Aquinas the question of how general empirical truths may be abstracted from sensory information and introduced a new distinction between intuitive knowledge and abstractive knowledge, the former being knowledge of objects in the material world and the latter concerning universal principles.[61]

The distinction between intuition and abstraction was maintained and developed by William of Ockham. His idea of intuition was more radical than that of Duns Scotus and led him to the rejection of "species" as a useful concept for understanding perception and cognition. Instead material objects and facts about them were perceived directly. He also introduced some novelty into the debate about the nature of the agent intellect by suggesting that the mind understood not only universals but also singular, or particular, knowledge.[62]

The debate on the nature of human intellect and cognition continued until the end of the Middle Ages. In the early fifteenth century for example, John Sharpe in his De Anima was debating the rival merits of the positions of Aquinas, Duns Scotus, and William of Ockham on such questions as whether intelligible species are required for rational thought and whether the human intellect can know both material and immaterial things.[63] Despite this long period of sustained interest, however, the medieval debate has left few traces on present-day psychology. Issues related to those discussed by medieval scholars are considered by contemporary philosophers, for example, by philosophers of mind, but not in general by psychologists. Whether this state of affairs is desirable is perhaps open to debate. On the one hand it might be argued that the issues do have psychological importance and thus should not be simply ignored. On the other hand, many, perhaps most, contemporary psychologists would claim that psychology should restrict itself to matters that can be investigated empirically, and it is difficult to see how the nature of the agent intellect, for example, could be studied experimentally or even empirically. At any rate, the division between modern philosophy and psychology[64] has effectively left much of the medieval discussion of cognition without a present-day referent in psychology.

MEMORY

Some aspects of memory have already been discussed fleetingly in the earlier parts of this chapter, and even from this brief discussion it might be inferred that medieval scholars posited more than one kind of memory. Two of the inner senses, the imagination, which stored visual images in the front ventricle, and the memory itself, which stored "intentions" or patterns of behavior, for example, the learned association made by a dog that it has been beaten by a stick or the instinctive knowledge of a sheep that wolves should be fled, in the rear ventricle, were clearly defined as types of memory. Moreover, in addition to these bodily memories, common to humans and animals, some thinkers suggested that the mind itself contained a storehouse of innate ideas or principles. All this suggests what in fact occurred; that a number of different mnemonic processes rather than simply one might be considered in medieval accounts of memory. In part the postulation of more than one kind of memorial process may reflect the rather fragmentary nature of the discussion of memory in the Middle Ages. Unlike theories of cognition or the nature of the agent intellect, the process and nature of memory does not seem to have been an important issue in the Middle Ages, perhaps because no critical theological issues were tied up with it. Indeed, of all the early Christian and medieval scholars only Augustine gives the impression of really being interested in the question of what memory is. Most other writers seem either to have restricted themselves to one aspect of memory, for example, mnemonic techniques, or to discuss it in a fragmented way. Aquinas, for example, discussed different aspects of memory in widely different places in the *Summa Theologiae*.

Much of the basis of the medieval discussion of memory was derived, along with the rest of psychology, from Aristotle. His main contribution is contained in the *De Memoria et Reminiscentia*,[65] which was studied in the Middle Ages as part of the *Parva Naturalia*. The work is divided into two chapters, one of which deals with remembering and the other with recollection.

Aristotle begins his discussion of remembering by distinguishing memory from perception; memory required the passage of time. To remember requires an image, which is perceived through the common sense, and imprinted in the imagination "as people do who seal things with signet rings."[66] The memory has a bodily substrate and is not part of the mind, first, because it is possessed by some animals and, second, because the very young and very old have poor memories which are related to difficulties in imprinting the image. The image is treated as a copy of the original perception and not the original object itself, but as a rule it is used to relate to the object originally seen rather than to the original act of perception.

Recollection, which involves the association of ideas, arises because the images themselves are stored in order, either naturally or by design. The search for a particular image requires a start point that is similar to, opposite of, or neighboring the particular image sought. It is particularly good to start in the middle of a series of ideas because from there one can go in several different directions. Hence, for Aristotle, as indeed for many present-day accounts of memory, the images are stored in an associative network and retrieved by the association of ideas.[67] Retrieval is easiest when the ideas are arranged in a fixed order, like successive demonstrations of geometry, and more difficult when they are badly arranged. The associations need not, however, follow a mathematical or even obvious order. One can, to use one of Aristotle's examples, recollect autumn starting from the idea of milk: milk suggests white, white mist, mist moist, and moist finally leads to autumn. The discussion of recollection concludes by pointing out that the process involves a kind of reasoning and hence does not occur in animals, but that the image sought is in the body not in the mind. An extra demonstration of this is that

it upsets some people when they are unable to recollect in spite of applying their thought hard, and when they are no longer trying they recollect none the less. . . . The reason for recollecting not being under their control is that just as it is no longer in people's power to stop something when they throw it, so also he who is recollecting and hunting moves a bodily thing in which the affection resides.[68]

Aristotle's insistence that memory has a physiological basis and that the mind was incapable of remembering on its own[69] was echoed also by Avicenna.[70] Augustine, however, held that mind itself contained memory, although he also conceded the existence of other kinds of memory.[71] He distinguishes, in fact, at least three different kinds of memory. One, which we share with animals, contains images of material objects, a second stores remembered emotions, while a third contains the mind itself.[72] In Book Ten of his *Confessions*, Augustine discusses memory in some detail; indeed one gains the impression that the processes and nature of memory fascinated the author. Augustine's discussion is frequently metaphorical and at times almost mystical, but mixed in with the metaphor are some profound thoughts on the nature of memory. Augustine's idea that memory contains innate as well as empirically derived ideas has been discussed above. Another point he makes concerns memory for emotion: "How does it happen that when I am joyful I can still remember past sorrow? Thus the mind has joy, and the memory has sorrow ... [yet] is not sad."[73] This observation illustrates Augustine's division of memory as well, perhaps, as recalling the Aristotelian point that the image or copy in memory can be rather different from the original perception or feeling.

Augustine uses memory to explain the nature of time. According to Augustine, the measurement of time takes place in the mind rather than, for example, being derived from some physical process such as the movement of the sun or planets.[74] As it passes time is "stretched out into some space of time" by the mind.[75] The process necessarily involves memory, because if we are comparing the durations of two intervals that have occurred successively (the syllables of a poem, for example), at least one interval must be remembered. The measurement then takes place using the images left by past events. Even silent intervals, or those in which no external events occur, can be measured in this way, because we continue to think in such intervals, and the thoughts, or more accurately the impressions left by the thoughts, can be remembered too.[76] We can also predict future durations, but then the estimates are derived from expectations based on past or present experience, rather than directly from the images left by past events.[77]

Perhaps the most interesting phenomenon discussed by Augustine is that of metamemory, as it is sometimes termed today.[78] That is, how is it that sometimes we know that we know something but cannot remember what it is? Augustine's example of the phenomenon, which is still that most commonly cited today, is the inability to remember the name of someone just seen or thought about.[79] As present-day psychologists have also noted, there is something of a paradox to the existence of metamemory. Augustine's formulation of the problem is as follows:

What happens when the memory itself loses something, as when we forget anything and try to recall it? And ... if by chance one thing is offered for another we refuse it until we meet with what we are looking for; and when we do, we recognize that this is it. But we could not do this unless we recognized it, nor could we have recognized it unless we remembered it. Yet we had indeed forgotten it.[80]

Augustine's solution to the paradox, again also used today, is that the memory itself is partially but not wholly retrieved: "Perhaps the whole of it had not slipped out of our memory; but a part was retained by which the other lost part was sought for."[81]

The phenomenon of metamemory was also known to Aquinas who uses it as a proof that memory resides in the mind as well as in the faculties of imagination and memory.

Memory, properly speaking does not belong to the intellectual part, but only to the sensitive . . . but . . . the term memory can be broadened to include the knowledge by which one knows the object previously known in so far as he knows he knew it earlier, although he does not know the object.[82]

In Aquinas' account of memory the actual images and intentions are retained in the physically based stores, but references to these images, as well as intellectual aptitudes that also have a mnemonic component, for example, the learned ability to perform mental arithmetic quickly, are in the mind. Thus Aquinas produced a rather clever synthesis of the differing positions of Aristotle and Augustine that is in good agreement with what it feels like to remember, or not to be able to remember, something.

That mnemonic processes in general might involve some interplay between the mind and the faculties of the inner senses was also suggested to Aquinas and other medieval scholars by their knowledge of the classic art of memory or mnemonic techniques.[83] The art of memory involves the conscious use of mnemonic techniques to improve one's memory of, for example, lists of unrelated objects. In classic times, training in its use was part of the art of rhetoric, and it was especially used to help orators deliver long speeches from memory without resorting to written aids.

There are a number of different techniques, best known of which was—and still is—the method of loci. To use this technique one has first to imprint on the memory an ordered series of places, for example, an ordered walk through the rooms of a mansion or scenes passed when one walks home from work every day. A list of objects or concepts that one wishes to remember is memorized by forming an image of the first object at the first previously memorized locus, the second object at the second locus, and so on. When one wishes to recall the objects in order, one imagines one's ordered walk and can then visualize in turn each object in its locus. The most important ingredient of the technique, which incidentally has been experimentally shown to be effective,[84] is the formation of appropriate images when memorizing the objects or concepts. The images must be both concrete and easily referenced to the objects or concepts they represent. Quintillian's use of a visualized anchor to represent the navy is a good example of this.[85]

The technique seems to have been common knowledge in classic times. It is referred to by Aristotle, and indeed his associative theory of recollection bears a marked resemblance to the technique, and was perhaps suggested by it or a similar technique.[86] It was also later the subject of treatises by Quintillian and Cicero.[87] Its use in the Middle Ages dates at least from the twelfth century, because Hugh of Saint Victor wrote a treatise on it and other mnemonic techniques then. Hugh not only described these techniques but also indicated how they could have practical medieval applications for tasks such as memorizing the psalms.[88] The method of loci also seems to have been familiar to both Albertus Magnus and Aquinas.[89] It is easy to see how the method, which uses not only images and hence the faculties of the front ventricle, but also some intellectual effort and hence the abilities of the mind, suggests that human memory generally might involve both physiological and intellectual processes. Aguinas, in fact, seems to have reasoned in just this way. Memory is described as a part of prudence, one of the faculties of the mind, because mnemonic techniques show that the ability can be improved by teaching and experience.[90]

Mnemonic techniques had another impact on the Middle Ages unconnected with either scholasticism or oratory. The techniques suggest that memory and learning can be aided by imagery and hence by visual decoration. From this derived in turn a justification for the extensive use of didactic painting, sculpture, and architecture in the Middle Ages.[91] The existence of mnemonic techniques thus served as a practical psychological example of the symbolic nature of reality that Bonaventure and others proposed: art could be used to teach or to remind one of, for example, scriptural stories in the same way that the world itself was supposed to indicate the nature of eternal reality.

CONCLUSIONS

What are described by contemporary psychologists as cognitive processes were divided by medieval scholars into the processes mediated by the physiological mechanisms of the cerebral ventricles and processes taking place in the rational soul or mind. The mind-body division thus divided cognition into two. On general grounds, one might expect such a division to produce an unsatisfactory, and in places confusing and contradictory, account of cognition. Strangely, though, this impression is not given, even in accounts of memory, which was often regarded as having both physiological and purely mental components. Probably the reason why the overall impression given is not one of an account cobbled together from two totally disparate parts is that the medieval scholars themselves were aware of the problem and were unremitting in their attempts to solve it. As one of the most successful of these attempts— that of Aquinas—considered mind as always operating in close coordination with, and indeed being dependent on, bodily processes, the theoretical effect was to reduce the problems potentially inherent in the division. It should also be remarked that postulating two different sorts of processes could occasionally be of theoretical advantage. Aquinas' account of metamemory and the apparent operation of the method of loci provide good examples of this.

On the whole the medieval account of cognition could be considered reasonably successful. It provided a reasonable description of the apparent operations of memory, observed patterns of animal behavior, and the effects of brain injury or illness on human functioning. In addition it was in good agreement with the physiological beliefs of the day, and provided a description of what people report they are doing when they think about, or remember, or imagine something. Unlike contemporary cognitive psychology, it did not attempt to do more.

Given this success it is perhaps surprising that the nature of the account is radically different from the approach taken by present-day cognitive psychology. True, both the present approach and that taken by the medieval doctrine of the inner senses can be considered as theories of information processing; true, also, that some of the phenomena studied in the experimental laboratory today, for example, visual imagery and metamemory, were also studied in the Middle Ages; but, on the other hand, there is no modern equivalent at all of the agent intellect or the division between singulars and universals. Nor has any modern account dared to specify the physiological basis of the ability to form mental images as the medieval scholars so blithely did.

Overall these major differences can probably be ascribed to differences in both empirical and theoretical approaches between the two eras. Modern theories of cognition are mainly concerned with accounting for the results of experimental investigations; in contrast, introspective accounts of thinking processes are generally regarded as being of minor importance. In the Middle Ages, on the other hand, experiments were not undertaken at all. Differences in theoretical approach can also be identified, most obviously in that modern accounts are under no theoretical obligation to be consistent with Christian theology. On the other hand, it is also true that modern cognitive psychologists are generally less keen to seek out an underlying physiological basis for cognitive processes than medieval scholars were. Finally we should note that the cognitive phenomena studied by present-day cognitive psychologists tend to be those believed in the Middle Ages to be carried out in the cerebral ventricles and not those carried out by the incorporeal mind. For example, there has been a plethora of recent research devoted to the study of visual imagery or pattern recognition, and very little to the psychological study of how mathematical principles are acquired. The functions supposedly performed by the medieval agent intellect, for example, how one acquires mathematical knowledge or how one might understand God, have been little investigated by modern psychology.

NOTES

1. An historical account of the doctrine of the inner senses is given by E. Ruth Harvey, *The Inward Wits: Psychological Theory in the Middle Ages and the Renaissance* (London: Warburg Institute, 1975). See also J. V. Brown, "Henry of Ghent on Internal Sensation." *Journal of the History of Philosophy* 10 (1972): 15–28; and Nicholas H. Steneck, "Albert the Great on the Classification and Location of the Internal Senses." *Isis* 65 (1974): 193–211.

2. Aristotle, *De Anima*, 3.2–8; Galen, *On the Usefulness of the Parts of the Body*, 413–432.

3. Aristotle, *De Partibus Animalium*, trans. W. Ogle. In W. D. Ross, ed., *The Works of Aristotle*, Vol. 5 (Oxford, UK: Clarenden, 1931), 1.10.656a.

4. Galen, *On the Doctrines of Hippocrates and Plato*, Book 7.

5. Augustine, *The Literal Meaning of Genesis*, 7.18.24.

6. Nemesius, *A Treatise on the Nature of Man*, 320–323, 338–343.

7. Lanfranc, *Science of Cirurgie* (London: Early English Text Society, O.S. 102, 1894), 113–114.

8. Nemesius, *A Treatise on the Nature of Man*, 341.

9. Steneck, "Albert the Great on the Internal Senses"; Bartholomaeus Anglicus, *On the Properties of Things*, 98; and Lanfranc, *Science of Cirurgie*, 113–116.

10. Avicenna, *Avicenna's Psychology*, 30–31.

11. John XXI, *Scienti Libri De Anima*, 7.1–5; Steneck, "Albert the Great on the Internal Senses"; and Bacon, *Opus Majus*, 421–429.

12. Different translators occasionally use different words to translate the original Latin, so that various English terms have been used to describe the different faculties. Even more confusingly, the same word is often used by different translators to refer to different faculties. The present use of terms is, I hope, the closest to the original Latin. The reader who wishes to go beyond my brief account is advised to consider the descriptions given of each faculty rather than the word used to denote it.

13. For example, Augustine, *On the Trinity*, 10.2.3; and Bacon, *Opus Majus*, 422. The metaphor is found in Aristotle, see Aristotle, *De Anima*, 2.12.424a; Aristotle, *De Memoria et Reminiscentia*. In W. R. Ross, ed., *The Works of Aristotle*, Vol. 3 (Oxford, UK: Clarendon, 1931), 1.450b, but he in turn seems to have obtained it from Plato. See Plato, *Theaetetus*, trans. John McDowell (Oxford, UK: Clarendon, 1973), 191C–195B.

14. Stephen M. Kosslyn, *Image and Mind* (Cambridge, Mass.: Harvard Uni-

versity Press, 1980), 1. In theory the imagination should also store images of other modalities, e.g., a particular melody, but I have come across no medieval account that refers to other than a visual image.

15. Kosslyn, *Image and Mind*, 6.

16. Augustine, *On the Trinity*, 11.3.6.

17. See John R. Anderson, "Arguments Concerning Representations for Mental Imagery." *Psychological Review* 85 (1978): 249–277; Z. W. Pylyshyn. "What the Mind's Eye Tells the Mind's Brain: A Critique of Mental Imagery." *Psychological Bulletin* 80 (1973): 1–24; and Roger N. Shephard, "The Mental Image." *American Psychologist* 33 (1978): 125–137.

18. Avicenna, *Avicenna's Psychology*, 45.

19. Aristotle, *De Somniis*.

20. Augustine, *The Literal Meaning of Genesis*, 12.18.39.

21. Averroes, *Epitome of Parva Naturalia*, trans. Harry Blumberg (Cambridge, Mass.: Medieval Academy of America, 1961), 41–42.

22. Sigmund Freud, *The Interpretation of Dreams*, trans. James Strachey (London: Allen & Unwin, 1957).

23. David Foulkes, *Dreaming: A Cognitive-Psychological Analysis* (Hillsdale, N.J.: Erlbaum, 1985).

24. Bacon, *Opus Majus*, 426.

25. Aquinas, *Summa Theologiae*, 1.78.4.

26. Avicenna, *Avicenna's Psychology*, 31.

27. E.g., Augustine, *On the Trinity*, 10.

28. Harvey, *The Inward Wits*, 38.

29. Nemesius, *A Treatise on the Nature of Man*, 342. This example was frequently quoted by medieval physicians.

30. Aquinas, *Summa Theologiae*, 1.78.4.

31. Steneck, "Albert the Great on the Internal Senses."

32. See R. L. Atkinson, R. C. Atkinson, E. E. Smith, and E. R. Hilgard, *Introduction to Psychology*, 9th ed. (San Diego: Harcourt Brace Jovanovich, 1987), 246–248.

33. Aristotle, *De Anima*, 3.4.429a.

34. Ibid.

35. Avicenna, *Avicenna's Psychology*, 39.

36. Ibid., 41–46.

37. Augustine, *Confessions*, 10.10.

38. See Bowman, "Agent Intellect in the Franciscan School."

39. Bonaventure, *The Mind's Road to God*.

40. Avicenna, *Avicenna's Psychology*, 56.

41. Something that, incidentally, the medieval scholars themselves often seem either to have ignored or taken for granted.

42. E.g., Augustine, *Confessions*, 10.12. The example is mine.

43. In *Confessions*, Augustine, in fact, moves straight on from considering memory to how the soul comes to know God.

44. The example is mine.

45. Aristotle, *De Anima*, 3.4–5.

46. For example, Avicenna, *Avicenna's Psychology*, 35.

47. For example, Averroes, *Conjunction with the Active Intellect*.

48. For example, Thorndike, *University Records*, 80.

49. Aquinas, *Commentaria*, 3.7.689–699.

50. Moody, *Studies in Medieval Philosophy*, 66–72; and Bowman, "Agent Intellect in the Franciscan School."

51. Patrick Lee, "St. Thomas and Avicenna on the Agent Intellect." *Thomist* 45 (1981): 41–61, gives a good summary of how Avicenna and Aquinas interpreted Aristotle's cognitive theory. Aquinas' own views are given both in his *Commentaria* and *Summa Theologiae*.

52. Aquinas, *Summa Theologiae*, 1.79.2–3.

53. Ibid., 1.76.2; 1.79.5.

54. Ibid., 1.84.2–4.

55. Ibid., 1.84.7. The imagination is particularly important in Aquinas' psychology since no cogitative faculty is supposed.

56. Ibid., 1.85.5.

57. Ibid., 1.84.7.

58. Ibid., 1.85.1.

59. Ibid., 1.88.1–3.

60. James A. Weisheipl. *Friar Thomas D'Aquino: His Life, Thought, and Work* (New York: Doubleday, 1974), 331–350.

61. Duns Scotus, *Philosophical Writings*, ed. and trans. Allan Wolter (Edinburgh, UK: Nelson, 1962), 96–132; and Christopher Devlin, *The Psychology of Duns Scotus* (Oxford, UK: Blackfriars, 1950).

62. Leff, *William of Ockham*, 1–123.

63. Leonard Kennedy, "The *De Anima* of John Sharpe." *Franciscan Studies* 29 (1969): 248–270.

64. There are, of course, attempts to bridge this division. See e.g., E. R. Valentine, *Conceptual Issues in Psychology* (London: Allen & Unwin, 1982).

65. See R. Sorabji, *Aristotle on Memory* (London: Duckworth, 1972), which contains both *De Memoria* and a substantial commentary on the work and of Aristotle's thinking on memory generally.

66. Aristotle, *De Memoria*, 1.450a.

67. See John R. Anderson, *Cognitive Psychology and its Implications*, 2nd ed. (New York, Freeman, 1985), chapt. 7.

68. Aristotle, *De Memoria*, 2.453a.

69. See also Aristotle, *De Anima*, 3.5.430a.

70. Avicenna, *Avicenna's Psychology*, 41ff.

71. In *On the Trinity*, 10, Augustine discusses memory as a power of the mind along with understanding and will.

72. Augustine, *Confessions*, 10.25.

73. Ibid., 10.14.

74. Ibid., 11.21–27.

75. Ibid., 11.27.

76. Ibid.

77. Ibid., 11.18; 11.28.

78. See J. H. Flavell and H. M. Wellman "Metamemory." In K. V. Kail and J. W. Hagan eds., *Perspectives on the Development of Memory and Cognition* (Hillsdale, N.J.: Erlbaum, 1977).

79. Augustine, *Confessions*, 10.19.

    80. Ibid.
    81. Ibid.
    82. Thomas Aquinas, *The Teacher and the Mind, (Truth, Questions X, XI)*, trans. James V. McGlynn (Chicago: Henry Regnery, 1965), 77.
    83. See Frances A. Yates, *The Art of Memory* (London: Routledge and Kegan Paul, 1966) on which the following discussion is based.
    84. See Gordon H. Bower, "Analysis of a Mnemonic Device." *American Scientist* 58 (1970): 496–510; and Simon Kemp and Christopher D. van der Krogt, "Effect of Visibility of the Loci on Recall Using the Method of Loci." *Bulletin of the Psychonomic Society* 23 (1985): 202–204.
    85. Yates, *The Art of Memory*, 1–26.
    86. See Sorabji, *Aristotle on Memory*, 22–31.
    87. Yates, *The Art of Memory*, 1–26.
    88. Grover A. Zinn, "Hugh of Saint Victor and the Art of Memory." *Viator* 5 (1974): 211–234.
    89. Yates, *The Art of Memory*, 61–81.
    90. Aquinas, *Summa Theologiae*, 2.2.49.1.
    91. Yates, *The Art of Memory*, 82–104.

5

Emotion and the Will

Previous chapters have considered contributions made to medieval psychology by a number of different writers. In this chapter, by contrast, only the thought of Thomas Aquinas on emotion and the will is presented. The principal reasons for this are, first, that no other medieval writer seems to have approached the complexity of discussion that Aquinas achieved on these two related issues and, second, that the issues do not seem to have been matters of great theoretical or theological controversy in the Middle Ages.

Although Aquinas' account exceeds in attention to detail and in coherence those of his predecessors and immediate successors, it was not formed in a vacuum. Rather, as is evident from the references he cites, his work is largely a synthesis, and in places an extension, of ancient and early Christian writings. Foremost among these influences was undoubtedly that of Aristotle, and in particular his *Nicomachean Ethics* and *Rhetoric*. Other important influences on his account of emotions and the will were Augustine, Nemesius,[1] and St. John of Damascus (ca. 675–749 A.D.).

AQUINAS ON EMOTION

Aquinas' theory of emotion, which is contained in the *Summa Theologiae*, considers, first, the nature of emotion in general and, second, the nature of particular, individual emotions. Emotions are experienced by the soul as part of the appetitive rather than the cognitive faculty.[2] Moreover, emotions belong to the sensory appetite, that shared by humans and animals, rather than the intellectual appetite or will. The major reason given by Aquinas for this view is that emotion is invariably accompanied by some kind of physiological change, but the will has no bodily organ and no physiological process is required for its functioning.[3] Here, as elsewhere, Aquinas has thoroughly committed himself to the existence of a physiological basis for the emotions, a commitment incidentally also held by many present-day psychologists investigating the field of emotion.[4]

A further general point about Aquinas' theory of emotion should be noted. Modern psychology often differentiates motivation—what drives or causes behavior—from emotion—what we feel in different situations. Aquinas, like other medieval and ancient writers, does not really distinguish these concepts at all: the appetites are both feelings and motivating forces.

Emotions can be classified into one of two faculties of the sensory appetite. The affective emotions—for example, joy, sorrow, love, and hatred—relate simply to pleasurable or aversive objects. On the other hand, the spirited emotions—for example, courage, fear, and hope—involve striving to obtain a pleasurable outcome or to avoid an aversive one.[5] Aquinas' distinction, which was by no means idiosyncratic,[6] is a useful one, and has some echo in present-day accounts of emotion. The spirited emotions all by definition require some form of arousal, as it is described in the modern idiom. The affective emotions, on the other hand, do not; rather they bear some resemblances to drives, forces sometimes believed to motivate behavior.[7] Aquinas distinguishes eleven separate emotions. There are six affective emotions, arranged in contrary or opposing pairs; these are love and hatred, desire and aversion, and pleasure and sadness. There are two pairs of spirited emotions: hope and despair, and fear and courage. In addition, anger, which has no contrary, is a spirited emotion.[8]

Most of the rest of Aquinas' account is concerned with the individual analysis of these eleven emotions. In the interests of brevity, only four of the emotions, two affective and two spirited, will be considered here: love, pleasure, fear and anger. Aquinas' general approach to each of the other emotions follows much the same pattern as to these four.

Love may involve either the sensory appetite or the intellectual appetite depending on its object. Aquinas distinguishes various kinds of love, for example, love of friendship and love of desire.[9] Love may arise from knowledge and also from similarity; thus we tend to like people who resemble ourselves.[10] Love is also in a way a cause of other emotions, because love consists of a sense of attraction to some object. This attraction causes the movement toward or remaining with the object, which is a necessary part of all the other emotions.[11] Love in its most general sense is then the cause of all action, as it is the desired or loved goal that motivates all behavior.[12] Usually the effects of love are beneficial. It is frequently a unifying emotion, particularly where there is mutual affection between friends. Moreover love is capable of providing ecstasy. On the other hand the emotion can also have less desirable effects. Jealousy, for example, or even hatred may arise when some real or perceived obstacle comes between the person and the desired object. The physiological effects of love, too, may be undesirable. Pleasure accompanies the possession of the object loved, but languor or fever can arise in its absence.[13]

Pleasure is experienced by both animals and man, but joy, which is a pleasure of the mind, is experienced only by human beings.[14] Intellectual pleasure is more durable and more highly prized than physical pleasure; the latter is, however, more intense, particuarly when it involves the sense of touch.[15] Pleasures may arise from a variety of causes, from activity, hopes, and memories; the actions of others; helping others; wondering; or even from sorrow. Change too may be a source of pleasure, because well-being is dependent on moderation. If something normally enjoyable is continued past a certain point, like sitting beside a fire for too long, it is the removal of the object or the cessation of the activity that is pleasant.[16] The idea that change itself may be a source of pleasure has reemerged in modern psychology. There is now a large body of research, recently summarized by Marvin Zuckerman, which indicates that both people and animals indulge in sensation seeking— the search for and exploration of new and stimulating situations.[17]

The effects of pleasure are to create a feeling of expansion and a desire for more. Under certain circumstances it may impede one's ability to reason, for example, by distracting one from a course of action, or when the physiological reactions that accompany pleasure impair one's ability to reason.[18]

"The object of fear," according to Aquinas, "is future, disagreeable, and escapes the control of the fearful person."[19] It is clear that a rather broad definition of fear is considered: one may, for example, refrain from undertaking a task from fear of the work involved, or fear the possibility of future disgrace, as well as fear death.[20] In addition one can fear other emotions such as guilt or even fear itself.[21] In particular we fear what cannot be avoided.[22] Fear is linked with love because it is inspired by the threatened withdrawal or unattainability of what is loved.[23] Finally, fear can be produced in the absence of any external cause, as happens in the case of people suffering from melancholy. The

occurrence of this phenomenon is for Aquinas proof that emotion involves bodily changes: in this case the fear results from a humoral imbalance.[24]

One of the effects of fear is an internal contraction and concentration
of heat and vital spirits in the internal organs, but away from rather
than toward the region of the heart. This process in turn causes the
fearful to fall back rather than to go forward.[25] In daring, by contrast,
body heat is raised in the area of the heart.[26] Fear also causes trembling,
because body heat is transferred to the digestive tract from the limbs
and head as well as from the heart.[27] Fear may interfere with one's ability
to reason. Aquinas' thinking on this point is worth quoting in full:

If the fear is moderate and does not excessively disturb the processes of reasoning, it is a help in acting well. Fear then will make a man more careful and
more attentive to what he is doing and to the need for deliberation. But if fear
should develop to the point where it upsets reason, then even mental functioning
will be disturbed.[28]

In this passage Aquinas clearly anticipates a frequent result in present-
day experimental psychology sometimes referred to as the Yerkes-
Dodson Law after the experimenters who called attention to it.[29] The
law states that, in general, best performance on a task results from
intermediate levels of arousal. Thus a moderate amount of arousal im-
proves performance but once a certain limit has been reached further
increases in arousal result in performance deterioration. The result is
reasonably general and has been demonstrated for different kinds of
tasks and different means of arousal. For example, a frequently demonstrated variant is that both people and animals perform simple tasks
best under relatively high levels of motivation or arousal but perform
complex tasks best under lower levels of arousal.[30] Aquinas also seems
to have believed the result was reasonably general because he posits
that anger might have a rather similar effect as fear.[31]

For Aquinas, anger is fundamentally a desire for revenge, and generally includes a rational component, at least in human beings, because
the emotion involves the consideration of repayment of injury with
punishment.[32] Thus considerations of justice and of whether one has
been fairly treated are important in understanding the nature of anger.[33]
Anger arises when we ourselves are injured or slighted; indeed the
motive for all anger is some kind of unjust slight or injury. Curiously,
one is more likely to be angered if one's own character is near perfection,
because then the slight or injury is less likely to be deserved.[34] Another
apparently unchristian aspect of Aquinas' discussion of anger is that
one feels pleasure when the revenge is obtained.[35] Aquinas was actually
being true to the beliefs of his time here, as well as to Aristotle from

whom much of this reasoning derives. The capacity to bear ill will, if necessary for a long time, and revenge oneself on one's enemies was regarded as a positive virtue in the Middle Ages, particularly by the knightly, upper class. In the twelfth-century *Perceval*, one of the most popular of the courtly medieval romances, Chrétien de Troyes states that "a man does ill to forget a shame or injury done to him—the pain passes but the shame remains in a staunch and vigorous man, but in a man of little worth it dies away and cools."[36] It is actually a sign of Perceval's essential nobility in the romance that he does, as he has promised, eventually take revenge on Kay for striking one of the Queen's maids, the injury to which the preceding quotation refers.

The physiological effect of anger is heating of the blood and vital spirits around the heart, caused by the evaporation of bile. This disturbance often produces effects on the limbs and also often interferes with the use of reason. Anger may in fact become so strong as to leave one speechless, because one is unable to control the necessary bodily functions.[37]

The main features of Aquinas' account emerge from this summary of his views. Essentially his account is based largely on empirical observation and common knowledge or report of what emotion feels like. Interestingly, recent research on what ordinary people think about emotion has turned up some rather similar results to Aquinas, for example, the perceived importance of the heating of blood when anger is felt.[38] Aquinas' account is, however, extended beyond the purely common-sense level by deduction and logic. An example of such an extension is his deduction that people who approach perfection are more readily angered. In addition, a common framework is provided for the emotions into which they can be easily fitted and related to each other. Nor is the account trivial; Aquinas' anticipation of the Yerkes-Dodson Law is sufficient counterevidence for that.

Physiological aspects of emotion are taken into account by Aquinas but these are seen as of secondary importance. Aquinas does not discuss the physiology involved in much detail, and, moreover, the physiological accompaniments of emotion—for example, the activity of the blood in the region of the heart—are clearly seen as effects rather than as causes or as the underlying biological reality of emotion. In this he would clearly disagree with the approach taken by some modern theorists of emotion who have thought of the experience of emotion as either a kind of epiphenomenon accompanying physiological activity or even, as suggested by William James, as the perception of the physiological activity.[39]

Present-day accounts of emotion are themselves rather diverse so that it is difficult to make comparisons between Aquinas' and modern theories. Overall his prime concern was with the phenomenology of feeling and explaining what we feel in terms of external causes. He was also concerned with the interplay between emotion and reason, and in this perhaps anticipated some rather recent theorizing that has tended to stress the role of cognitive processes in emotion.[40] One similarity between his and modern approaches is perhaps more surprising. Aquinas' description of the emotions is almost free of moral, ethical, or theological considerations, sometimes, as, for example, in his account of anger, to a rather surprising extent. This is not because Aquinas is uninterested in such considerations; indeed, he is more concerned with them than he is with psychological theory, and devotes more space overall in the *Summa Theologiae* to discussing them. Rather it is because he wishes the solutions to moral issues to be based on what man can be empirically shown to be than on what man ought to be. Aquinas' psychology was primarily worked out to provide the framework for his attempted solution of moral and theological problems.

Probably the biggest difference between Aquinas' and modern accounts is that he is relatively unconcerned with behavior. In contrast, many modern theories are almost exclusively concerned with behavior and consider emotional feelings of little importance.[41] The cause of this difference is clear. In Aquinas' account, as in all medieval theories of psychology, the consequences of emotions for behavior are mediated, at least in human beings, by the operation of the will. Whereas animal behavior was believed to be directly caused by the appetites, modified to some extent by the operation of the instinctive faculty in the central ventricle, human behavior—except for some physiologically based behavior such as trembling with rage or fear—was believed to be the result of conscious choice. Thus while behavior might be indirectly influenced by the emotions, it was not determined or directly caused by them. Aquinas then had no expectation that behavior could be simply predicted from emotional state.

THE WILL

The will was acknowledged by all Christian medieval scholars to be that part of the rational soul, or mind, that was responsible for choice and initiation of behavior. It was commonly agreed throughout the Middle Ages that man was free to choose, particularly between good and evil, and had control of his own individual actions and hence of his own immortal soul. The historical origins of this belief seem to lie in the origins of Christianity itself, and particularly in its early struggle with the rival, more deterministic beliefs prevalent in the Roman Empire. Some aspects of this struggle and its aftermath, particularly with reference to astrology, are considered in the next chapter. For now, however, it should be noted that the belief in free will was one of the most important and basic beliefs of medieval psychology. Moreover it was one on which the Church, following the lead of its early Fathers, was not prepared to compromise. Among the errors condemned by the Bishop of Paris in 1270, for example, we find the beliefs that man's will is moved by necessity, that terrestrial actions depend on the necessity of the celestial bodies, and that free will is moved necessarily by the appetite.[42]

The will, like the mind of which it formed a part, is found in humans but not animals. Thus emotions and the operations of the inner senses are directly causal of behavior in animls but not in man. In the context of discussing the nature of despair and demonstrating its presence in the animal kingdom, Aquinas remarks that the existence of emotions in animals is implied by the behavior they display. A dog, he states, will run after a hare that is near at hand. On the other hand, if the hare is a long way away it will not be pursued, implying that the dog has no hope or expectation of catching it.[43]

Aquinas' discussion of the will is, naturally enough for a theologian, concerned more with the ethical and moral than the purely psychological aspects of the will. The latter are considered, however, and it is with them that we are concerned here. Perhaps chief among the psychological issues addressed is the question of how the will itself is set in motion. According to Aquinas it may be set in motion by a number of different faculties, by the mind, by the sensory appetite or emotion, by itself, or by an external object presented to the senses.[44] The question of the autonomy of the will then becomes a rather difficult one. If, for example, an external cause sets the will in motion and this in turn brings about the action, what causal role is played by the will and freedom of choice at all? Aquinas' solution to this problem seems to depend in part on the distinction between ends and means. Suppose, for example, it is a hot day and I see a shop selling ice creams and my sensory appetite is stimulated. Between the stimulation of my appetite and my finally obtaining and eating an ice cream there is a chain of mental and behavioral processes that bring the desired end about. Thus the mind deliberates whether I have the money in my pocket to pay for it, a decision is made by the will as to whether this is the best use of my money. Deliberation and decision may also be involved in deciding what type of ice cream to buy. The will is then also necessary to initiate the physical actions that take me to the shop counter, ask for the ice cream and pay the vendor. Thus the complexity of human behavior needed to attain ends suggested by the sensory appetite appears to guarantee a place for the will in Aquinas' philosophy.[45]

A rather different and more philosophical argument is advanced when the question of whether the will is moved of necessity by its object is considered. The point made by Aquinas is that the value of an object usually depends on the standpoint taken when evaluating it. If an object had only favorable and no unfavorable aspects, then the will would necessarily have to decide for it. Generally, however, objects have both good and bad aspects and so the will may decide either for or against an object depending on the point of view actually taken.[46] The choice of points of view is in turn suggested by reason, which of its nature involves the consideration of opposites.

The relationship of the will to the sensory appetite is complex. In general the appetites influence the will but do not control it. However, it is possible for reason to be completely bound by passion. This may happen, for example, when people are driven out of their minds by rage or as a consequence of a physical disorder, because, as Aquinas reminds his readers, emotion accompanies physiological change. When people are overpowered by passion so as to deprive them of reason and will, they effectively become animals whose behavior is always determined by their appetites.[47]

Thus the appetites can be resisted except in cases where both reason and will are bound by passion and do not operate at all. This concession, that in exceptional circumstances the will and reason do not operate and that in these circumstances people are not rational and not responsible for their own actions, is by no means unique to Aquinas. It had, as will become apparent later, important consequences for the consideration of mental disorder.

Aquinas goes on to describe the process involved in action. This involves the formation of an intention or intentions by an act of will, an act of free choice, deliberation about the means to be employed in attaining the end, consent by the will to employing the means suggested by reason, and finally application or execution of the plan, by commanding the activity of the body. This complex process, which is responsible only for the initiation of human and not animal action, involves reason and the will in constant interaction with each other, as even the relatively simple example of buying an ice cream suggests.[48]

An interesting question considered by Aquinas is that of which faculties are capable of being commanded. The answer to this is mixed. We can control the activity of our limbs and other bodily members but not, on the other hand, acts issuing from the vegetative soul, for example, digestion or generation.[49] Rather more problematic is whether the emotions can be directly controlled. The answer to this seems to be partly. As emotions result from perception and imagination that are partially under rational control, some degree of command is possible. On the other hand, the will cannot stop a sudden arousal of emotion by something just seen or perhaps remembered, nor can the will command bodily dispositions.[50] In summary, Aquinas suggests, following Aristotle, that "the reason governs the appetites of desire and contention, not by the despotic rule of a slave master, but by the civil and royal rule which governs free men who are not entirely subject to dictate."[51]

Aquinas' use of this comparison between the will and a liberal ruler, which is made more than once in his account of the will,[52] illustrates the important point that he does not see emotions themselves as evil. Even anger, as we saw above, is not seen as particularly harmful, and some human acts which are initiated by emotions, for example, those involving courage, are seen as particularly virtuous.[53] Emotions generally are a necessary part of the human being and, provided they are properly governed by reason and the will, they are both useful and moral. Certainly feelings are not invariably to be denied or ruthlessly repressed.

How does Aquinas' concept of the will compare with that offered by present-day psychology? The answer is that there is little to compare it to: the will, and the psychological processes involved with the initiation of action that Aquinas suggested, are not frequently investigated at all by modern psychologists. Partly this reflects the fact that Aquinas' processes are not easily investigated by laboratory experimentation; partly it reflects the hostility frequently shown by psychologists in this century to theorizing about unobservable variables. An extreme case of this hostility was demonstrated by B. F. Skinner who argued that concepts such as will, freedom, or consciousness had no explanatory power at all, and that an adequate account of human behavior could be constructed without reference to them.[54] Indeed it is only in the last decade or so, with the increased interest in cognitive psychology, that visual imagery or reasoning ability or consciousness have again become respectable objects of scientific enquiry in psychology. The revival of interest in these topics has, however, not yet been accompanied by very much interest in the will.

An exception to the general lack of interest may be found in George Mandler's speculations on the role of consciousness in human behavior, which in fact have some resemblance to Aquinas' ideas. Mandler suggests that consciousness is of key importance in choice and in the selection of action, particularly action in novel situations or actions that have not previously been performed. In addition consciousness serves to organize disparate action components to perform parts of a higher plan. This happens, to use one of Mandler's examples, when, in planning a drive to a new destination, different sections of the route are considered. Thus for both Mandler and Aquinas it is relatively complex behavior that requires conscious or willful action.[55]

Although there has been little modern interest in the will, there has been a large amount of contemporary research into choice and decision making. The emphasis of such research, however, has often been rather different. Characteristically, such studies have examined the effect of externally manipulated variables on choices made. One frequently studied experimental situation, for example, which has obvious economic implications, requires subjects to choose between two gambles, one of which might have a low potential return but relatively little risk attached to it, while the other has a higher potential return but also greater risk. In such a situation the potential returns and the risks can be manipulated and the results obtained from the experiment compared with those that would be predicted if the subject was following a particular type of strategy.[56]

Another aspect of modern choice research is the frequent use of animal subjects. For example, animals may be rewarded in different ways for responding in different places. The animal's distribution of responses between the different places is a kind of choice, and the changes in distribution when reward rates are varied have been shown by operant psychologists to follow rather regular laws.[57] An important aim of this research is to attempt to uncover regularities in choice behavior that apply to both humans and animals. Aquinas, in contrast, was largely concerned with processes he believed unique to human beings, processes perhaps more complex than those investigated in animal experiments, and ones that are at least partly accessible to introspection.

NOTES

1. Nemesius' work is (erroneously) attributed by Aquinas to Gregory of Nyssa.

2. Aquinas, *Summa Theologiae*, 1.2.22, 1–2. The translator of questions 22–39 in the Blackfriars edition of the *Summa Theologiae* translates the Latin *appetitus* as "orexis." As, however, *orexis* is not a frequently used word, even by the other translators of the *Summa*, I have rendered it as the more usual "appetite." There is, in fact, a very general problem in describing emotions not only in Aquinas' account or translations of it but also in present-day psychology. See K. T. Strongman, *The Psychology of Emotion*, 3rd ed. (London: Wiley, 1987), 1–8.

3. Aquinas, *Summa Theologiae*, 1.2.22.3.

4. See E. Gellhorn, and G. N. Loufbourrow, *Emotions and Emotional Disorders* (New York: Hoeber, 1963); and J. Panksepp, "Towards a General Psychobiological Theory of Emotions." *The Behavioral and Brain Sciences* 5 (1981): 407–467.

5. Aquinas, *Summa Theologiae*, 1.2.23.1

6. For example, Nemesius, *A Treatise on the Nature of Man*, 350–351.

7. Strongman, *The Psychology of Emotion*, 21–27, 56–86, etc.

8. Aquinas, *Summa Theologiae*, 1.2.23.2–4.

9. Ibid., 1.2.26.4.

10. Ibid., 1.2.27.3.

11. Ibid., 1.2.27.4.

12. Ibid., 1.2.28.6.

13. Ibid., 1.2.28.1–5; 1.2.29.2.

14. Ibid., 1.2.31.3.

15. Ibid., 1.2.31.5–6.

16. Ibid., 1.2.32.2.

17. Marvin Zuckerman, *Sensation Seeking: Beyond the Optimal Level of Arousal* (Hillsdale, N.J.: Erlbaum, 1979).

18. Aquinas, *Summa Theologiae*, 1.2.33.1–3.

19. Ibid., 1.2.41.4.

20. Ibid., 1.2.41.4; 1.2.42.2.

21. Ibid., 1.2.42.3–4.

22. Ibid., 1.2.42.6.

23. Ibid., 1.2.42.1.

24. Aquinas, *Commentaria*, 1.2.22.

25. Aquinas, *Summa Theologiae*, 1.2.44.1.

26. Ibid., 1.2.45.3. As with the effects of fear, the physiology is derived from Aristotle.

27. Ibid., 1.2.44.3.

28. Ibid., 1.2.44.4.

29. R. M. Yerkes and J. P. Dodson, "The Relation of Strength of Stimulus to Rapidity of Habit-Formation." *Journal of Comparative Neurology and Psychology* 18 (1908): 459–482.

30. See Patricia M. Wallace, Jeffrey H. Goldstein, and Peter Nathan, *Introduction to Psychology* (Dubuque, Iowa: Brown, 1987), 272–275; J. W. Kling and Lorrin A. Riggs, eds. *Woodworth and Schlosberg's Experimental Psychology*, 3rd ed. (New York: Holt, Rinehart, and Winston, 1971), 826–845.

31. Aquinas, *Summa Theologiae*, 1.2.48.3.

32. Ibid., 1.2.46.4.

33. Ibid., 1.2.46.7.

34. Ibid., 1.2.47.1–3.

35. Ibid., 1.2..48.1.

36. Chrétien de Troyes, *Perceval: The Story of the Grail*, trans. Nigel Bryant (Cambridge, UK: D. S. Brewer, 1982), 32.

37. Aquinas, *Summa Theologiae*, 1.2.48.1–4.

38. Phillip Shaver, Judith Schwartz, Donald Kirson, and Cary O'Connor, "Emotion Knowledge: Further Exploration of a Prototype Approach." *Journal of Personality and Social Psychology* 52 (1987): 1078.

39. William James, "What Is an Emotion?" *Mind* 9 (1984): 188–205.

40. For example, R. S. Lazarus, "On the Primacy of Cognition." *American Psychologist* 39 (1984): 124–129.

41. See Strongman, *Psychology of Emotion*, 21–34.

42. Thorndike, *University Records*, 80–81.

43. Aquinas, *Summa Theologiae*, 1.2.40.3.

44. Ibid., 1.2.9.1–4.

45. Ibid. See 1.2.8.1–3; 1.2.8.4. The ice cream example is, of course, mine, but the process is mapped out by Aquinas.

46. Ibid., 1.2.10.2.

47. Ibid., 1.2.10.3.

48. Ibid., 1.2.12–17.

49. Ibid., 1.2.17.8–9.

50. Ibid., 1.2.17.9; see also 1.2.10.3.

51. Ibid., 1.2.17.7.

52. See also ibid., 1.2.9.3. Compare also to William of Auvergne's metaphor describing the soul at the end of chapter 2.

53. Ibid., 1.2.56.4.

54. See especially, B. F. Skinner, *Beyond Freedom and Dignity* (New York: Knopf, 1971).

55. George Mandler, *Mind and Emotion* (New York: Wiley, 1975). See especially 41–64.

56. See W. Edwards and A. Tversky, eds. *Decision Making* (Harmondsworth, UK: Penguin, 1967); and D. Kahneman, P. Slovic, and A. Tversky, eds. *Judgement under Uncertainty; Heuristics and Biases* (Cambridge, UK: Cambridge University Press, 1982).

57. See R. J. Herrnstein, "On the Law of Effect." *Journal of the Experimental Analysis of Behavior* 13 (1970): 243–266.

6

Individual Differences

The study of individual differences in present-day psychology is the study of the way in which mental processes and behavior differ from person to person. Particularly interesting are those differences that appear to be characteristic of a given person and are manifested in different kinds of situations. Probably the most important and well-known category of psychological differences is that of personality differences, but differences in intelligence and cognitive abilities have also been frequently studied.

In the Middle Ages both of these kinds of individual difference were recognized. Moreover it was recognized that differences between people might be due to differences between their incorporeal minds or differences that appeared to have a physical basis. Most of this chapter is concerned with two well-elaborated accounts—those given by astrology and the doctrine of the humors—that traced psychological differences to physical causes. Before considering these, however, it is worth briefly examining Thomas Aquinas' account of dispositions (*habitum*), which embraced mental as well as physiological differences.

Dispositions, according to Aquinas, are quasi-permanent qualities that are generally manifest in behavior of some kind. It is essential to Aquinas' notion that there is a range of possible behaviors or types of behavior available for choice.[1] Dispositions are then either qualities of the intellect or will alone, for example, the tendency to act justly, or of the lower faculties such as the inner senses acting under the command of reason, for example, one can train oneself to remember something quickly.[2] A consequence of Aquinas' approach is that animals, which have no will, and hence no power to choose from a range of behaviors, do not have dispositions naturally, although they can be trained by human beings.[3]

Dispositions, although generally of a rudimentary kind, may be innate, thus some people are inclined by their physiological makeup to be chaste or even tempered. Strictly speaking, however, dispositions are learned or acquired gradually by repeated action.[4] Similarly, dispositions can be weakened or lost through disuse. When, for example, an intellectual disposition is not used, one may be distracted by irrelevant or confusing images. If the appearance of these images is not prevented by applying the intellectual disposition, errors of judgment may be made.[5]

The key features of Aquinas' account of dispositions are that they are generally acquired as a result of one's past actions, that they exist in the mind rather than in the body or the lower faculties of the soul, and that they do not totally determine behavior. By contrast both the theory of astrology and the doctrine of the humors stressed causal factors in individual differences that were outside of the control of the individual. Yet, in the Middle Ages, belief in these theories was widespread. Furthermore considerable intellectual effort went into making these theories compatible with each other and with Christian thinking as a whole.

ASTROLOGY

Both the discovery of the five planets known to the ancient and medieval world (Mercury, Venus, Mars, Jupiter, and Saturn) and the astrological theory that linked their movements and those of the Sun and Moon to terrestrial events appear to have originated in Babylon. The evidence suggests that astrological reasoning was at first restricted to mundane astrology and applied to events of worldwide or at least Babylonian significance. Only later was astrology used to attempt to predict the behavior or fate of individual people. The first known horoscope for an individual was drawn up in 409 B.C. in Babylonia; like all its successors it consists of a list of the positions of the Sun, Moon, and planets at birth, together with predictions derived from those positions.[6]

Ancient astrology incorporated both what we now call astronomy, including geometry and cosmological theory as well as observation of the movement of the planets, and religious belief. According to the cosmological theory of the time, which extended into the Middle Ages, the planets are supposed to circle the earth and, in increasing distance from the Earth, are arranged in the order: Moon, Mercury, Venus, Sun, Mars, Jupiter, and Saturn. The motion of the planets and the fixed stars is held to be eternal and unchanging. The warmth of the planet is de-termined by its distance from the Sun. Thus, for example, Saturn is cold and Mars hot. The moistness is determined partly by its proximity to the drying influence of the Sun, and partly by its proximity to moisture rising from the Earth. Thus the Moon is moist, while Saturn is rather dry, and Mars very dry.[7] This cosmological account was, as we shall see, of psychological as well as physical importance because it placed the planets on the dimensions of hot-cold and wet-dry, dimensions that were important in ancient and medieval medicine as well.

It was a common ancient belief to regard the planets either as divine in themselves, as did Plato for example,[8] or as under the control of a divinity. These planetary divinities were often called demons (*daimones*), and they were regarded as intermediaries between god (or the gods) and man.[9] Linked to this belief was the idea that human souls ascended into heaven after death. Plato believed, for example, that human souls were originally assigned stars before being placed in bodies on earth. Souls who lived virtuously were returned to their native star at death, those who did not were placed into the bodies of women or animals.[10] In the Hermetic writings, probably written in the first two centuries A.D. and so called because they are written in the form of dialogues with Hermes Trismegistus, the soul when incorporated took on a mixture of planetary essences that determined its character. At death, the soul, if virtuous, ascended to a heaven beyond the planets, divesting itself of the seven types of planetary essence on the way.[11]

Astrology flowered under the Roman Empire. Many of the emperors, for example Tiberius and Hadrian, were personally interested in astrol-ogy and frequently took astrological advice. Astrology was also popular with the Roman people generally. Virgil, Horace, Ovid, Seneca, and Petronius all mention horoscopes and astrology, and the frequent purges and proscriptions of astrology in Rome seem to have been motivated by fear of its effects rather than scorn at its accuracy. Nor was this fear totally misplaced: astrological prophecies encouraged Vespasian success-fully and other aspirants unsuccessfully to seek the imperial throne.[12]

The spread of astrological ideas led to a number of works on astrology; some were religious but some were essentially manuals for the astrologer and dealt with issues such as how to draw up horoscopes and how to interpret the resulting chart. Two such manuals were the *Tetrabiblos* of Claudius Ptolemy, probably written about 150–170 A.D., and the *Mathesis* of Julius Firmicus Maternus, written about 334 A.D.[13] Both manuals were available in manuscript in later medieval Europe and influenced medi-eval writing and thinking about astrology.

Two features of Roman astrology ensured the hostility of the early Christians. The first was that astrology was inextricably linked to existing religious beliefs, which the early Christians opposed. Hence directly the

Christian diatribes against demon worship. The second feature was that Roman astrology tended to be deterministic. Roman astrology was extensively used for foretelling, rather than, say, determining propitious times for doing things. This type of astrology, later known as judicial astrology, arose from the view that all earthly events, including those involving human behavior, were controlled by the stars (or their presiding deities) and thus could in theory be astrologically predicted.

It is worth noting that astrological determinism was a very rigid system indeed. The course of the stars was not only predictable but could also be seen to be unchanging. Comets could provide an element of randomness but their visits were of course infrequent; moreover, as Seneca quite correctly suggested, it was likely that their courses too would be discovered.[14] Another possibility was that clouds might exert a mitigating effect as suggested earlier by the Babylonians.[15] This suggestion, however, seems to have been ignored by Roman and medieval astrologers, although Henry of Hesse took up, or more likely rediscovered, the notion in the fourteenth century.[16] Some idea of the rigidity of astrological determinism can be gained by comparing it to Skinnerian behaviorism. While B. F. Skinner's theories are among the most deterministic advanced in contemporary psychology, these theories clearly recognize the practical impossibility of predicting the future in detail. Furthermore, if the environment is held to determine behavior, it is central to Skinner's thinking that the organism can modify the environment.[17] Astrologers, on the other hand, have generally denied that human behavior could alter the course of the stars. Curiously, this denial is not universal: an early Christian gnostic sect held that Christ had freed the stars from their courses and Paracelsus (1493–1541) later suggested that terrestrial events might alter the course or influence of the stars.[18]

The early Christian writers were often prepared to concede the possibility of stellar influence, especially where this was thought to be useful, as in the case of medicine or agriculture. On the other hand, they were implacably hostile to judicial astrology, largely because, as we have seen, they were determined to give a prominent place to free will in deciding human action. One of the most hostile critics was Augustine. In *The City of God*, he made use of Cicero's arguments against judicial astrology, objecting, particularly, that twins such as Jacob and Esau have different destinies although born under the same constellations. He also extended the attack to cover the astrological methods for deciding propitious times.[19] Later he stated that "when astrologers give replies that are often surprisingly true, they are inspired in some mysterious way, by spirits, but spirits of evil."[20] Yet Augustine was not able to demonstrate that there was no stellar influence on terrestrial events, particularly faced with the obvious effects of the sun and moon: "Now it could be maintained, without utter absurdity that some influence from the stars had an effect on variations confined to the physical realm [but] it is not conceivable that the decisions of man's will are subject to the stars."[21] A more moderate stance was taken by Origen: he was hostile to judicial astrology, which he described as a "delusive system," but he was prepared to concede that the stars might predict "the approach of lightnings, and fruits, and all manner of productions."[22] Similarly he accepted that the planets were living, rational beings, and that some souls on earth had descended from places in the heavens.[23]

One effect of the adoption of Christianity as the official religion of the Roman Empire was to curb the power of astrology. However, the Church did not attempt to forbid its practice altogether. Perhaps most important from the point of view of medieval psychology was that a rigidly deterministic model of human behavior was rejected in favor of one that advocated the primacy of free will. The practice of astrology in the early Middle Ages seems to have been limited not so much, however, by the hostility of the Church, as by the fact that few, if any, Western Europeans knew very much about it. One recent scholar concluded that the cause of the disappearance of "scientific" (i.e., mathematical) astrology was "not persecution or prosecution, but the lack of proper manuals."[24]

Revival of interest in astrology accompanied the dissemination of astrological literature and manuals in the eleventh and twelfth centuries, and for the rest of the Middle Ages and, indeed, up until the seventeenth century, belief in the fundamental tenet of astrology, that the positions of the planets have significant effects on terrestrial events, was nearly universal among educated Europeans.[25] Medieval astrology was not confined to dealing with psychological issues, as astrological considerations were widely believed to be important in agriculture, geology, chemistry or alchemy, the weather, medicine, and historical and sociological occurrences. In the medieval period it was common to ascribe the outbreak of epidemics to planetary courses. This tradition was strengthened with the appearance of the Black Death, first in 1348 and then at frequent intervals for many centuries after, and many astrological writers tried to link recurrences of the plague with planetary conjunctions.[26] By the end of the fourteenth century, astrologers were in regular demand as advisers in many of the European courts, and, for example, produced predictions regarding the Hundred Years War between England and France.[27]

In general, the attitude of medieval scholars and churchmen to astrology during the later Middle Ages was rather less hostile than that of Augustine. Aquinas summarized a common view of his time when he stated that change to earthly conditions must be causally determined by changes in heavenly conditions.[28]

On the other hand the stars are unable to affect the will.[29] The reconciliation of these apparently opposing positions was, as usual, elegantly achieved.

Most men follow their passions, which involve changes in sense-desire, and in these changes the heavenly bodies can play a part. On the other hand, those wise enough to be able to resist these passions are few and far between. Consequently, astrologers are able to foretell the truth in the majority of cases, especially in a general sense. However, they cannot do so in particular cases, for nothing stops a man from resisting his passions by his free-will.[30]

The use of astrology for divination was thought by Aquinas to be evil in itself as well as laying one open to the possibility of diabolic intervention. On the other hand, it was permissible to predict future events with physical causes such as the weather.[31] Similar views are expressed by Albertus Magnus, from whom Aquinas probably derived his own.[32]

Two features of Aquinas' account are noteworthy. First, he was prepared to concede that astrology often works. Second, it is clear that his view of astrology, which he shared with most (although not all) of his contemporaries differed radically from that of classic astrology in its conception of the nature of the stellar forces. For classic astrologers, the forces were essentially divine and operated on the human soul or spirit. Most medieval writers saw the forces as physical and operating on the human body, and in particular on its humors, while the mind and the will were not directly affected. Thus it was possible both to enjoy the imagined scientific benefits of astrology and even to allow the determinism of many terrestrial events while at the same time allowing for human free will.

The main astrological doctrine of psychological consequence in the Middle Ages, as now, was the method of nativities, which attempted to predict future behavior from the position of the planets at birth. The astrological systems of both Ptolemy and Firmicus Maternus, for example, suggested rules for obtaining personal predictions from horoscopes, generally on the basis that each planet represented or controlled a personality trait or group of traits. There was also reasonable agreement about which planet represented which trait or traits. For example, Ptolemy believed Mercury to produce people who are "wise, shrewd, thoughtful, learned, inventive . . . inquirers into nature, speculative, gifted, emulous,"[33] Firmicus suggested that "those who have Mercury as ruler of the chart are clever, talented, students of all things, modest, they desire to learn the secret of all skills,"[34] while Bartholomaeus Anglicus remarked that being born under Mercury is a token of wit and wisdom.[35] Similarly Mars was held to produce active, fierce, and often rather bad-tempered individuals; Venus was associated with the love of pleasure; and Jupiter with lordliness.[36] Agreement of attributes was not always clear-cut: Alexander of Neckham (1157–1213 A.D.) described Mars as bestowing the gift of counsel,[37] while the attributes ascribed to Saturn were always rather debatable.[38]

Although medieval scholars such as Aquinas and Bacon knew of astrology and were even sympathetic to some of its less deterministic claims, they do not seem to have shown much interest in it. Rather more discussion of astrology is found in more popular writings of the later Middle Ages. In *Secretum Secretorum* (*The Secret of Secrets*), for example, which is written in the form of apocryphal (and often rather unlikely) advice given by Aristotle to Alexander the Great, there is frequent mention of astrological ideas, and an example given of a child's horoscope that "shewed that the child should be wise, curious of his hand, and of good and convenient counsel."[39] However, when his father tried to have him taught science, this was ineffective as the child's astrological bent was to be a smith.

Both John Gower (ca. 1327–1408) and Geoffrey Chaucer (ca. 1343–1400) reveal in their poetry a detailed knowledge of astrology. Gower regarded astrology, which he called astronomy, as one of the sciences that a king should know and, in his *Confessio Amantis*, discussed at some length the nature of the planets and the zodiac signs.[40] He remarks of Mercury, for example,

> That under him who that bore is,
> In boke he shall be studious,
> And in writinge curious,
> And slowe and lustles to travaile
> In thing which elles he might availe.[41]

In Chaucer's *Canterbury Tales*, astrology often plays an important role. The planets, particularly Saturn, determine the events of "The Knight's Tale" and astrological magic is worked in "The Franklin's Tale." The wife of Bath attributes her lust and lechery to the natal influence of Venus and her hardiness to Mars, and remarks that her ascendant (i.e., the zodiac sign on the eastern horizon at the time of her birth) was Taurus and contained Mars.[42]

THE DOCTRINE OF THE HUMORS

Astrology developed from a combination of astronomy and religious belief; the doctrine of the humors, however, was a medical theory. According to the classic tradition of medicine that originated with Hippocrates of Cos (ca. 460–377 B.C.), illness arose from disturbances (*dyscrasia*) to the balance of the four bodily fluids or humors. These four humors were the blood, phlegm, black bile (melancholy), and yellow bile (choler). [43] The general features of the model seem to have been widely accepted by ancient, as indeed they were by medieval, physicians, although there were occasional dissenting voices: the Methodist sect of physicians, for example, seem to have made little use of it. [44] Precisely how disturbances of the humors were related to the different illnesses was frequently a matter of debate, and different post-Hippocratic physicians introduced or supported different versions of the theory. [45]

There were also developments in the way the humors themselves were regarded. One development was the introduction of subtypes of the four humors. For example, Galen, who notes that Praxagoras distinguished ten humors in addition to blood, himself distinguished a normal and a pathenogenic type of each of black bile, yellow bile, and phlegm. [46] The pathenogenic forms arose from combustion of the normal humors. Avicenna, whose *Canon of Medicine* was a commonly used medieval medical text, distinguished two types of black bile (one normal and one abnormal), three types of yellow bile (two abnormal), and no less than eight abnormal types of phlegm. [47] Thus in later medical theory, an imbalance of a normal humor was not generally a cause of illness, rather illness was caused by the appearance of an abnormal variant of the humor. A second development in the theory of the humors was the linking of the humors with the system of physical qualities. The four simple qualities were hot, cold, dry, and moist, and Galen, for example, reckoned these to be the basic and most important of the medical principles. The four normal humors are typified by the four permissible combinations of these qualities. Thus blood is hot and moist, yellow bile hot and dry, black bile cold and dry, and phlegm cold and moist. [48] A third development of the theory of the humors was the perceived correlation between the humors and the constitutions and physiognomy of healthy as well as unhealthy individuals. In Galen's system of temperaments there were four simple (one for each physical quality) and four mixed temperaments (one for each humor), and these temperaments were related to character differences. Hence arose the idea of temperaments in which one or other of the humors predominated. The sanguine temperament was dominated by blood, the melancholic by black bile or melancholy, the choleric by yellow bile, and the phlegmatic by phlegm. According to Galen's system, a preponderance of yellow bile was responsible for acuteness and intelligence, black bile for steadiness, and blood for simplicity. [49]

Although the basic idea that the humors determined, or were correlated with, character survived Galen, his particular pairing of characteristics with humors did not. Subsequent writers tended to regard the sanguine humor as producing an ideal, good-natured individual, yellow bile as responsible for bad temper, phlegm as producing stolidity, while black bile took on rather negative characteristics, resembling the melancholic illness.[50] In Gower's *Confessio Amantis*, for example, the cold and dry or melancholic is described as the worst of the temperaments, and he who has it is suspicious, wrathful, and anxious. Phlegmatic individuals are slow and lethargic, while the choleric are ingenious, active, and bad tempered. The best temperament is, however, that of the blood.[51] Bartholomaeus Anglicus describes a very phlegmatic man as listless, heavy, and slow, dull of wit and thought, and forgetful, with a tendency to sleep a lot. Such men are fat and short, and have a white complexion.[52] Choleric men are wrathful, hardy, light, unstable, and impetuous, tending to be tall and lean with a brown complexion and black hair.[53] Bartholomaeus Anglicus does not recognize a sanguine man as such, but comments that those with pure blood are glad and prone to love, and that it gives a good color to the body.[54] He also distinguishes a natural and pathological black bile or melancholy, but the character description given of the person dominated by this humor is in the pathological terms of the medieval mental disorder of melancholy (considered in the following chapter) which was held to be caused by abnormal, pathenogenic black bile. Such people are characterized by having causeless fears or sorrows.[55] This tendency to confuse the melancholic character with the melancholic mental disorder was not restricted to Bartholomaeus Anglicus and seems, in fact, to have been common in the Middle Ages.[56]

A particularly idiosyncratic theory of the humors was produced by Hildegard of Bingen (1098–1179), in her medical work *Causae et Curae*. She distinguished temperaments based on four kinds of phlegm: dry, moist, frothy, and lukewarm. Those dominated by dry phlegm tend to be fat and dark, and although often industrious are also irascible, hardheaded, tyrannical, and greedy. Moist phlegm predominates in people who are cheerful and gentle but rather slow, while frothy phlegm is found in those who are generally good-humored but quick to anger. The lukewarm type is similar to black bile in producing sorrow and fear.[57] An interesting feature of Hildegard's medicine is her frank and lengthy discussion of human sexuality, which extends into her discussion of personality. She distinguished four types of men and also of women on the basis of their attraction to, and need for, the opposite sex. For example, there are especially virile men who are distinguished by their reddish, hot-blooded complexion and strong build. They enjoy the company of women more than men and are generally healthy and cheerful except when sexually frustrated. Correspondingly there are women who are naturally lovable and finely built. They are healthy when they have men but sicken without them; they are also prone to premenstrual tension.[58]

Individual differences in cognitive abilities in the Middle Ages were often held to be due to differences in the workings of the inner senses. These differences in turn were commonly believed to be due to their temperature and moistness. The origin of this notion, as for the idea of the inner senses as a whole, is Aristotelian. In *De Memoria et Reminiscentia*, Aristotle comments that the texture of some people's memory is too soft and moist to retain impressions while that of others is too hard and dry to enable the imprint to occur in the first place.[59] The elaboration of the doctrine of the inner senses also enabled the elaboration of this explanation of individual differences in them. Averroes maintains that good memory occurs in people who have a relatively dry back of the brain, because, although dry surfaces receive the imprint of forms with difficulty, they retain it for a long time. If this region is relatively moist, the impressions will not be retained and forgetting will occur. On the other hand, quickness of actual retrieval is improved by moisture.

Consequently, one who is excessive in dryness will be short in understanding but long in remembering; one who is excessive in moisture will be quick at grasping that which he retains, fast in forgetting, and slow in remembering. Those whose complexion is a medium will combine within them good power of grasping that which is retained and good power of memory.[60]

Averroes continues by using the theory to explain differences in memory between the young and the old. The former, who have naturally moist brains, are quick at grasping what is retained but have less long memories.[61]

Superiority of imagination, according to Averroes, is possessed by those who have a cold and dry, i.e., melancholic, balance of humors. This is because the proper functioning of the imagination requires images of relatively long duration and good definition that do not change too frequently. Coldness delays the motion which changes the image while dryness causes the image to endure. Melancholic people tend, for this reason and also because the vapors of black bile tend to bring on sleep, to have more frequent and "truer" dreams. Indeed, they often perceive in waking what others dream when they are asleep.[62]

The four qualities and the humors then could be theoretically combined with the doctrine of the inner senses. Another medieval development was the attempt to combine the doctrine of the humors with astrological theory. That this should be attempted is not surprising given, first, that the qualities of the planets, that is their temperature and moistness, were already determined in ancient astrology and, second, that the qualities of the humors were well established.

Furthermore, in the field of medicine, there was in the Middle Ages a well-established body of opinion that held that the planets and, in particular the moon, had a great influence on the flow of bodily fluids, as clearly happened in the case of tides. Pliny, for example, had stated that the Moon increased and decreased blood,[63] and it was commonly held that menstruation depended on the phase of the Moon.[64] Hence it was often believed that the day chosen for phlebotomy or bloodletting should be influenced by the lunar cycle.[65] A related belief was that epilepsy, which was generally believed in the Middle Ages to be caused by phlegm or bile obstructing the passage of spirit in the brain, was also correlated with the lunar cycle. The Moon was held to influence the movement of the obstructing humors.[66]

The first explicit suggestion of a link between the planets and the humors seems to occur in the writings of Abu-Masar (d. 885 A.D.) who discussed proposals that the stars, elements, and humors, as well as colors, were all interrelated: Saturn, which was cold and dry, was linked to black bile; Mars was linked with "red" bile (i.e., choler); Jupiter, with blood; and the Moon, with phlegm.[67] The idea of a causal link between the stars and the humors, which could provide an essentially physical rather than religious explanation of astrology and in which the terrestrial effects were mediated by the heat and light of the stars, was often favorably received by Christian writers in the later Middle Ages. Such a model was theologically and psychologically acceptable because the astrological causes were thus linked to the body and physiological mechanisms that could be overridden by the will.

There were, however, some difficulties with it, even when the lack—to modern eyes—of a plausible causal process linking a planet to a particular humor was ignored. Nicholas Oresme (d. 1382), for example, argued that if the influence of the stars was indirect then knowledge of the inferior but more direct causes (i.e., the qualities or the humors) was much more important than knowing about the positions of the planets. Moreover, he argued, why should planets have more influence in one aspect than in another?[68] Furthermore, in practice it was not easy to work the seven planets and the four humors into one system, and different writers produced rather different accounts. For Hildegard of Bingen, who followed a medical tradition, the Moon alone was the main cause of change in the humors and hence behavior.[69] A more usual scheme, however, assigned a particular planet to each humor with some left over. For example, Bartholomaeus Anglicus describes Saturn as having mastery over the melancholic humor, Jupiter over the sanguine, and Mars over the choleric. The Moon is described as cold and moist but is designated as having power over all the humors, and phlegm is actually left unassigned to any planet.[70] In The Book of Secrets of Albertus Magnus, (whose authorship is unknown but is almost certainly not that of Albertus Magnus himself), the phlegmatic humor is ascribed to Venus, but the other pairings are maintained.[71] Such models, of course, leave it unclear how Mercury or the Sun could exert their influences on personality.

Despite these theoretical difficulties, however, it is clear that the combination of astrology and the doctrine of the humors could provide a more or less unified account of individual differences, so long as the account was not subjected to too detailed an analysis. In the next section, some of the more psychological characteristics of both the initial theories and their combination are considered.

THEORY OF PERSONALITY IN ASTROLOGY AND THE DOCTRINE OF THE HUMORS

The theory of astrology and the doctrine of the humors, and even more so the combination of the two accounts, have certain features that are important not only for the causal explanation of how individual differences arise but also for the perceived nature of the differences. That is, a particular way of looking at individual differences is made necessary if one adopts an astrological, or for that matter a humoral, viewpoint. We now consider in detail what constraints were imposed.

In the first place, the astrological account of personality, like that resulting from the humors model, had to be either a trait theory or a typology. A trait theory is one that supposes personality to be structured around a relatively stable and enduring handful of *traits* or basic dimensions of possible personality difference. A simple trait theory, for example, is contained in the idea that people can be placed on the two dimensions of hot-cold and dry-moist, and how warm and how dry they are determines a large part of their behavior. As we have seen this simple trait theory was quite popular in the Middle Ages and could be used to predict people's cognitive abilities and personality.

That the astrological account should be a trait theory follows naturally because there were only seven planets known, and hence seven possible dimensions of personality available. Such a trait theory could be quite sophisticated. Ptolemy's system had both positive and negative aspects for each dimension and he believed most personalities to reflect the combination of the seven planets and their associate traits. Indeed, his account is rather more complex than some present-day trait theories. Eysenck's account, for example, which by his own admission bears strong resemblance to the ancient and medieval model of the qualities, makes use of only two basic dimensions of personality: extraversion-introversion and neuroticism.[72] In practice, however, seven dimensions of personality may be thought of as a theoretical maximum in ancient and medieval astrology. The solar and lunar dimensions were usually rather poorly defined—the Sun was held to have a general beneficial influence, while the Moon usually had special significance for bodily health rather than for personality.[73] Moreover, tying the astrological to the humoral system effectively gave only four possible personality dimensions (two, if the underlying hot-cold and dry-wet dimensions of quality are used instead of the humors), with Mercury providing an extra dimension close to that of present-day intelligence.

In practice, the medieval account tended to be even further simplified into a typology, in which people's personalities were classified into distinct types, rather than being represented as points in a space defined by continuous dimensions. In astrology this occurred when only the ruling planet and its associated personality characteristics were considered; in the humoral model when the dominant humor for the individual was deemed of primary importance.

Again the extent of the simplification depended on the sophistication of the theorist. While the briefer humoral accounts, for example, that of Bartholomaeus Anglicus, considered only the dominant humor, that of Hildegard of Bingen considered the effects of all the possible combinations. For example, people in whom there is a large quantity of luke-warm phlegm with a moderate amount of dry and less of the other two types tend to exhibit unusual emotional swings while those who have a large amount of lukewarm moderated by frothy phlegm tend to be hard, inconsiderate and discontented.[74]

Second, in the astrological method of nativities the mixture of traits is determined by the planetary positions at birth. Hence the personality of the individual is predicted to remain largely unchanged throughout life. Consideration of the humors provided some potential for change, however, because these could be affected by other factors, especially diet.

Third, because the planets were believed to affect not only personality, but also, for example, life span, occupation and physical characteristics, the astrological account predicted correlations between personality traits and these other variables, particularly the physical characteristics. Similar predictions follow naturally from the theory of humors, where the balance of humors was often supposed to be diagnosed from an individual's appearance. Such predicted correlations tend to enhance the tendency to stereotyping which results from classifying people into planetary or humoral types. For example, according to Ptolemy, Jupiter tends to produce light-skinned, relatively tall men with curling hair; the planet also makes people magnanimous, generous, honorable, dignified, and affectionate and imbues qualities of leadership.[75] It follows logically that light-skinned, tall men with curly hair should also tend to have the personality characteristics of Jupiter. Similarly if one meets someone possessed of the dark complexion supposedly resulting from an excess of the melancholic humor, one might also expect them to show melancholic character attributes such as suspicion. The idea that people's characters may be inferred from their appearance is seen at its logical development in some versions of The Secret of Secrets, which contain a complete section outlining how character may be inferred from physiognomy.[76] Although both astrological and humoral references appear in the book, the section on using physiognomy to infer personality does not contain them, so it is unclear from where the predictions derive. Some of the physiognomic signs, however, have earlier astrological references. A striking example in *The Secret of Secrets* is a belief still sometimes encountered today: the idea that red-haired people have fiery tempers.[77] This connection is found in Firmicus Maternus, who states that people who are ruled by the red planet Mars tend to have red hair and be bad tempered, as it is in *The Book of Secrets of Albertus Magnus*, where it is again attributed to Martian influence.[78] In theory, a wide variety of stereotypes of this kind could have been deduced and fixed in medieval, or for that modern, culture. One factor probably acting to prevent this was that there was often some disagreement over details of astrological or humoral predictions. For example, although Ptolemy and Bartholomaeus Anglicus agree that Mars produced a quick temper, neither associates the planet with red hair. Ptolemy associates Mars with fair hair, and Bartholomaeus makes no association with hair color at all.[79]

Implicit in the preceding discussion is the possibility that an astrological model of personality might be employed that is not really dependent on the physical positions or properties of the planets at all. Such a view was articulated, although somewhat hesitantly, in the fifteenth century by Marsilio Ficino (1433–1499), who seems to have been led to this view, in part, from considering astrological magic.

Briefly, the use of astrological magic involved the contemplation of astrological images or talismans.[80] These images were supposed to capture the spirit of a planet. A medieval Arab text called *Picatrix*, for example, recommends that the spirit of Saturn might be captured by making an image in "the form of a man standing on a dragon, clothed in black and holding in his right hand a sickle and in his left a spear."[81] The medieval Church, as one might expect, disapproved of such practices, although astrological magic was known in Western Europe— Chaucer describes it in "The Franklin's Tale." Ficino tried to provide a Christian rationale for astrological magic.

Ficino's main motivation for using astrological magic was medical. He believed illness to arise from overdomination by a particular kind of planetary influence, especially melancholy, which, as we have seen, was linked to Saturn. Those who suffered from this influence could counter it by attracting influences from more cheerful planets, such as the Sun and Jupiter. This could be done by contemplating the right astrological images, by surrounding oneself with precious stones or fragrant herbs related to the appropriate planet, or by listening to particular sorts of music.[82]

A feature of this rather charming therapy is that it is unclear whether the magic is supposed to work because actual planetary influences are captured or because the images and music work directly on the imagination or memory of the perceiver. Ficino himself seems to have been undecided on this point, although it is clear that he recognized the second possibility.[83] Similarly Ficino believed that one might become melancholy, not by virtue of a horoscopic influence of Saturn, but because one's occupation might bring one under the influence of Saturn. Students, and other people engaged in contemplative activities, were particularly susceptible.[84] Furthermore, as Ficino wrote in a letter to Lorenzo d'Medici, the planets and their qualities could be conceived as internal: "We have an entire sky within us, our fiery strength and heavenly origin: Luna which symbolizes the continuous motion of soul and body, Mars speed and Saturn slowness, the Sun God, Jupiter Law, Mercury reason, and Venus humanity."[85] Thus as a whole Ficino's psychology, although theoretically grounded in astrology, is effectively independent of the truth or otherwise of astrology, as he himself occasionally recognized.

MEDIEVAL AND PRESENT-DAY ACCOUNTS OF PERSONALITY

It has been shown that the medieval account of personality differences contained in astrology and the doctrine of the humors was a trait theory or a typology. In this it resembles a number of present-day accounts of personality, one of which, Eysenck's, has already been mentioned. The existence of a close relationship between physical and psychological characteristics is also proposed by some present-day theorists, most notably William Sheldon. According to Sheldon's constitutional psychology, which is, it should be noted, not currently in great favor, people's body types are related to personality. Plump people (endomorphs) are supposed to be sociable and outgoing; tall, thin people (ectomorphs) to be restrained and solitary; and muscular people (mesomorphs) to be aggressive and active.[86] Endomorphs could perhaps be thought of as phlegmatic and ectomorphs as melancholic in the medieval view although the correspondences are not exact and, moreover, the mesomorphs could be assigned to either the choleric or the sanguine temperament.

It is important to realize, however, that theories of individual differences do not have to posit the existence of a correlation between physical and psychological characteristics, nor do they even have to be trait theories at all. A number of modern theories do not make use of traits or personality dimensions;[87] moreover, Aquinas' account of dispositions is not a theory of this type. In this theory, it will be recalled, dispositions, or tendencies to act in a particular way, are generally learned, have no necessary connection with any physical characteristics, and do not have to be limited to a small number of basic, underlying dimensions of disposition. Yet on the whole Aquinas' approach seems to have had relatively little impact outside of the scholarly world, while the less academic theory of personality contained in astrology and the doctrine of the humors persisted and prospered well beyond the Middle Ages. It seems likely, too, that in the Renaissance and early modern era, knowledge of these theories spread to a greater proportion of the population. Some indication of this spread is given by the relative frequency of detailed astrological and humoral references—presumably meant to be understood by their audiences—in the works of the Elizabethan dramatists.[88]

A possible reason why the astrological and humoral theories proved so durable is that the account of personality they contain closely resembles that uncovered by present-day research into person perception. The study of person perception concerns how people perceive and make judgments about one another.[89] An important aspect of this study is the way in which people assess one another's personality, sometimes referred to as "implicit personality theory." It has been shown that the medieval account of personality predicted differences in a small number of very stable traits, which were linked to physical characteristics. It so happens that people gauge one another's personality in a very similar way.[90]

A number of recent studies have shown that people do make personality judgments on the basis of physical appearance and that such judgments tend to be based on stereotypes, for example, thin people tend to be suspicious and ambitious or fair-haired people tend to be kind.[91] Moreover, while people make personality judgments using a vast variety of trait terms, the judgments appear to be based on a stable structure or implicit theory that is organized around a few basic traits.[92] There are even parallels between these basic traits and those used in the Middle Ages. For example, the warm-cold dimension seems to often be of great importance in these naive personality theories, as it was in the medieval accounts.[93]

Thus there is good evidence of similarity between the medieval account and the personality theories implicit in the way present-day ordinary people or *naive perceivers*, as they are called by research workers in the area, assess other people. Why do these similarities arise? There seem to be a number of possibilities, not necessrily mutually exclusive.

One possibility is that the correspondence simply arises because both medieval theorists and present-day naive perceivers base their judgments on personality traits or regularities in behavior that are real as well as perceived or, simply stated, that everyone has been right for 2,000 years. Clearly an important question to answer in this context is:

How good are naive perceivers at observing regularities in behavior or real personality traits? A definite answer to this question would require a generally agreed on theory of the "real" structure of personality. In its absence, however, it is apparent that in some situations naive perceivers are quite good at predicting the behavior of other people, although there are also systematic inaccuracies in their predictions.[94] Also, of course, it is quite possible that real personality varied along the same dimensions in the past as it does today.

There is, however, good reason to doubt that the correspondences arise solely because real personality structure today is the same as in the Middle Ages. First, it is difficult to see why the same personality structure should be explained by the same implicit personality theory in two different cultures. A particular reason for this difficulty is that many personality descriptions have a rather loose relationship to behavior—what behaviors, for example, are associated with a "warm" or a "cold" personality? Second, it seems improbable that stereotypes of the "red hair equals bad tempered" kind have any actual basis, although I know of no systematic investigation of this question. Finally, but most important, is the fact that there is a parallel between one of the systematic inaccuracies of naive perceivers and astrological doctrine. The systematic inaccuracy is known as the fundamental attribution error. It has been shown in a number of studies that over a range of situations people attribute more behavior to perceived personality traits and less to situational influences than they should, that is, they mistakenly attribute behavior to the individual rather than the circumstances.[95] For example, if an observer sees someone arguing heatedly, the observer is likely to conclude that the disputant is bad tempered or touchy rather than that he has been the victim of unfair treatment of some kind. A surprising but common case of the attribution error is the tendency of television watchers to identify the actors in long-running television series with the characters they play; an actor who plays a lawyer, for example, is likely to receive letters asking for legal advice. The similar "error" in astrological writings is that the fate or behavior of individuals is almost invariably attributed to planetary rather than chance or environmental influence. For example, Firmicus Maternus stated that "Those who are born with this star [Belva] rising will be fishermen, but of large fish. They will catch sea-dogs, sword-fish, tunnies, and crocodiles."[96] The obvious environmental explanation that fishermen tend to be born into fishing families in fishing villages is ignored. This tendency to ignore environmental influences did not pass unnoticed in the Middle Ages, and astrology was frequently criticized for this reason.[97]

These considerations suggest that similarities between the medieval account and present-day research into implicit personality theory cannot be entirely explained by reference to real personality structures. Two further possibilities can be considered. The first is simply that people generally perceive personality in much the same way, regardless of the times they live in. Obviously this possibility could explain the correspondences found above. Moreover, it would account for some of the apparent popularity of astrology and the doctrine of the humors: they were believed in part because the personality theory contained in them accorded with the commonsense views that people have about personality.

The other possibility is more radical and to my mind more unlikely, but I do not think it can be totally ruled out. Perhaps the way in which people assess one another's personality today has been conditioned, at least in part, by the long history of belief in astrology and the doctrine of humors in European culture. Certainly it seems plausible that a stereotype of the kind that links red hair with an explosive temper could have been transmitted in this way.

Causal mechanisms aside, it is clear that the medieval account of personality has clear resemblances to that used by ordinary people today. This, in itself, is interesting, indicating as it does both that human behavior has remained relatively unchanged and that the way in which we evaluate each other personally has not altered appreciably.

NOTES

1. Aquinas, *Summa Theologiae*, 1.2.49.1–3.
2. Ibid., 1.2.50.3–5.
3. Ibid., 1.2.50.3 ad. 2.
4. Ibid., 1.2.50.1; 1.2.51.1–3.
5. Ibid., 1.2.53.3.
6. Jack Lindsay, *Origins of Astrology* (London: Frederick Muller, 1971), 1–62.
7. Claudius Ptolemy, *Tetrabiblos*, trans. F. E. Robbins (London: Heinemann, 1938), 1.4–5.
8. Plato, *Timaeus*, 54–55.
9. Plutarch, *De Iside et Osiride*, trans. J. G. Griffiths (University of Wales, 1970), 157–159; and Walter Scott, ed. and trans., *Hermetica Vol. 1: Texts and Translation* (Oxford, UK: Clarendon, 1924), 269–271, 293–295.
10. Plato, *Timaeus*, 57–58.
11. Scott, *Hermetica*, 129, 305, 349.
12. Frederick H. Cramer, *Astrology in Roman Law and Politics* (Philadelphia: American Philosophical Society, 1954), 83–125, 135; and Lindsay, *Origins of Astrology*, 258–291.
13. Ptolemy, *Tetrabiblos*; and Julius Firmicus Maternus, *Ancient Astrology: Theory and Practice*, trans. J. H. Bram (Park Ridge, N.J.: Noyes, 1975).
14. Cramer, *Astrology in Roman Law*, 121.
15. Lindsay, *Origins of Astrology*, 4.
16. Thorndike, *A History of Magic and Experimental Science*, Vol. 3, 486.

17. Skinner, *Beyond Freedom and Dignity*; B. F. Skinner, *Science and Human Behavior* (New York: Macmillan, 1953).

18. Lindsay, *Origins of Astrology*, 395; and F. R. Jevons, "Paracelsus's Two-Way Astrology." *British Journal for the History of Science* 2 (1964): 139–155.

19. Augustine, *Concerning the City of God Against the Pagans*, trans. Henry Bettenson (Harmondsworth, UK: Penguin, 1972), 5.1–10.

20. Ibid., 5.7.

21. Ibid., 5.6.

22. Origen, *The Writings of Origen*, Vol. 2, trans. F. Crombie (Edinburgh, UK: T and T Clark, 1910), 280, 423.

23. Origen, *First Principles*, trans. G. W. Butterworth (London: Society for Promoting Christian Knowledge, 1936), 61–62, 305.

24. L. W. Laistner, "The Western Church and Astrology During the Early Middle Ages." *Harvard Theological Review* 34 (1942): 275.

25. Thorndike, *History of Magic and Experimental Science*, Vols. 2–4; and Wedel, *The Medieval Attitude toward Astrology*.

26. See Thorndike, *History of Magic and Experimental Science*, Vol. 3, 224–232; 290–293, 303.

27. Ibid., Vol. 3, 585–601, Vol. 4, 88–100.

28. Aquinas, *Summa Theologiae*, 1.115.3.

29. Ibid., 1.115.4.

30. Ibid., 1.115.4. ad 3.

31. Ibid., 2.2.95.5.

32. Albertus Magnus, *Ausgewahlte Texte*, trans. Albert Fries (Darmstadt, West Germany: Wissenschaftliche Buchgesellschaft, 1981), 97–117.

33. Ptolemy, *Tetrabiblos*, 3.13.

34. Firmicus, *Ancient Astrology*, 141.

35. Bartholomaeus Anglicus, *On the Properties of Things*, 483.

36. Ibid., 480–483; Firmicus, *Ancient Astrology*, 139–141; and Ptolemy, *Tetrabiblos*, 3.13.

37. Thorndike, *History of Magic and Experimental Science*, Vol. 2. 203.

38. Compare Firmicus, *Ancient Astrology*, 138 and Ptolemy, *Tetrabiblos*, 3.13. The question of the nature of Saturn is discussed in detail in Raymond Klibansky, Erwin Panofsky, and Fritz Saxl, *Saturn and Melancholy* (London: Nelson, 1964).

39. M. A. Manzalaoui, ed. *Secretum Secretorum* (Oxford, UK: Early English Text Society, O.S. 176, 1977), 76.

40. John Gower, *Confessio Amantis*, ed. Henry Morley (London: Routledge, 1889), 349–358.

41. Ibid., 350.

42. Geoffrey Chaucer, "The Wife of Bath's Prologue." In *The Tales of Canterbury*, ed. Robert A. Pratt (Boston: Houghton Mifflin, 1966), lines 609–616.

43. Hippocrates, *The Nature of Man*. In *Medical Works*, trans. J. Chadwick and W. N. Mann (Springfield, Ill.: Charles C. Thomas, 1950).

44. Caelus Aurelianus, *On Acute Diseases and on Chronic Diseases*, trans. I. E. Drabkin (Chicago: University of Chicago Press, 1950).

45. See Galen, *On the Natural Faculties*, trans. Arthur J. Brock (London: Heinemann, 1916), 2.8–9; and Helmut Flashar, *Melancholie und Melancholiker in den Medizinischen Theorien der Antike* (Berlin: Walter de Gruyter, 1966).

46. Galen, *On the Natural Faculties*, 2.9.

47. Avicenna, *The General Principles of Avicenna's Canon of Medicine*, trans. Mazhar H. Shah (Karachi, Pakistan: Naveed Clinic, 1966), 38–46.

48. Galen, *On the Natural Faculties*, 2.9. It may be questioned how a fluid can be dry. Galen's answer is that some fluids act as drying agents, as salt water preserves meat.

49. See Klibansky, Panofsky, and Saxl, *Saturn and Melancholy*, 57–58; and Rudolph E. Siegel, *Galen on Psychology, Psychopathology, and Function and Diseases of the Nervous System; An Analysis of His Doctrines, Observations, and Experiments* (Basel, Switzerland: Karger, 1973), 173–219.

50. See Klibansky, Panofsky, and Saxl, *Saturn and Melancholy*, 60–66.

51. Gower, *Confessio Amantis*, 345–346.

52. Bartholomaeus Anglicus, *On the Properties of Things*, 157.

53. Ibid., 159.

54. Ibid., 153.

55. Ibid., 161.

56. Klibansky, Panofsky, and Saxl, *Saturn and Melancholy*, 65.

57. Hildegard of Bingen, *Heilkunde*, trans. Heinrich Schipperges (Salzburg: Otto Muller, 1957), 95–97.

58. Ibid., 137–144. There is no simple relationship between her humoral system and the "sexual personality" types.

59. Aristotle, *De Memori et Reminiscentia*, 1.450b.

60. Averroes, *Epitome of Parva Naturalia*, 31.

61. Ibid.

62. Ibid., 50–51.

63. Pliny, *Natural History*, trans. H. Rackham (London: Heinemann, 1938), 2.102.

64. For example, Bartholomeus Anglicus, *On the Properties of Things*, 155; Sharpe, "Isidore of Seville," 48.

65. See Arnold of Villanova, *Parabeln der Heilkunst*, trans. Paul Diepgen (Leipzig: Barth, 1922), 26–28.

66. For example, Bartholomaeus Anglicus, *On the Properties of Things*, 353–354; W. G. Lennox, "Bernard of Gordon on Epilepsy." *Annals of Medical History*, Third Series 3 (1941): 372–383; Edna P. Von Storch and Theo J. C. Von Storch, "Arnold of Villanova on Epilepsy." *Annals of Medical History*, New Series 10 (1938): 251–260.

67. Klibansky, Panofsky, and Saxl, *Saturn and Melancholy*, 127–133.

68. Thorndike, *History of Magic and Experimental Science*, Vol. 3, 308–423.

69. Hildegard, *Heilkunde*, 56–70.

70. Bartholomaeus Anglicus, *On the Properties of Things*, 479–494.

71. Michael R. Best and Frank H. Brightman, eds. *The Book of Secrets of Albertus Magnus* (Oxford, UK: Clarendon, 1973), 66–72. Although, while most of the book was written about the time of Albertus Magnus, the astrological sections may be additions from the end of the Middle Ages or the early sixteenth century.

72. H. J. Eysenck, *The Structure of Human Personality*, 3rd ed. (London: Methuen, 1970).

73. The different nature of the Sun and Moon is explicit in Firmicus, *Ancient Astrology*, 117–118; 138–144.

74. Hildegard, *Heilkunde*, 116.

75. Ptolemy, *Tetrabiblos*, 3.11, 3.13. I have considered Jupiter in only its positive aspects.

76. For example, Manzalaoui, *Secretum Secretorum*, 89–113.

77. Ibid., 92.

78. Firmicus, *Ancient Astrology*, 140; and Best and Brightman, *The Book of Secrets of Albertus Magnus*, 68.

79. Ptolemy, *Tetrabiblos*, 3.11; Bartholomaeus Anglicus, *On the Properties of Things*.

80. For a fuller description see D. P. Walker, *Spiritual and Demonic Magic from Ficino to Campanella* (London: Warburg Institute, 1958); and Frances A. Yates, *Giordano Bruno and the Hermetic Tradition* (London: Routledge and Kegan Paul, 1964).

81. Yates, *Giordano Bruno*, 75.

82. Moore, *The Planets Within*; Yates, *Giordano Bruno*, 62–82.

83. Walker, *Spiritual and Demonic Magic*, 1–80.

84. Yates, *Giordano Bruno*, 63.

85. Moore, *The Planets Within*, opening quotation on the frontispiece.

86. William Sheldon, *The Varieties of Temperament: A Psychology of Constitutional Differences* (New York: Harper, 1942).

87. See Calvin S. Hall and Gardner Lindsay, *Theories of Personality*, 3rd ed. (New York: Wiley, 1978).

88. See J. Parr, *Tamburlaine's Malady and Other Essays on Astrology in Elizabethan Drama* (Westport, Conn.: Greenwood, 1971). For humoral references one need not look past the title of Ben Jonson's *Every Man in His Humor*, ed. M. Seymour-Smith (London: Benn, 1966).

89. See D. J. Schneider, A. H. Hastorf, and P. C. Ellsworth, *Person Perception*, 2nd ed. (Reading, Mass.: Addison-Wesley, 1979).

90. Much of the following argument is also contained in Simon Kemp, "Personality in Ancient Astrology." *New Ideas in Psychology* 6 (1988): 267–272.

91. S. Roll and J. S. Verenis, "Stereotypes of Scalp and Facial Hair as Measured by the Semantic Differential." *Psychological Reports* 28 (1971): 975–980; and W. D. Wells and B. Siegel, "Stereotyped Somatotypes." *Psychological Reports* 8 (1961): 77–78.

92. J. M. Digman and J. Inouye, "Further Specification of the Five Robust Factors of Personality." *Journal of Personality and Social Psychology* 50 (1986): 116–123; and S. Rosenberg, C. Nelson, and P. S. Vivekanathan, "A Multi-Dimensional Approach to the Structure of Personality Impressions." *Journal of Personality and Social Psychology* 9 (1968): 283–294.

93. S. E. Asch, "Forming Impressions of Personality." *Journal of Abnormal and Social Psychology* 41 (1946): 258–290; and Rosenberg, Nelson, and Vivekanathan, "A Multi-Dimensional Approach."

94. See M. P. Zanna, E. T. Higgins, and C. P. Herman, eds. *Consistency in Social Behaviour: The Ontario Symposium* (Hillsdale N.J.: Erlbaum, 1983).

95. See L. Ross, "The Intuitive Psychologist and His Shortcomings: Distortions in the Attribution Process." In L. Berkowitz, ed., *Advances in Experimental Social Psychology*, Vol. 10 (New York: Academic Press, 1977); and M. Ross and G.J.O. Fletcher, "Attribution and Social Perception." In G. Lindzey and E. Aronson,

eds., *The Handbook of Social Psychology*, Vol. 2, 3rd ed. (New York: Random House, 1985).

   96. Firmicus, *Ancient Astrology*, 280.

   97. Wedel, *The Medieval Attitude toward Astrology*.

7

Mental Disorder I: Medical and Legal Aspects

So far we have been concerned with what is today called "pure" psychology, that is to say psychology as the more or less disinterested study of the human mind or behavior. Theoretical accounts or models of psychology have, however, often been applied to practical purposes; in our own day, to take just a few examples, in the fields of ergonomics, organizational and management studies, advertising, and consumer behavior. The most important and best known of these applied areas is, however, the study of the causes, diagnosis, and treatment of mental or behavioral disorder. This chapter and the following one consider medieval approaches to mental disorder.

Pure psychology in the Middle Ages was studied and written about mainly by academics, as, of course, it is today. Mental disorder, however, had, and still has, practical consequences for society as a whole and could not remain the preserve of intellectual speculation. Thus there was in the Middle Ages not only an intellectual medical tradition of mental disorder, but also a largely pragmatic medical approach as well as legal and religious approaches. The coexistence of these different approaches in the Middle Ages should not be surprising, because it is common today to find rather different approaches to mental disorder or, for that matter, to many other imperfectly understood problems of practical concern. Today mental disorder is commonly studied and treated by psychiatrists and clinical psychologists who may adopt a bewildering array of different viewpoints as to the cause and treatment of any disorder. In addition to these official health professionals, there also exist psychoanalysts, hypnotherapists, scientologists, color therapists, religious healers, and other "fringe" practitioners. Finally, there is a legal aspect to mental disorder, for example, with respect to determining the moral responsibility of an individual for crimes committed, which also shows differences from the modern psychiatric or psychological approaches. Fundamentally these different approaches reflect the fact that we do not have a very good understanding of the causes and nature of mental disorders, nor very reliable treatments for them. The same could be, and in fact was, said of mental disorder in the Middle Ages.

THE MODERN MYTH OF MEDIEVAL MENTAL DISORDER

Before examining what the different medieval approaches to mental disorder were, it is useful to consider briefly what they were not. In particular the modern myth of medieval approaches to mental disorder—that the mentally disordered in the Middle Ages were harshly treated because they were generally regarded as witches or possessed by demons or both—needs to be examined.

A common source of the myth is Zilboorg's book, *A History of Medical Psychology*. Briefly Zilboorg's view can be summarized by two propositions. First, mental illness in the Middle Ages was generally attributed to demonic possession. Second, the mentally ill, particularly women, were very likely to be tried, tortured, and executed as witches. By the end of the Middle Ages, Zilboorg claims, "almost all mentally sick were considered witches, or sorcerers, or bewitched."[1]

In brief, the first of Zilboorg's propositions is partly true, the second almost completely false. There is no doubt that some individuals who exhibited abnormal behavior in the Middle Ages were regarded as possessed by demons, and this attribution is considered in detail in the following chapter. On the other hand, as is outlined in the following sections, the dominant medieval medical model of mental disorder was physiological and stressed physical causes and treatments. Neither those regarded as possessed nor those supposed to be suffering from problems of physiological origin were harshly treated as a rule; moreover, the legal system, at least in England, generally regarded the insane as unfortunate rather than as malefactors.

Zilboorg's idea that those prosecuted for witchcraft were themselves mentally disordered derives in large part from the confessions of supposed witches reported in *Malleus Maleficarum*, a "witch-hunters manual" written by two Dominican monks, Heinrich Kramer and James

Sprenger, and first published about 1486. "The hallucinatory experiences ... of the psychotic women of the time are well described by Kramer and Sprenger," wrote Zilboorg.[2] It is certainly true that many of the bizarre confessions extracted from the supposed witches and described in *Malleus Maleficarum* are most unlikely to have had any basis in fact. However, in view of the frequent and recommended practice of torturing the suspects,[3] there is a simpler explanation of the oddness of the confessions than supposing the suspects to be psychotic. Interestingly, the confessions of witches in England, where torture was not practiced, were rather less bizarre and elaborate than some of their continental counterparts.[4]

European witch-hunts have been extensively studied by modern historians, and although there is considerable academic controversy over the cause of their upsurge, some historical features seem fairly clear. First, witchcraft trials and persecutions were rather rare prior to the fifteenth century and attained their greatest frequency in the sixteenth and seventeenth centuries. Thus they were not really a medieval phenomenon at all, but rather an early modern one. Second, the evidence suggests that those accused tended to be old, poor, unpopular, and female. It was not improbable that this group had a higher incidence of mental and behavioral problems than most, but it seems most likely that they were persecuted because they were vulnerable and hence likely scapegoats. Overall, when the low number of prosecutions for witchcraft in medieval Europe is considered together with the virtual certainty that the majority of those accused were not mentally disordered, it seems that very few of the mentally ill could have been hanged or burned at the stake for witchcraft.[5]

Both of Zilboorg's propositions regarding attitudes to mental disorder in the Middle Ages are frequently reiterated in present-day introductory texts in psychology.[6] Moreover, although Zilboorg was careful to separate the two propositions, some later writers have not been so careful. For example, "In the fifteenth and sixteenth centuries madness was considered evidence of witchcraft and devil possession. . . . Any uncommon behavior, such as having hallucinations and delusions, was seen as a sign of witchcraft. This conclusion then justified the medieval mode of 'treatment': burn the body and save the captive soul."[7] And in another text:

Those who were thought to be unwilling hosts for evil spirits were subjected to curses or insults designed to persuade the demons to leave; if this approach had no effect, exorcism was tried, to make the person's body an unpleasant place for demons to reside, through beatings, starving, near-drowning, and the drinking of foul-tasting concoctions. Many people who were perceived as having accepted their condition voluntarily—as being in league with the devil—actively participated in their own prosecution and conviction.[8]

Both these accounts misinterpret the relationship that was believed to exist between witchcraft and demonic possession in medieval as well as early modern Europe. Witches themselves were never believed to be either insane or possessed by the devil. They were, however, believed to have the power to induce madness or to cause demonic possession in their victims (although cases of madness or demonic possession believed to be instigated by witches were rather rare in the Middle Ages). In reality, while the suspected witches, particularly in early modern Europe, were often subjected to torture or other ill-treatment, their presumed victims, for example, the possessed, were usually treated with sympathy. Certainly the possessed, regardless of whether their possession was attributed to witchcraft or held to result from some other cause, were not themselves tortured or burned.

MEDICAL MODELS OF MENTAL DISORDER

In the twentieth century, mental and behavioral disorders have been usually thought of rather differently to more "physical" disorders. The clearest evidence for this difference is in the separation of the institutions in which the patients are treated: those suffering from "ordinary" ailments are housed in general hospitals, while the mentally disordered are often placed in special mental hospitals. In addition, those suffering from mental disorders are examined and treated by different practitioners, usually psychiatrists or clinical psychologists.

The approach taken in medieval medicine to mental disorder, as portrayed in medieval medical writings, contrasts with the modern approach in two related ways. In the first place, there appears to have been no real distinction made between "mental" and "physical" disorders. Second, almost all kinds of mental disorder were attributed to, or at least believed to be mediated by, the breakdown of some physiological process. Indeed, often "mental" and "physical" disorders were attributed to rather similar causes. In short, contrary to what is often argued, the medieval practitioner appears to have been more rather than less likely than a modern one to attribute mental disorder to a physiological cause.[9]

In their approach to mental disorder, medieval physicians relied heavily on the traditions established by the Greeks and Romans. Hippocrates did much to establish the tradition of physiological explanation, and promulgated the humoral account of disease as due to an imbalance of blood, phlegm, yellow bile, and black bile in the body.[10] In his work on *The Sacred Disease*, Hippocrates firmly rejected supernatural explanations of epilepsy, stating that its cause was in the brain, as indicated by the fact that in animals suffering from the disease the brain was found to be moist and evil smelling when the head was cut open.[11] In fact he suggested that the corruption of the brain might be caused either by an excess of phlegm or bile, the cases being differentiated by their behavior: patients suffering from an excess of bile were noisier and more restless.[12]

More directly influential on medical thinking in the Middle Ages were the medical writers of the Roman Empire, and in particular Galen. Galen followed Hippocrates in giving a physiological and in particular humoral account of mental disorder.[13] He did, however, suggest that failure to control one's passions, particularly anger, might also be a cause of a kind of madness, and that ungoverned passion might increase to the point of becoming an incurable disease of the soul.[14] Losing one's temper with a servant and causing him injury—a vice to which the Romans seem to have been prone—"is the act of someone slightly insane or of an irrational, wild animal. Man alone . . . has the special gift of reason, if he casts this gift aside and indulges his anger, he is living and acting like a wild animal rather than a man."[15] Clearly for Galen insanity might arise not only through some physiological cause impairing the control of the mind or rational soul, but also through a voluntary failure to exercise willpower.

In general, the Christian medical tradition seems to have paid little attention to this idea, but a similar notion is found in the medical writings of the Jewish philosopher Moses ben Maimon (Maimonides), who lived in Mohammedan Spain in the twelfth century. Maimonides suggested that virtues and vices are acquired by frequent repetition. The soul then becomes diseased if the acts performed then incline one to extreme behavior. If this happens, for example if someone becomes extremely avaricious, the "patient" should resort to a philosopher, just as he would visit a physician if he were suffering from some physical ailment.[16] Maimonides also stressed the importance of the emotions in physical disorder, and recommended education in philosophy and ethics as a means of controlling the emotions and hence helping to maintain good health.[17]

Although the medieval medical approach to mental disorder does not appear to have been characterized by much debate or controversy, the ancient writers from whom most of their models and theories derived often were in some disagreement. While many physicians at the time of the Roman Empire followed the Hippocratic model of ascribing disorders to humoral imbalance; for example, in attributing melancholy to the action of black bile and in using a range of pharmaceutical treatments for this and other disorders, others adopted rather different approaches. In the writings of Caelus Aurelianus, (ca. 255–320 A.D.), who described himself as a member of the Methodist sect of physicians, mental (and other) disorders are defined almost wholly in terms of their symptoms. Discussion of their causation or possible underlying physiological processes is limited largely to the criticism of the theories of other sects. For example, of melancholy it is said that it derives its name from the fact that the patient often vomits black bile, and not because black bile is itself responsible for the disorder.[18] Caelus Aurelianus was also critical of many of the treatments used by other physicians: he condemns the frequent use of music and opium in treating mania, for example.[19] As so often occurred, however, the medieval reaction to this diversity of ancient opinion was to attempt to minimize it. This process of reconciliation was aided not only by the relative obscurity of some of the ancient writers (such as Caelus Aurelianus himself) but also by the fact that there was rather less disagreement between ancient physicians about the categories and definitions of the different disorders than about their causes and treatments.[20]

In the early Middle Ages, there seems to have been a decline in the sophistication of medical thinking about mental disorder. In the Byzantine Empire, medical writings continued but even there physicians such as Paulus Aegineta (ca. 625–690 A.D.) essentially produced condensed versions of the doctrines of earlier physicians, adding little and omitting much.[21] In Western Europe the situation was rather worse, and it is probable that in places the ancient lore was either unavailable or unknown. Isidore of Seville mentions and defines the more common categories of mental disorder more or less accurately in his medical writings, but his definitions are clearly too brief to have had any possible practical value.[22] From the eleventh century onward, however, medical learning revived with the translation and greater availability of both ancient and Arabic texts.

In general, medieval physicians followed the Hippocratic tradition and, in particular, Galen and Avicenna in attributing mental disorder to humoral imbalance, but the humoral account was often supplemented by another tradition in which different disorders were often linked to different areas of the brain. The latter tradition is clearly linked to the doctrine of the inner senses and appears to have originated with Posidonius in the fourth century A.D.[23] In the Middle Ages, as is discussed in more detail below, mental disorders were often associated with disturbances of function in one or more of the cerebral ventricles.

A problem arises for the modern reader who wishes to discern the medieval medical categories of mental disorder. Although there was reasonable agreement in the Middle Ages as to what the different categories of disorder were and how they might be distinguished, they did not clearly distinguish mental from other forms of disorder. Some disorders, however, meet two criteria that might be used to identify mental conditions: first, they were clearly seen as arising from malfunction of the brain or its ventricles and, second, they were characterized by abnormal behavior, emotion, or thinking. Four such disorders—the list is not exhaustive—which seem to have been commonly distinguished by medieval, as by ancient, medical writers were melancholy, mania, phrenitis, and epilepsy.[24]

The word *melancholy* is derived from the Greek word for black bile.[25] Thus from the beginning the disorder was associated with a particular physiological cause, an imbalance or excess of black bile. Ancient physicians seem to have been in some disagreement about the precise nature of the physiological process involved in the disorder, and, as we have seen, the Methodist school did not accept the physiological explanation at all.[26] The most influential of the physiological accounts, which derived from Rufus of Ephesus and was later endorsed by both Galen and Avicenna, suggested that there were really two forms of black bile, one of which was a more or less harmless substance responsible for the melancholic temperament, while the other, sometimes known as the atrabilious humor, was pathological. The pathological form arose from the combustion within the body of one of the four "normal" humors, and was responsible for mental and many other forms of disorder.[27]

An influential medieval account of melancholy was given by Constantinus Africanus, whose *De Melancholia* derived largely from an Arabic text of Ishaq ibn Imran.[28] Melancholy is defined either as a belief in some imaginary evil or as dominating suspicion, from which arises fear and sorrow.[29] The symptoms are extremely variable, but characteristically of long duration. They include depression, unreasonable fears, brooding over unimportant things, and frightening hallucinations. Some see black men who want to kill them; some believe they have lost their heads; some hear booming sounds or smell unpleasant odors; some believe the sky might fall on them. Patients might suffer either from sleeping too much or too little. Similarly some overeat while others actually starve themselves to death. Social behavior too can be very variable, with either immoderate laughter or weeping, and either sociability or (more usually) withdrawal from company.[30]

Constantinus' definition of melancholy would include a large proportion of modern psychiatric patients. Many of those presently diagnosed as schizophrenic, particularly those suffering from paranoid schizophrenia, would presumably have been diagnosed melancholic, along with a large number of those recognized as suffering from endogenous depression (i.e., depression with no apparent external cause). It is perhaps possible to criticize Constantinus' notion of melancholy as covering too wide a range of possible complaints and behaviors. Such a criticism would however miss the point that for Constantinus the unifying feature of the disorder is not in its symptoms but in its presumed cause.

According to Constantinus all the varied symptoms of melancholy derived from the different operations of black bile mounting to the head or the heart. For example, withdrawal and alienation were caused by black bile affecting the heart or vital spirits, fear of the future by vapors of black bile literally darkening the imagination. Even apparently contrary symptoms could be explained in this way: excessive sleepiness resulted from a direct effect of black bile on the brain, while sleeplessness occurred if the brain dried following clogging of its pathways by the black bile.[31]

The distinction between *mania* and melancholy does not seem to have been an easy one for either ancient or medieval physicians. Galen appears to have mentioned mania only rarely, and attributed it to the effects of yellow bile on the brain.[32] On the other hand, Caelus Aurelianus, whose discussion of melancholy was rather brief, gave considerable attention to mania, defining it as a chronic impairment of reason with a variety of symptoms, many indistinguishable from those that Constantinus described as occurring in melancholy, for example, the fear of harmless things.[33] In the later Middle Ages, however, a distinction was introduced between the two disorders that was based on the doctrine of the inner senses rather than the humoral theory. According to this new distinction, mania was held to be a disorder affecting primarily the imagination in the front cerebral ventricle, while melancholy was a disorder affecting the cogitative or reasoning power in the central ventricle. A third disorder, lethargy, in which the memory was affected, was supposed to be due to an impairment of the rear ventricle.[34]

From the theoretical point of view, the new account had the advantage of parsimoniously reconciling the doctrine of the inner senses and the ancient categories of mental disorder. Moreover it enabled a useful distinction of cases where clearly there was some disorder of imagination or perception, for example, a patient who imagined he had no head, and cases where imagination or perception appeared normal and reasoning was impaired. Galen's sick man who threw glass vessels out of a window, but was able to name each one correctly, was an often quoted example.[35] On the other hand, the new account was not really compatible with the older medical tradition in which the disorders were related to humoral disturbance. It must also have been practically difficult clinically to categorize mental disorders into those of impaired imagination and impaired thinking; some indication of this difficulty is given by the fact that the medieval writers often discussed mania and melancholy side-by-side. Bartholomaeus Anglicus, for example, includes mania and melancholy under the subheading of amentia, or madness, and makes no distinction in recommended remedies between them.[36] Whatever the difficulties associated with the new account, it seems nonetheless to have been popularly accepted even outside the medical profession.

Chaucer refers to it in "The Knight's Tale," when he describes Arcite's lovesickness as resembling mania produced by black bile:

Nat oonly lyk the loveres maladye
of Hereos, but rather lyk manye [mania]
Engendred of humour malencolyk,
Biforen, in his celle fantastyk.[37]

Phrenitis, from which derives the English "frenzy," was for ancient physicians an acute (i.e., not lasting) disorder characterized by mental derangement and fever.[38] Caelus Aurelianus distinguishes it symptomatically from mania and melancholy by the presence of fever and by a characteristic kind of plucking movement with the fingers. Like mania and melancholy, however, the disorder was accompanied by rather varied behavior; some patients wept, some raged, some laughed, while others showed symptoms of anxiety or complained of noises in the head. Violent behavior often occurred. Phrenitis could be distinguished from pneumonia or pleurisy because the delirium was not aggravated by pain.[39] Both Caelus Aurelianus and Galen believed that in phrenitis, as opposed to other kinds of delirious disorder, the locus was in the head.[40] Generally in ancient medicine, the disorder was believed to result from the action of yellow bile on the brain.[41] Galen distinguished different varieties of phrenitis, whose severity was determined by the kind of yellow bile responsible. Phrenitis caused by pale yellow bile was milder than that caused by dark yellow bile. Paraphrosyne, a "bestial and melancholic delirium," was produced only by overheated dark yellow bile.[42]

Phrenitis was commonly mentioned in the medical writings of the Middle Ages and usually attributed to the action of yellow bile on the brain.[43] Bartholomaeus Anglicus distinguished two forms: "frenesis," which he attributed to the actions of yellow bile, resembled cholera, and "parafrenesis," which was usually a less serious and shorter lasting condition.[44] Phrenitis was recognized as a distinct condition not only by the more learned medical writers of the later Middle Ages but also in earlier texts such as the Anglo-Saxon *Leechbook of Bald*, where separate herbal remedies are recommended for the possessed, the lunatic, and the frenzied,[45] and in more popular medical and even literary writings of the later Middle Ages.[46] Thus it seems to have been a commonly recognized condition in Medieval Europe and quite probably one that was frequently encountered.

It is clear from its description that the medieval syndrome of melancholy would today be regarded as some type of mental disorder. How those suffering from phrenitis would be regarded is rather less clear. It has been argued, for example, that Galen's account of phrenitis would today be recognized as meningitis or even possibly as typhoid fever.[47]

More likely, however, when the broadness of the ancient and medieval definition is considered together with its variability between physicians, is that a wide range of present-day disorders, including both psychiatric and more physical ones, were referred to as phrenitis in the Middle Ages.[48]

The final disorder considered here, that of epilepsy, is one that is regarded today almost wholly in physical terms rather than as a mental disorder. Historically, however, the disorder is interesting because in ancient and medieval times it was actually one of the less likely to be understood in physiological terms: there was a strong tendency, apparent particularly in the New Testament and the early Middle Ages, either to identify it as, or to confuse it with, demonic possession. This tendency, explored in more detail in the next chapter, was, however, almost completely absent from the medical tradition, which, from the time of Hippocrates, attempted a physiological explanation for the disorder.

Hippocrates himself regarded the disorder as due to the movement of either phlegm or bile to the brain.[49] In the later Middle Ages, following the doctrines of Galen,[50] epilepsy was held to arise from an occlusion of the ventricles or passages of the brain by phlegm or, more rarely, black bile or blood.[51] It was common to distinguish different types of epilepsy. For example, Arnold of Villanova (ca. 1234–1311) distinguished true epilepsy, caused by phlegm already present in the brain itself; analepsy, in which fumes rose from the stomach; and catalepsy, in which blood, phlegm, or melancholy reached the ventricles from the limbs. Diagnosis of these different kinds was aided by the phase of the Moon, which was believed to affect the humors in different ways.[52] Rather similar accounts and descriptions are given by other medieval medical writers, and even by a religious chronicler at the shrine of St. Bartholomew.[53]

The preceding discussion shows that the prevailing model of mental disorder among the learned medical writers of antiquity and later Middle Ages was physiological, and that this model was derived from the Hippocratic theory of the humors, the anatomy of Galen, and the late Roman and medieval doctrine of the inner senses. It is, however, open to question how much of this model was actually known to the majority of medical practitioners. It should be remembered that the model was essentially an academic one, instruction in which was given principally at universities, and the majority of practitioners, particularly in England, were not university educated even by the end of the Middle Ages.[54] Although knowledge of the basic academic categories of disorder, like phrenitis, seems to have been comparatively widespread, these categories appear to have coexisted with categories such as lunacy and demonic possession, which were not a major part of the academic medical tradition. It is possible, as has been argued by one recent historian, that in the later Middle Ages there was actually a considerable gulf between the academic tradition and what was known and practiced by the majority of medieval practitioners.[55]

TREATMENT

Ideally the treatment of a disorder should be closely related to, indeed perhaps even suggested by, the etiology of the disorder. In practice, although some medieval treatments were clearly related to the perceived physiological cause of the disorder, many of the treatments were not. One reason for this rather loose connection between treatment and etiology can be found in the fact that most of the treatments, like the theories, of mental disorder were derived from the synthesis of the views of ancient physicians. Whereas, however, the ancient physicians often disagreed about treatment on theoretical grounds, the medieval medical writers tended to simply list the different treatments regardless of their original theoretical basis.[56] This seems to have occurred even when the writers themselves were somewhat sceptical about the merits of the remedies. Bernard of Gordon writing about epilepsy, for example, listed a number of suggested remedies, particularly herbal concoctions, despite stating that he had never seen a case of adult epilepsy cured by himself or anyone else except when the disease could be attributed to a poor health regime of recent origin.[57]

Yet one should not be too critical of medieval writers for their lack of rigor in recommending treatments that lacked a generally accepted scientific basis. In the first place, such treatments might be clinically effective, or believed to be effective, in the absence of any such basis. Second, it should be borne in mind that many present-day treatments for mental disorder also have no generally accepted basis. Electroshock therapy is a fairly well known and controversial example. Less controversial, probably because of the proven effectiveness of the remedy, is the use of phenothiazines such as chlorpromazine to alleviate the symptoms of schizophrenia. Not only was chlorpromazine initially used in the absence of any neurochemical theory of the nature of schizophrenia, but also its usefulness was discovered largely by chance. The phenothiazines were discovered to have sedative properties in the course of research into their possible use as antihistamines.[58] In this context, incidentally, it is noteworthy that the use of treatments to attack symptoms rather than postulated underlying causes also has medieval antecedents: Constantinus Africanus, for one, recommended this approach in the treatment of melancholy.[59]

There was a broad range of types of treatment recommended in the Middle Ages, some having a theoretical base and some not. In the first place, we might distinguish treatments that had the objective of allowing excess noxious humors to escape. In this category were the widely recommended measures of purgatives and venesection, also known as phlebotomy and bloodletting. Thus, for example, one recommended treatment for phrenitis was to be bled from the middle vein of the forehead.[60] Venesection was also employed, although rather more rarely, for melancholy and epilepsy.[61] Related to venesection were the use of leeches, also used to draw blood, and cupping, by which blood could be drawn to a point or small area on the surface of the body.

Medieval physicians followed their Greek and Roman predecessors, in stressing the roles of diet, climate, exercise, and surroundings, both in promoting health and in the treatment of disorder. In part the recommendations were based on humoral theory. For example, Arnold of Villanova stated that care should be taken with the diet of epileptics to avoid food such as beef or beans that were held to produce phlegm or black bile.[62] A change of climate could also be beneficial, because it was generally believed, following the doctrine of Hippocrates, that each humor was strongest in a particular season or combination of weather conditions.[63] According to Constantinus Africanus the house in which melancholics were treated should face east to obtain a more equable climate.[64] A similar recommendation was made by Maimonides, who also pointed out that the intake of bad air polluted the spirit, in particular the animal spirit in the brain.[65] Constantinus also recommended hard exercise to produce sweating followed by bathing as a means of releasing noxious humors.[66]

The careful attention to matters of diet, exercise, and surroundings does not, however, seem to have been wholly motivated by etiological considerations. The best indication of this is probably in the fact that the Methodist sect, which almost completely eschewed theoretical explanations of disorders, relied heavily on detailed regime in their treatment, and, by contrast with Galen for example, were reluctant to use pharmaceutical remedies.[67] At least some of their specific remedies and recommendations, which were derived from pragmatic rather than theoretical grounds, were employed in the Middle Ages. For example, the injunction that paintings should not be hung in rooms where patients suffering from phrenitis are housed is mentioned by Bartholomaeus Anglicus.[68]

Most of the medieval remedies for mental disorder given in both the writings of the academic physicians and in apparently more popular works are recipes of herbs or mixtures of herbs. An electuary recommended by Arnold of Villanova for epilepsy, for example, comprised a dram of each of almond, sticha, physeleos, and chrysanthemum; two drams each of fresh cardamom, aristolochia rotunda, asphodel root, asses' cucumber, licorice, corpobalsam, and peony root; and six drams of agaric. This mixture was to be further mixed with water and honey and cooked.[69] The *Leechbook of Bald* recommended that lunatics be given a mixture containing costmary, goutweed, lupin, betony, attorlothe, cropleek, field gentian, and hare fennel.[70] In the *Book of Quinte Essence*, the reader learned that frenzy or madness could be assuaged by the application of a mixture of popilion, vinegar, and rue to the hands, feet, and nostrils.[71] Frequently writers mentioned more than one of these recipes and, in the case of academic writers on epilepsy, dozens of them were given. As a general rule, the theoretical reason, if any, for using a particular recipe was not given, even in the more academic accounts. Many of the herbs and mixtures, however, were derived from Greek and Roman prescriptions; for example, "poppy juice" and hellebore appear to have been widely used by both ancient and medieval physicians.[72]

Yet another category of remedies could be loosely described as behavioral. It was occasionally recommended, for example, that manic and melancholic patients could be helped by playing soothing music to them.[73] Similarly they might be aided by participating in elevating conversations or listening to the speeches of Plato.[74] Maimonides stated that "one who suffers from melancholia may rid himself of it by listening to singing and all kinds of instrumental music, by strolling through beautiful gardens and splendid buildings, by gazing upon beautiful pictures and other things that enliven the mind and dissipate gloomy moods."[75]

Related to this category is the recommendation, found in the *Leechbook of Bald*, that lunatics be whipped.[76] The reason for this apparently bizarre and inappropriate treatment is not given by the Anglo-Saxon author, and it has been suggested that the intention was to drive out devils, although there is no evidence in this or any other medieval work of physical torture being used for this purpose.[77] Another possibility is that the whipping was intended as a punishment or deterrent: it was apparently the practice in some medieval German towns to whip the insane before expelling them.[78] A third, and to my mind more likely, possibility is that the treatment is an incomplete version of that employed by Titus Anfidius in the first century A.D. He recommended melancholics be moderately whipped and then encouraged to indulge in as much sexual activity as possible. The treatment was apparently popular with his patients.[79]

It seems to have been fairly common to bind or restrict the movement of patients, again following ancient precedent. Caelus Aurelianus recommends this only when necessary to stop patients hurting themselves.[80] In catalepsy, in which noxious humors were believed to ascend to the brain from the extremities of the body, the limbs were often tightly bound to prevent the movement of the humors.[81] More dramatic surgical interventions in which the skull itself was opened were occasionally recommended, with the object of releasing the humors directly.[82] Again ancient precedent was followed, particularly in the treatment of epilepsy.[83] An interesting sidelight on medieval surgery is the existence of a group of quacks known as the "stonecutters" who flourished in Flanders in the fifteenth century. They "cured" mental disorder by claiming to remove "headstones," which were actually produced by sleight of hand following a small incision in the head. Although lampooned at the time, the fact of their existence suggests fairly widespread acceptance of head surgery for psychological conditions.[84]

A number of the cures recommended, even by academic physicians, can be best categorized as magical. In the *Liber de Diversis Medicinis*, probably written about the mid-fifteenth century, we read that the falling evil can be cured by writing, in the patient's own blood, the names of the three kings (given as Jasper, Melchior, and Attro) on his forehead. Alternatively, the name could be written (again using the patient's blood) on a scroll that he was to hang around his neck.[85] Belief in the virtue of this cure was not, however, universal: Bernard of Gordon derided its value along with that of other magical and religious cures.[86] Some of the herbal cures seem to have been recommended for magical reasons, for example, the wearing of hellebore seed in a ring on the finger or using human skull bones in medicinal powder.[87] One medicine recommended for the treatment of epilepsy was made by heating a cuckoo in a closed urn until it was reduced to a powder. The rationale behind this cure, as outlined by John of Gaddesden, was that the cuckoo was believed by some to have epilepsy itself every month, and so its powdered remains drew the potentially harmful humors to themselves and away from the brain.[88]

No account of medieval treatments would be complete without mention of religious remedies. There seems to have been near-universal belief in the Middle Ages that illness or disorder of any kind might be cured as a result of prayer or saintly intervention or by a visit to a shrine. The chronicles of the shrine of St. Bartholomew in London, for example, record cures for a variety of disorders including mental disorders.[89] Similarly, the lives of the saints, particularly those from the early Middle Ages, contain numerous examples of cures of all kinds of disorder. There was even a special shrine at Gheel, in modern Belgium, where the mentally disordered prayed at the tomb of St. Dymphna. St. Dymphna, legend relates, died in the seventh century A.D. at the hands of her enraged father when she refused to marry him, and subsequently became the patroness of the insane.[90] Nor were the medical practitioners of the period immune from these beliefs. Although Bernard of Gordon regarded with derision the clerical treatment of epilepsy, in which mass was sung and the Gospel of the Ember Days describing Christ's cure of an apparent epileptic recited, John of Gaddesden seems to have accepted the practice as possibly useful.[91] John Mirfield, who wrote a medical text, *Breviarium Bartholomaei*, at the end of the fourteenth century, mixed descriptions of surgical techniques with formulas for charms and prayers.[92]

It is probably tempting for a twentieth-century reader to dismiss medieval therapies as a heterogeneous mishmash. Such a conclusion, however, should be tempered by two considerations. First, it should be remembered that modern therapies are also very diverse. Widely employed in the treatment of mental disorder, for example, are various forms of pharmaceutical remedy, behavioral therapies, counseling and insight therapies, plus the occasional use of electroconvulsive therapy or even of surgical procedures such as prefrontal leucotomy. Second, although there was no controlled evaluation of different therapies in the Middle Ages, at least some physicians seem to have been aware that mental disorders were difficult to cure and that their remedies were not always successful. Bernard of Gordon's pessimism about the treatment of epilepsy has already been mentioned. Constantinus Africanus, too, recognized that melancholy was difficult to treat.[93] The diversity and number of recommended treatments may in fact be a result of recognition that none of them was reliably effective.[94]

ENGLISH LEGAL AND INSTITUTIONAL RESPONSES TO MENTAL DISORDER

There are two major legal aspects to mental disorder in the Middle Ages, as indeed there are today. First, there was the question of whether mental disorder might be viewed as a defense in a criminal charge. Second, there was the question of whether the community had a responsibility to care for the mentally disordered. These aspects are not, of course, totally independent of one another: restricting the freedom of the mentally disordered might be claimed to serve the dual function of protecting the community and caring for the patient. In the Middle Ages, however, the two aspects seem to have been rather more distinct than they are today, perhaps because there were few medieval equivalents of the modern mental hospital.

Differing answers to the question of how responsible the mentally disordered were for crimes they committed depended in the early Middle Ages on different legal viewpoints. In Roman law, which had a great influence on medieval, and particularly canon (or Church) law, the state of mind of a wrongdoer was important. Persons suffering from mental disorder were not regarded as free citizens, had reduced property rights, and were not held responsible for their actions.[95]

In Anglo-Saxon law on the other hand, a general rule of strict liability for wrongs or damage done was applied. However, Anglo-Saxon crimes were punished not by imprisonment or physical harm but by the payment of a fine to the victim or, in the case of murder, the victim's family. When the perpetrator of the crime was mentally disordered, his kinsmen paid the fine and presumably kept him under close watch thereafter.[96] This seems to be the explanation of why a madman named Hwaetred, who slew three men with an axe in the seventh century, could be later brought by his parents to St. Guthlac for healing.[97]

From about the tenth century in England, the ecclesiastical viewpoint seems to have had some legal influence. In the laws of Henry I (r. 1100–1135), which do not seem to have been revolutionary in this respect, provision was made for persons to be not guilty on the grounds of their state of mind.[98] In the thirteenth century, by which time the system of fines for murder had been replaced by the death penalty, there were some legal cases that show that insanity was available as a legal defense. In 1270, Richard of Cheddestan was confined to jail after killing his wife and children in a frenzied seizure. An enquiry six years later to determine whether he might be safely released was answered in the negative.[99] In 1285, a clerk named Richard who was "rendered frantic and mad by his sickness" slew a Brother Walter who was tending him, and then, covered with his blood, laughed and told the other brothers what he had done. He was imprisoned indefinitely.[100]

The thirteenth-century practice of taking intention and state of mind into account did not occur in a theoretical vacuum. Henry Bracton, a leading thirteenth-century jurist who was well versed in canon law, argued in his De Legibus et Constuetudinibus Angliae (On the Laws and Customs of England) the Roman case that madmen should not be held responsible for their actions:

But what shall we say of a madman bereft of reason? And of the deranged, the delirious and the mentally retarded? . . . Quare whether such a one commits a felony de se [if he commits suicide]. It is submitted that he does not, nor do such persons forfeit their inheritance or their chattels, since they are without sense and reason and can no more commit . . . a felony than a brute animal.[101]

Although Bracton's argument seems to have been ridiculed by much later jurists who believed him to have equated the mentally disordered with "wild beasts," the argument actually derives from the generally understood principles of medieval psychology.[102] According to those principles, as we have seen in the preceding chapters, man is distinguished from the animals by his possession of a rational soul or mind. In mental disorder, some physical defect prevents the mind from exerting its usual control. The resulting psychological state, and consequent behavior, then resembles that of an animal. Thus both legal practice and theory in thirteenth-century England were in good agreement with the psychological theory current at the time.

As in ancient Rome, medieval England made provision for the management of the estates of those considered insane. At least from the thirteenth century, the king was responsible for the management of the estate of "natural fools" or "idiots," that is, those mentally defective from birth, and enjoyed the surplus revenue of the estates after making provision for the proper treatment and maintenance of the fool. On the other hand, the king did not profit from the estates of those deemed to be *non compos mentis* (later, lunatics), who became mentally impaired at some later time. The actual determination of mental impairment and whether this was foolishness or lunacy was determined by a jury acting under a writ issued by the Court of Chancery.[103]

Official examiners employed by the court seem to have determined idiocy by simple tests of competence and memory. Individuals were asked, for example, to perform simple calculations, often with money, to name how many days were in the week, and so forth.[104] Lunacy investigations, of which there were few prior to the sixteenth century, probably because they were not profitable, seem to have concentrated more on determining the existence of behavioral abnormality.[105]

Occasionally either the examiners or the petitioners requesting a person be declared mentally incompetent suggested a cause of the impairment. In only one case, that of Emma de Beston in 1383, was an impairment put down to "the snares of evil spirits."[106] Perhaps more surprising is that the medical categories of mental disorder seem to have also been seldom employed. Instead the disorders were attributed to causes such as a "blow received on the head," or following a grave illness, or "induced by fear of his father."[107] Overall both the criteria for determining mental disorder and the causes held to produce it were commonsense, everyday ones, and seem to have been relatively uninfluenced by specialist religious or medical viewpoints.

When individuals are certified as insane today, they are often committed to mental hospitals that are maintained by public funds. Those deemed idiots or lunatics by the Court of Chancery, however, were placed in the care of private guardians who were responsible for their welfare and the maintenance of the estate. They were paid from the revenues of the estate.[108]

In Latin Europe in the Middle Ages there were few special institutions for the mentally disordered. Indeed there were very few public welfare institutions of any kind. In this respect Western Europe differed from both the Christian Byzantine Empire and the Islamic countries, where some mental hospitals were maintained at public expense.[109] Presumably the vast majority of mentally disordered individuals in the Middle Ages were, like Hwaetred, cared for by their immediate or extended families, or within the village communities in which most medieval people lived. They would have received such medical attention as was available locally or at the nearest town. An extended stay in a hospital or other institution, however, would have been very unlikely. Some hospitals, for example, that of St. John Baptist at Oxford, excluded those suffering from mania or epilepsy, not so much because of objections to treating cases of mental disorder but because they did not want to house patients suffering from chronic disorders. Such individuals were treated as outpatients.[110] The religious houses too were often unwilling to accept the mentally disordered, although the frequent complaints made by medieval English nunneries suggest that there were attempts to thrust mentally disordered or retarded novitiates on them.[111] Even at Gheel, where the shrine of St. Dymphna attracted a mentally disordered colony, the sufferers boarded with peasant families and were not housed together.[112]

In the later Middle Ages some hospitals provided wings or special facilities for mentally disordered patients, as, for example, at the Hotel-Dieu in Paris, at the Georgshospital at Elbing in 1326, and in some other German towns.[113] In England, the Hospital of St. Mary of Bethlem (later, Bedlam) in London provided facilities for six inmates from the late fourteenth century: the facilities seem to have consisted mainly of chains and manacles.[114] The first hospital built specifically for the mentally disordered seems to have been the Hospital of Innocents at Valencia, Spain in 1409.[115] It seems likely that the gradual provision of special facilities at this time was linked to the growth of medieval towns, and the presence in them of increased numbers of mentally disordered people whose family and kin were either untraceable or in distant villages. It is likely that many of the towns accepted this new responsibility with reluctance. Some of the German towns followed the practice of banishing the insane from their walls. Occasionally they were whipped first, presumably to discourage them from returning.[116] The towns along the Rhine sometimes shipped those believed to be mentally disordered out on boats, thus giving rise to the idea of the "ship of fools," which was celebrated in medieval literature, notably in Sebastian Brant's satire, *The Ship of Fools*.[117]

NOTES

1. Zilboorg, *History of Medical Psychology*, 153.

2. Ibid., 160.

3. Heinrich Kramer and James Sprenger, *Malleus Maleficarum*, trans. Montague Summers (London: Arrow, 1971). There are fairly frequent procedural references to torture. See Pt. 3, Qu. 13.

4. Nicholas P. Spanos, "Witchcraft in Histories of Psychiatry: A Critical Analysis and an Alternative Conceptualization." *Psychological Bulletin* 85 (1978): 417–439.

5. For discussions of prosecutions for witchcraft and their causes, see Cohn, *Europe's Inner Demons*; Richard Kieckhefer, *European Witch Trials: Their Foundations*

in Popular and Learned Culture, 1300–1500 (Berkeley: University of California Press, 1976); Spanos, "Witchcraft in Histories of Psychiatry"; and Thomas Szasz, *The Manufacture of Madness* (New York: Delta, 1970).

6. For example, Atkinson et al., *Introduction to Psychology*, 527; and Henry Gleitman, *Psychology* (New York: Norton, 1981), 656–657. See also notes 7 and 8 below. A similar phenomenon exists in textbooks of abnormal psychology, where one recent study counted eleven out of nineteen of these volumes producing Zilboorg's identification of witches with the mentally ill: Thomas J. Schoeneman, "The Role of Mental Illness in the European Witch Hunts of the Sixteenth and Seventeenth Centuries." *Journal of the History of the Behavioral Sciences* 13 (1977): 337–351.

7. G. A. Kimble, N. Garmezy, and E. Zigler, *Principles of Psychology* (New York: Wiley, 1984), 551–552.

8. N. R. Carlson, *Psychology: The Science of Behavior*, 2nd ed. (Boston: Allyn & Bacon, 1987), 953.

9. A number of modern writers provide good summaries of the medieval medical attitude to mental disorder. These include Basil Clarke, *Mental Disorder in Earlier Britain* (Cardiff: University of Wales, 1975); Stanley W. Jackson, "Unusual Mental States in Medieval Europe: I. Medical Syndromes of Mental Disorder: 400–1100 A.D." *Journal of the History of Medicine and Allied Sciences* 27 (1972): 262–297; and C. H. Talbot. *Medicine in Medieval England* (London: Oldbourne, 1967).

10. Hippocrates, *The Nature of Man*, 4–5.

11. Hippocrates, *The Sacred Disease*. In *Medical Works*, trrans. J. Chadwick and W. N. Mann (Springfield, Ill.: Charles C. Thomas, 1950), 14.

12. Ibid., 17–18.

13. Galen's account of mental disorder is chiefly contained in his work *On the Affected Parts*, trans. Rudolph E. Siegel (Basel, Switzerland: Karger, 1976). See also, Stanley W. Jackson, "Galen—On Mental Disorders." *Journal of the History of the Behavioral Sciences* 5 (1969): 365–384; G. Roccatagliata, *A History of Ancient Psychiatry* (Westport, Conn.: Greenwood, 1986); and Siegel, *Galen on Psychology*.

14. Galen, *On the Passions and Errors of the Soul*, trans. P. W. Harkins (Columbus: Ohio State University Press, 1963), 10.

15. Ibid., 5.

16. Moses ben Maimon (Maimonides), *The Eight Chapters of Maimonides on Ethics*, trans. Joseph I. Gorfinkle (New York: Columbia University Press, 1912), 51–59.

17. Moses ben Maimon (Maimonides), *Regimen Sanitas*, trans. Sussmann Muntner (Frankfurt: Akademische Verlag, 1966), 3.12–14.

18. Caelus Aurelianus, *Chronic Diseases*, 1.180.

19. Ibid., 1.173–177.

20. Discussions of ancient theories of mental disorder can be found in Flashar, *Melancholie und Melancholiker*; Klibansky, Panofsky, and Saxl, *Saturn and Melancholy*; and Roccatagliata, *History of Ancient Psychiatry*.

21. Paulus Aegineta, *The Seven Books of Paulus Aegineta*, trans. Francis Adams (London: Sydenham Society, 1844). Mental disorders are discussed in Books 3, 6, 9, 13–16.

22. Sharpe, "Isidore of Seville," 56, 58.

23. Roccatagliata, *A History of Ancient Psychiatry*, 142–143.

24. For example, each of these is discussed briefly in Bartholomaeus Anglicus, *On the Properties of Things*, 348–355.

25. See Klibansky, Panofsky, and Saxl, *Saturn and Melancholy*, 9.

26. It is, in fact, arguable that Caelus Aurelianus did not view melancholy as a mental disorder but as a disorder of the esophagus. Caelus Aurelianus, *Chronic Diseases*, 1.180–183.

27. Avicenna, *Canon of Medicine*, 41; Galen, *On the Affected Parts*, 3.9; and Galen, *On the Natural Faculties*, 2.9. For an overview of ancient theories of melancholy, see Flashar, *Melancholie and Melancholiker* or Klibansky, Panofsky, and Saxl, *Saturn and Melancholy*.

28. In Ishaq ibn Imran, *Magala fi L-Malihuliya*, and Constantini Africani, *Libri Duo de Melancholia*, ed. Karl Gabers (Hamburg: Helmut Buske, 1977). See also, Heinrich Schipperges, "Melancolia als ein mittelalterlicher Sammelbegriff fur Wahnvorstellungen." *Studium Generale* 20 (1967): 723–736.

29. Constantine, *Libri Duo de Melancholia*, 87–88.

30. Ibid., 120–127.

31. Ibid., 127.

32. Siegel, *Galen on Psychology*, 273.

33. Caelus Aurelianus, *Chronic Diseases*, 1.144–179.

34. For example, Bartholomaeus Anglicus, *On the Properties of Things*, 349–351. See also Clarke, *Mental Disorder in Earlier Britain*, 89–98; and Klibansky, Panofsky, and Saxl, *Saturn and Melancholy*, 90–93.

35. See Nemesius, *A Treatise on the Nature of Man*, 342; and Klibansky, Panofsky, and Saxl, *Saturn and Melancholy*, 93.

36. Bartholomaeus Anglicus, *On the Properties of Things*, 349–350.

37. Chaucer, "The Knight's Tale." In *The Tales of Canterbury*, ed. Robert A. Pratt (Boston: Houghton Mifflin, 1966), lines 515–518.

38. Caelus Aurelianus, *On Acute Diseases*, 1.1–53; and Galen, *On the Affected Parts*, 3.9.

39. Caelus Aurelianus, *On Acute Diseases*, 1.31–53.

40. Ibid., 1.56; Galen, *On the Affected Parts*, 3.9.

41. Roccatagliata, *History of Ancient Psychiatry*, 167–168, 185–187, etc.

42. Galen, *On the Affected Parts*, 3.9.

43. Bartholomaeus Anglicus, *On the Properties of Things*, 348–349; Clarke, *Mental Disorder in Earlier Britain*, 89–95; and Jackson, "Unusual Mental States," 268–274.

44. Bartholomaeus Anglicus, *On the Properties of Things*, 348–349.

45. *Leechbook of Bald*, 1.63. In Oswald Cockayne, ed. *Leechdoms, Wortcunning, and Starcraft of Early England* (London: Longman, 1864). The *Leechbook of Bald* comprises most of Volume 2.

46. For example, Furnivall, *Book of Quinte Essence*, 22; and J. Bazine, ed. *The Metrical Life of St. Robert of Knaresborough* (London: Early English Text Society, Old Series 228, 1953), 72, line 981.

47. S. E. Jelliffe, "Notes on the History of Psychiatry: VII." *Alienist and Neurologist* 33 (1912): 307–322.

48. Jackson, "Galen," 373.

49. Hippocrates, *The Sacred Disease*, 18.

50. Galen, *On the Affected Parts*, 3.9–11.

51. For example, Bartholomaeus Anglicus, *On the Properties of Things*, 352–355; W. G. Lennox, "Bernard of Gordon"; W. G. Lennox, "John of Gaddesden on Epilepsy." *Annals of Medical History* Third Series, 1 (1939): 283–307; and E. P. Von Storch and T.J.C. Von Storch, "Arnold of Villanova."

52. Von Storch and Von Storch, "Arnold of Villanova," 253.

53. Sir Norman Moore, ed. *The Book of the Foundation of St. Bartholomew's Church in London* (London: Early English Text Society, Old Series 163, 1923), 47.

54. Robert S. Gottfried, "English Medical Practitioners: 1340–1530." *Bulletin of the History of Medicine* 58 (1984): 164–182. The university teaching of medicine was, however, much less advanced in England than, for example, in Italy.

55. John M. Riddl, "Medieval Medicine." *Viator* 5 (1974): 157–184.

56. Caelus Aurelianus gives a number of examples of treatments disparaged or recommended on theoretical grounds. See *Chronic Diseases*, 1.117–134.

57. Lennox, "Bernard of Gordon," 376.

58. See Anthony Hordern, "Psychopharmacology: Some Historical Considerations." In C.R.B. Joyce, ed., *Psychopharmacology: Dimensions and Perspectives* (London: Tavistock, 1968).

59. Constantine, *Libri Duo de Melancholia*, 139–140.

60. For example, Bartholomaeus Anglicus, *On the Properties of Things*, 349; and Caelus Aurelianus, *Acute Diseases*, 1.70–76.

61. For example, Clarke, *Mental Disorders in Earlier Britain*, 91; and Von Storch and Von Storch, "Arnold of Villanova," 253.

62. Von Storch and Von Storch, "Arnold of Villanova," 254.

63. Hippocrates, *The Nature of Man*, 5.

64. Constantine, *Libri Duo de Melancholia*, 143.

65. Maimonides, *Regimen Sanitas*, 4.1.

66. Constantine, *Libri Duo de Melancholia*, 140.

67. Caelus Aurelianus, *Chronic Diseases*, 1.98–100, 1.173.

68. Caelus Aurelianus, *Acute Diseases*, 1.59; and Bartholomaeus Anglicus, *On the Properties of Things*, 349.

69. Von Storch and Von Storch, "Arnold of Villanova," 257.

70. *Leechbook of Bald*, 1.63.

71. Furnivall, *Book of Quinte Essence*, 22.

72. For example, Caelus Aurelianus, *Chronic Diseases*, 1.170–173; Bartholomaeus Anglicus, *On the Properties of Things*, 349; Celsus, *De Medicina*, trans. W. G. Spencer (London: Heinemann, 1938), 3.18; and Von Storch and Von Storch, "Arnold of Villanova."

73. Caelus Aurelianus, *Chronic Diseases*, 1.175–176; Bartholomaeus Anglicus, *On the Properties of Things*, 350; and Schipperges, "Melancolia," 732.

74. Schipperges, "Melancolia," 732. Again the therapy was practiced by the Methodists. Caelus Aurelianus, *Chronic Diseases*, 1.162–164.

75. Maimonides, *The Eight Chapters*, 70.

76. *Leechbook of Bald*, 3.40.

77. Wilfred Bonser, *The Medical Background of Anglo-Saxon England: A Study in History, Psychology, and Folklore* (London: The Wellcome Historical Medical

Library, 1963), 259; and Stanley Rubin, *Medieval English Medicine* (Newton Abbott, UK: David & Charles, 1974), 127.

78. George Rosen, *Madness in Society* (London: Routledge and Kegan Paul, 1968), 140.

79. Caelus Aurelianus, *Chronic Diseases*, 1.177–179; and Roccatagliata, *History of Ancient Psychiatry*, 124.

80. Caelus Aurelianus, *Acute Diseases*, 1.65.

81. Lennox, "Bernard of Gordon," 379; Galen, *On the Affected Parts*, 3.11; and Von Storch and Von Storch, "Arnold of Villanova," 253.

82. Bartholomaeus Anglicus, *On the Properties of Things*, 350; and Clarke, *Mental Disorder in Earlier Britain*, 89.

83. Caelus Aurelianus, *Chronic Diseases*, 1.118; and Owsei Temkin, *The Falling Sickness* (Baltimore, Md.: Johns Hopkins, 1945), 75–76.

84. James M. Grabham, "The Witch of Mallegem," *Journal of the History of Medicine and Allied Sciences* 30 (1975): 384–385.

85. Margaret S. Ogden, ed., *Liber de Diversis Medicinis* (London: Early English Text Society, Old Series 207, 1938), 42.

86. Lennox, "Bernard of Gordon," 376.

87. Von Storch and Von Storch, "Arnold of Villanova," 256, 258–259.

88. Lennox, "John of Gaddesden," 297.

89. Moore, *The Book of the Foundation of St. Bartholomew*.

90. S. Baring-Gould, *The Lives of the Saints*, Vol. 5 (May) (Edinburgh, UK: John Grant, 1914), 207–211.

91. Lennox, "Bernard of Gordon," 376; and Lennox, "John of Gaddesden," 298.

92. John Mirfield, *Surgery [Breviarium Bartholomei, Part 9]*, trans. J. B. Colton (New York: Hafner, 1969).

93. Klibansky, Panofsky, and Saxl, *Saturn and Melancholy*, 85; and Schipperges, "Melancholia," 732–733.

94. Clarke, *Mental Disorder in Earlier Britain*, 92.

95. For example, T. C. Sanders, *The Institutes of Justinian* (London: Longmans, Green and Co., 1917), 74–76.

96. Nigel Walker, *Crime and Insanity in England: Vol. 1. Historical Perspective* (Edinburgh, UK: Edinburgh University Press, 1968), 15–16.

97. Felix, *Life of Saint Guthlac*, trans. B. Colgrave (Cambridge, UK: Cambridge University Press, 1956), 41.

98. Walker, *Crime and Insanity*, 17.

99. Ibid., 20–23.

100. Talbot, *Medicine in Medieval England*, 181–182.

101. Henry Bracton, *On the Laws and Customs of England, Vol. 2*, trans. Samuel E. Thorne (Cambridge, Mass.: Bellknap, 1968), 424.

102. Anthony M. Platt and Bernard L. Diamond, "The Origins and Development of the 'Wild Beast' Concept of Mental Illness and Its Relation to Theories of Criminal Responsibility." *Journal of the History of the Behavioral Sciences* 1 (1965): 355–367.

103. Richard Neugebauer, "Treatment of the Mentally Ill in Medieval and Early Modern England: A Reappraisal." *Journal of the History of the Behavioral*

Sciences 14 (1978): 158–169; and Richard Neugebauer, "Medieval and Early Modern Theories of Mental Illness." *Archives of General Psychiatry* 36 (1979): 477–483.

104. Neugebauer, "Treatment of the Mentally Ill," 161. Note that the determination of such impairment did not prove the condition to have been present at birth. Naturally, the Crown was financially concerned to obtain the broadest possible definition of idiocy.

105. Ibid., 192.

106. Neugebauer, "Medieval and Early Modern Theories," 481.

107. Ibid.

108. Neugebauer, "Treatment of the Mentally Ill," 162.

109. Michael Dols, "Insanity in Byzantine and Islamic Medicine." In J. Scarborough, ed., *Symposium on Byzantine Medicine*, Paper No. 38 (Washington, D.C.: Dumbarton Oaks, 1984).

110. H. P. Chomeley, *John of Gaddesden and the Rosa Medicinae* (Oxford, UK: Clarendon, 1912), 121.

111. Eileen Power, *Medieval English Nunneries* (Cambridge, UK: Cambridge University Press, 1922), 31–33.

112. Baring-Gould, *Lives of the Saints*, Vol. 5, 209–210.

113. Rosen, *Madness in Society*, 139.

114. Nigel Walker and Sarah McCabe, *Crime and Insanity in England. Vol. 2. New Solutions and New Problems* (Edinburgh, UK: Edinburgh University Press, 1973), 2.

115. Emilio J. Dominguez, "The Hospital of Innocents: Humane Treatment of the Mentally Ill in Spain." *Bulletin of the Menninger Clinic* 31 (1967): 285–297.

116. Rosen, *Madness in Society*, 140–141.

117. Sebastian Brant, *The Ship of Fools*, trans. Edwin H. Zeydel (New York: Dover, 1962).

8

Mental Disorder II:
Demonic Possession and
Other Religious
Disorders

In the preceding chapter it was shown that, contrary to the popular modern view of medieval mental disorder, there were well-developed medical and legal views of mental disorder that owed little to theology. Yet physiological and environmental causes were not the only ones admitted for mental disorder in the Middle Ages. "Among those who lack the use of reason," says Aquinas, "are the possessed."[1]

Reference to belief in demonic possession, and evidence that some people who exhibited strange behavior really were regarded as being possessed by devils is contained in a number of accounts. Here are three typical examples. The first was recounted by Bishop Gregory of Tours (ca. 540–594 A.D.):

A certain man named Aquilinus was practising hunting with his father in the woods of France. He incurred a very severe trembling when the Enemy trapped him. He had a palpitation of the heart, and was seen at times to be out of his senses. In truth his parents realized that he was being punished by the entrance of a devil. As is the custom of the rustics, they obtained bandages for him and potions from the fortune-tellers and soothsayers. But when, as is customary, these things had no power, forced by grief they readily sought the aid of St. Martin and said: "He can lay bare this ambush of evil since we have heard he exposed that wraith, worshipped with the false name of religion." They took him from that region and sent him to the sacred basilica. There he stayed with prayer and fasting and assiduously sought the aid of the saint. And when he had stayed for a long time in this faith, all his trembling was removed, and he recovered his senses as he had had them before.[2]

The second is from Felix's *Life of Saint Guthlac*, written 730–740 A.D.

At another time too a certain *gesith* of the before-mentioned exile Aethelbald, named Ecga, was miserably attacked by the extreme violence of an unclean spirit, so that he did not know what he was or where he dwelt or what he was about to do. Although the strength of his body and limbs remained unharmed, yet his powers of speech, discussion, and understanding failed him entirely. One day his relatives, fearing that perpetual madness would come upon him, took him to the abode of this same Guthlac, and as soon as he bound himself with the saint's girdle, he felt that all his madness had disappeared and his mind had wholly returned to him; and also, because he always girded himself with that same girdle, he suffered no molestation from Satan to the last day of his life.[3]

The third example is taken from a thirteenth-century biography of St. Francis of Assisi (1181–1226 A.D.), written by Thomas of Celano.

Also at Citta di Castello there was a woman obsessed by the devil. When the most blessed father Francis was in this city, the woman was brought to the house where he was staying. That woman, standing outside, began to gnash her teeth and, her face twisted, she began to set up a great howl, as unclean spirits do. Many people of both sexes from that city came and pleaded with St. Francis in her behalf, for that evil spirit had long tormented and tortured her and had disturbed them with his loud cries. The holy father then sent to her a brother who was with him, wishing to discover whether it was really a devil or deception on the part of the woman. When that woman saw him, she began to deride him, knowing that it was not Francis who had come out. The holy father was inside praying. He came out when he had finished his prayer. But the woman, unable to stand his power, began to tremble and roll about on the ground. St. Francis called to her and said: "In virtue of obedience, I command you, unclean spirit, to go out of her." Immediately he left her, without injuring her, but departing in great anger.[4]

This chapter considers the history of belief in demonic possession and how it and other religiously based concepts of mental disorder were applied in the Middle Ages.[5] The investigation begins, however, with a brief examination of some of the research into possession beliefs and psychiatric syndromes carried out by present-day anthropologists, psychologists, and psychiatrists.

POSSESSION IN MODERN PSYCHIATRY AND ANTHROPOLOGY

In 1921, Oesterreich, in his work *Possession: Demoniacal and Other*, defined what can be thought of as a psychiatric syndrome of possession.

This syndrome has, according to Oesterreich, several striking and dis-
tinctive characteristics. Most important of these is "that the patient's organism appears to be invaded by a new personality; it is governed by a
strange soul."[6] The apparent invasion—Oesterreich did not believe that
there was an actual takeover by an alien personality or intelligence—is
signaled by physiognomic changes, generally involving distorted gri-
maces; by changes in voice, usually it deepens; and by changes in
expression. The new personality uses expressions and ideas very unlike
those normally used by the patient: "the words uttered by the strange
voice generally betray a coarse and filthy attitude, fundamentally opposed to all accepted ethical and religious ideas."[7] In addition patients
often display very forceful and distorted body movement. Following the
possession "attack"—characteristically, there are repeated attacks inter-
spersed with intervals of more normal behavior—patients are either unable to recall anything of the attack or their behavior during it, or are
aware of everything that takes place but unable to control their behavior.[8]

Psychiatric cases with all these symptoms are rarely encountered today
by psychiatrists or psychologists, although they are occasionally reported.[9] Some of the symptoms occur somewhat more frequently in
other disorders, for example, in multiple personality disorder, and the
belief that one is possessed is sometimes encountered in schizophren-
ics.[10] Probably the disorder sharing the most common symptoms is Gilles
de La Tourette's syndrome, also rare and featuring involuntary tics and,
frequently, the compulsive utterance of obscenities.[11]

A probable reason why Oesterreich's possession syndrome is only
rarely encountered by present-day Western mental health professionals
is that a key factor in producing the syndrome seems to be a culture or
subculture that believes in the spiritual reality of possession. This factor
is remarked both by Oesterreich and other psychiatrists and also by
anthropologists interested in possession.[12] Thus the apparent rarity of
the occurrence of the syndrome today does not imply that it should have
been equally rare in the Middle Ages.

Some indication that the syndrome may have been more common in
medieval times is given by the fact that in Western society today the
possession syndrome is most commonly encountered in Christian fundamentalist and pentecostal sects. Belief in the reality of demonic possession is quite common in such sects and the characteristic symptoms
listed by Oesterreich are actually discussed by fundamentalist writers.[13]
Here is a description of one such case:

One of the elders of his church, who was unquestionably a believer, became so
demon possessed that his personality changed. He became vile and profane in
his language and extraordinarily strong. Some of the members of the church
locked him up in a room and sent for Hillis.

When Dick walked in the door, this man became violent and a strange voice shouted, "I know who you are."

Hillis said, "And I know who you are," and began to speak to the demon.

This was a case when a believer was actually possessed by a demon who spoke in another voice.[14]

Possession and possession trances have been studied by present-day anthropologists in a number of cultures: Erika Bourguignon has estimated that 360 of 488 known societies feature either a belief in possession or possession trances.[15] The results of these anthropological investigations have revealed, first, that the incidence of possession in a society is related to societal variables, and, second, that, depending on the society, the behaviors taken by the society as indicative of possession can be very variable. Overall, belief in possession, and behavior such as possession trance in which individuals appear to be possessed, has been shown to be more common in societies that have a relatively rigid social structure or those that practice slavery. Within a society, possessed individuals are more likely to have low status, or to be women in a male-dominated society. There are definite indications in fact that possession acts as some sort of societal safety valve, and permits individuals to behave in ways that would normally not be tolerated by the society.[16] Similar considerations probably also apply to members of Christian sects.[17]

Possession as diagnosed in such communities does not always involve the syndrome suggested by Oesterreich, but may cover a wide range of behavior. In present-day Christian sects, too, possession is often diagnosed as the cause of a wide range of disorders. Epilepsy is often regarded as being caused by demons. One member of a pentecostal church informed me that he had been exorcised to try to rid him of "a spirit of asthma."

Lewis distinguishes two different kinds of possession; one of these is "central" to the society, approved by it, and often accompanied by ritual, while the other is "peripheral" and occurs spontaneously.[18] Central possession does not appear to be pathological and is generally perceived favorably by the participants, while peripheral possession is generally regarded as a kind of mental disorder both by those possessed and by observers within the culture.[19] Moreover, individuals undergoing peripheral possession display more pathology in their normal state (i.e., in the intervals when they are not apparently possessed) than nonsuffering control subjects.[20] Thus Oesterreich's possession syndrome is a type of peripheral possession, but should not be mistaken for central possession.

A rather similar distinction is maintained in present-day Christian sects. One type of possession, usually marked by speaking in tongues (*glossolalia*), is believed to be caused by the Holy Spirit and is regarded favorably, even as a sign of divine favor. The other is believed to be of diabolical origin and regarded with horror. Curiously the two kinds are not always easy to distinguish even for members of the sect. "Perhaps no spiritual gift is more susceptible to Satanic counterfeit and confusion than the gift of tongues."[21] In one incident in an Apostolic church in Yucatan, parishioners who had thought they were possessed by the Holy Spirit changed their minds when it was pointed out that they had thrown their Bibles away.[22] On the other hand, in the few clinical cases reported, patients invariably complain of diabolical rather than divine influence.[23]

Although present-day understanding of the phenomenon of possession is incomplete, some hypotheses of possible relevance to the Middle Ages emerge. Was the attribution of demonic possession applied to a broad range of disorders or was it restricted to cases of Oesterreich's possession syndrome? To what extent did the attribution depend on the culture, or on the existence of alternative perceived causes for mental disorder? Was there trouble in distinguishing central possession, of presumably divine origin, from peripheral diabolic possession?

THE CHRISTIAN TRADITION

So far in this book, the origins of the different aspects of medieval psychology have been traced back to Greek scientific thought, particularly that of Aristotle. This does not apply to medieval ideas about possession. Although there was an ancient Greek tradition of possession, particularly divine possession, this had little influence on the concept of possession in the Middle Ages. Medieval ideas on demonic possession were derived from the Bible and the writings of the early Church Fathers.

On the other hand, it should not be thought that the early Christians were alone in believing in the reality of demonic possession. In the first few centuries after Christ belief in possession and other related phenomena seems to have been widespread in the Roman Empire. In the Hermetic writings, we find, for example, that "all man's thoughts are brought forth by his mind . . . bad thoughts, when it is impregnated by some demon."[24] Spiritual healing too was not the exclusive preserve of Christians. Appollonius of Tyana (ca. 0–50 A.D.) performed many such feats and was renowned for curing the demoniacally possessed.[25] In short the beliefs of the early Christians do not seem to have been any more superstitious or credulous or unscientific than those generally held under the Roman Empire.

The word *demon* itself originally had a more neutral flavor; it was used, by Plutarch, for example, to describe an order of beings between God and man.[26] These demons were often supposed to be the intelligences of the planets, described by Plato in *Timaeus* as inhabited by divine beings.[27] Thus part of the Christian horror of demons can be ascribed to their rejection of rival religious beliefs. In this context it may be remarked that it is not always clear whether someone described by an early Christian as under demonic influence was mentally disturbed or simply an adherent of a different religion.

Although references to the devil and demonic possession are relatively uncommon in the Old Testament, they are frequent in the New Testament, and both Jesus himself and the apostles are described as casting out devils.[28] As these descriptions were of substantial later influence it is worthwhile recounting two of them here.

As he stepped ashore, a man possessed by an unclean spirit came up to him from among the tombs where he had his dwelling. He could no longer be controlled; even chains were useless; he had often been fettered and chained up, but he had snapped his chains and broken the fetters. No one was strong enough to master him. And so, unceasingly, night and day, he would cry aloud among the tombs and on the hill-sides and cut himself with stones. When he saw Jesus in the distance, he ran and flung himself down before him, shouting loudly, "What do you want with me, Jesus, son of the Most High God? In God's name do not torment me." (For Jesus was already saying to him, "Out, unclean spirit, come out of this man!") Jesus asked him, "What is your name?" "My name is Legion," he said, "there are so many of us."[29]

A man in the crowd spoke up: "Master, I brought my son to you. He is possessed by a spirit which makes him speechless. Whenever it attacks him, it dashes him to the ground, and he foams at the mouth, grinds his teeth, and goes rigid. I asked your disciples to cast it out, but they failed." . . . So they brought the boy to him; and as soon as the spirit saw him it threw the boy into convulsions, and he fell on the ground and rolled about foaming at the mouth. Jesus asked his father, "How long has he been like this?" "From childhood," he replied; Jesus rebuked the unclean spirit. "Deaf and dumb spirit," he said, "I command you, come out of him and never go back!" . . .

Then Jesus went indoors, and his disciples asked him privately, "Why could not we cast it out?" He said, "There is no means of casting out this sort but prayer."[30]

Several features of these accounts deserve consideration. In the first place, while the first of these incidents describes a disorder like Oesterreich's possession syndrome, the second appears to describe a case of epilepsy. Note that here the victim does not talk and foams at the mouth. Moreover, the disciples are unable to help him, and Jesus himself seems to regard the case as somewhat different. The difference of this case did not go unnoticed by later Christians and probably formed the scriptural basis for the early medieval view that epilepsy was demoniacally caused.

Second, the demons are apparently clairvoyant: it is the demoniacally possessed who, in the Gospels, consistently proclaim Jesus to be the Son of God, as happens in the first of the biblical examples. In medieval times demonic utterances seem to have been chiefly used to attest the holiness of saints, but later on, in early modern England, for example, the utterances were often subjected to testing to see if there was a "real" possession.[31] At least one example of medieval scepticism about a particular case of possession has survived. The third of the opening examples of this chapter relates how Francis of Assisi had suspicions as to whether one woman was really possessed and sent a brother in his place to test her.[32]

Finally the power to exorcise demons was generally regarded at the time as a sign of the worth of a religion or of the holiness of the exorcist, and Jesus' ability as an exorcist clearly impressed his contemporaries. Jesus encouraged his disciples to follow his example and to cast out devils in his name.[33] Not everyone, however, succeeded in doing this and generally the ability to cast out devils was regarded in the Middle Ages as a sign of saintliness.[34] Hence a major reason why accounts of exorcisms feature so strongly in the lives of the saints or in the records of religious shrines: they were often treated as evidence supporting a case for canonization.[35]

The early Christians continued the demonic tradition of the New Testament. Tertullian (ca. 155–220 A.D.) stated that "the breath of demons . . . achieves the corruption of the mind in foul bursts of fury and insanity, or in savage lusts, along with every kind of delusion."[36] He also equated demonic possession with the religious and ecstatic experiences of believers in other religions.[37] John Cassian (360–435 A.D.), one of the founders of monasticism, discussed the nature of demons and of possession, stating that in possession the demon has power over the body but is not united to the soul.[38] Augustine discusses three cases of possession he had personally encountered that involved some kind of visionary experience. In one, a man on his sickbed predicted when the priest was coming to visit him and what stops he made on the way, while in another, a pain-wracked boy had visions of heaven and hell.[39]

The early Church paid close attention to the possessed. From the third century, exorcists were counted among the four lower orders of clergy. An exorcist was not an ordained priest, but was required to pray and fast. His duties included memorizing the forms of exorcism and laying hands daily on the possessed or *energumeni* and giving them their food. The possessed were supposed to sweep out the church.[40]

Demonic possession was also an early subject for canon law. The

Synod of Elvira (305 A.D.) excluded demons from participation in divine service, but allowed them to be baptized if dying.[41] Demonic possession, epilepsy and lunacy were held to be disqualifications for the priesthood. The Synod of Orange (441 A.D.) stated that "those who have been once publicly possessed by a demon shall not be ordained. If such have been already ordained, they shall lose their office."[42] Pope Gelasius in the fifth century prohibited epileptics from holy orders on the grounds that epileptic seizures arose from demonic possession.[43]

Epilepsy, lunacy, and demonic possession seem to have frequently been confused throughout the early Middle Ages. Seventh-century Latin texts identify *caducus* ("epileptic") with *demoniacus* and prescribed remedies "for epileptics i.e. demoniacs and those suffering convulsion."[44] An Anglo-Saxon herbarium describes herbal remedies "for witlessness, that is, for devil sickness."[45] Isidore of Seville remarked that epileptics were called lunatics by the common people, "since under the influence of the moon's cycle, *lunae cursus*, the snare of demons snatches them up."[46]

A tendency to ascribe a demonic cause to epilepsy and mental disorders is also found in the descriptions of miracles given by religious writers in this period. Neither Aquilinus' nor Ecga's disorder, the brief descriptions of which were given at the beginning of this chapter, really resembles Oesterreich's possession disorder. Aquilinus one might tentatively suggest to have suffered from some kind of anxiety disorder, while Ecga's behavior does not seem to have been active enough for Oesterreich's possession syndrome. Bede (ca. 672–735 A.D.) describes a man who "was suddenly seized by the devil and began to call and shout and grind his teeth, and the foam came from his mouth, and he began to twist his limbs with all sorts of movement."[47] The victim, who certainly sounds to have been epileptic, was cured by dust over which had been poured water that had washed the blessed Oswald's bones. This passage is illuminating because Bede himself can in no way be dismissed as simply an ignorant and credulous priest. He was perhaps the most learned European of his age; he could read Greek, for example, and used his knowledge to correct Latin translations.[48]

DEMONIC POSSESSION IN THE LATER MIDDLE AGES (1100–1500)

As was recounted in the previous chapter, the dominant ancient model of mental disorder was physiologically based, and, with the revival of medical learning that began in the eleventh and continued in subsequent centuries, knowledge of this model became more widespread. As this knowledge spread, physiological explanations came to be preferred to demonological ones for at least certain classes of disorder. The change in preference, however, was overall slow and uneven.

In general, Christian and Arabic medical writers of the Middle Ages ignored rather than argued against demonic or religious explanations of mental disorder. Thus, for example, although Bartholomaeus Anglicus discusses demons briefly in his encyclopedia, they are not mentioned at all in his treatment of mental disorder.[49] Similarly the accounts of epilepsy given by Bernard of Gordon and Arnold of Villanova do not mention demonic possession.[50] There are nevertheless exceptions. Abulqasim (ca. 1000 A.D.) discussed some cases that had helped to overcome his scepticism regarding demonic possession. "He had seen some people who fell down, whose appearance changed, who talked in a tongue formerly unknown to them and read books, wrote and talked about scientific matters of which they had hitherto had no knowledge."[51] Constantinus Africanus recommended a test for distinguishing epilepsy and demonic possession, in which a formula was spoken into the patient's ear.[52] The same procedure was suggested by John of Gaddesden: "Utter these words into the ear of the suspect: 'Depart demon and go forth.'" A demoniac was supposed to go into a coma while an epileptic would be unaffected.[53]

The existence of this test suggests that the general attitude of the medieval medical profession to demonic possession may not have been one of outright scepticism, although medical writers were sometimes critical of clerical attitudes to mental disorder and especially epilepsy. Rather it raises the possibility of a division of responsibility between the medical and religious professions, the former being responsible for physiologically based disorders and the latter for demoniacally caused ones. It should be noted in this context that the Second Lateran Council in 1139 A.D. resolved that monks and canons were not in future to study medicine for the sake of temporal gain. The practice of medicine, particularly when sick women had to be visited, was also discouraged. Other councils also imposed regulations restricting clerical practice and knowledge of medicine.[54]

The medieval church seems to have gradually abandoned the demonological explanation of epilepsy. St. Hildegard of Bingen, in the twelfth century, suggested that demonic and physiological factors might interact in epilepsy, but this suggestion does not seem to have found much later popularity.[55] In the twelfth-century records of the shrine of St. Bartholomew in London, for example, although demonic causes are frequently suggested for other disorders, the mechanism responsible for producing epilepsy in a sick child is clearly identified as the conventional medical one; that the disorder resulted from compression of the ventricles and the pathways of the brain.[56] Thomas of Celano describes how Francis of Assisi cured one of the brothers from the falling sickness or from a devil: "I do not know by what name [the infirmity] is called, though some think it is an evil spirit."[57] Clearly Thomas was aware of an alternative explanation to the demonic one but was uncertain which was correct in this case. Additional evidence of the progress of the physiological explanation of epilepsy is provided in *Malleus Maleficarum* where it is explicitly stated that, while witches have the power to induce epilepsy, it usually arises "from some long-standing physical predisposition or defect."[58]

It seems indisputable that the physiological account of epilepsy became more influential than the demonological one during the later Middle Ages. Far less clear is why it did so. In the first place, the physiological account actually employed in the Middle Ages that explained epilepsy as the result of congestion of the ventricles and passages of the brain is completely wrong. Second, and more seriously, the physiological account was useless: it did not lead to any cure. Although Bernard of Gordon might deride superstitious chants and the clerical methods of dealing with epilepsy he had nothing better to offer, as he was honest enough to admit. Presumably the physiological account was in the end preferred simply because of the great prestige accorded classical theorists like Galen, even by religious writers.

The frequency of attribution of disorders other than epilepsy to demonic possession seems to have depended on the orientation of the attributer. Such attribution was rare in the English courts and the medical profession. Moreover, although Aquinas acknowledged the reality of demonic possession, he also stated that in general the insane or mentally deficient are deprived of the use of reason because of some impediment of a bodily organ.[59] His view of mental disorder was clearly much the same as that of the physicians. On the other hand, an examination of the chronicles of English religious shrines and the biographies of the saints reveals a rather more frequent use of demonic explanation. One reason for this has already been mentioned: successful expulsion of devils was a sign of sanctity, regardless apparently of whether the candidate for canonization was dead or alive at the time of the exorcism. Hence, the frequency and rather biblical flavor of the exorcisms, such as that described at the beginning of this chapter performed by St. Francis.

Nine miraculous cures chronicled at St. Bartholomew's shrine appear to have been of mental disorder of some kind, and, of these, five seem to have been regarded as of diabolic origin.[60] Three of the five cases display some but not all of the symptoms of Oesterreich's possession syndrome, most notably a young waitress who showed great strength in breaking her bonds and blasphemed.[61] On the other hand, the fourth and fifth cases do not display these symptoms. One is of a man named Rayf who was "rauashid of a feende and made woid." He dismounted, tore his clothes, scattered money and threw stones at people.[62] This case is interesting as it clearly involved neither the possession syndrome nor epilepsy, and in this way resembles the much earlier accounts of Aquilinus' and Ecga's illnesses.

Twelfth-century records from Becket's shrine at Canterbury, and a fifteenth-century series from the tomb of Henry VI at Windsor also show a willingness to blame devils for mental disorder. Much of the demonic activity in the latter series, however, was not possession, nor was it regarded so at the time. For example, Agnes Alyn was set on and hit by "the raging fury of a most evil spirit . . . actually and by no means invisibly." Clearly Agnes was mugged. "A man out walking at night was attacked by an evil spirit in the form of a very black dog: at the mention of Henry it disappeared, confounded."[63]

There is some evidence that the confusion of the uneducated noted by Isidore of Seville regarding what was or was not demonic possession continued into the later Middle Ages. Johann Busch, a fifteenth-century subprior of Wittenburg recounted that "a man who was ploughing ran forth from the field and said that his wife was possessed with a devil . . . I found she had many fantasies, for that she was wont to sleep and eat too little, whence she fell into feebleness of brain and thought herself possessed by a demon; yet there was no such thing in her case."[64] Such attitudes among the peasantry persisted well beyond the Middle Ages: contemporary observers remarked that the early seventeenth-century scepticism of the Church of England toward possession cost it the support of the lower classes.[65]

That belief in the reality of possession should be most marked among the more powerless members of society is in line with the findings of present-day anthropological research. Studies of present-day Christian sects also indicate that there should have been some medieval confusion as to divine and demonic possession, that, for example, some of the saints should also have been regarded as possessed. Despite the frequently odd behavior of many of the saints, however, such confusion seems to have been rare—or else reports of it were rarely written. The only clear example I have found is that of St. Lidwyna (1380–1433 A.D.), who had the misfortune to be regarded as demented by her curate, Andrew of Marienward. Andrew refused to listen to her visions and prophecies and asked the congregation to pray for her as she was crazed and tempted by the devil. The congregation, however, refused to believe him and sided with Lidwyna.[66]

Overall three conclusions seem justified about demonic possession in the later Middle Ages. First, there seems to have been little doubt in any part of society that it could and did occur, although whether or not a particular case might be considered possession could be debated. In particular, it seems likely that patients displaying Oesterreich's possession syndrome were often considered to be possessed. Second, mental disorders in general, and epilepsy in particular, were less likely to be attributed to demonic possession in the fifteenth century than the eighth. Third, whether or not a particular person was held to be possessed depended heavily on who was observing him. A late fifteenth-century account of the illness of Hugo van der Goes makes this point clear:

Certain people talked of a peculiar case of *frenesis magna*, the great frenzy of the brain. Others, however, believed him to be possessed of an evil spirit. There were, in fact, symptoms of both unfortunate diseases present in him, although I have always understood that throughout his illness he never once tried to harm anyone but himself. This, however, is not held to be typical of either the frenzied or the possessed. In truth, what it really was that ailed him only God can tell.[67]

OTHER RELIGIOUS VIEWS OF MENTAL DISORDER

So far the only religiously derived cause of mental disorder that has been considered is that of demonic possession. There were, however, other ways in which demons could cause psychological problems; moreover, there was a potentially difficult issue in the possible relationship between sin and mental disorder.

In demonic possession the demon (or, more rarely, demons) was held to possess the victim essentially and to have almost total bodily control. On the other hand, as with Oesterreich's psychiatric syndrome, there was no possession of the mind although the sufferer's will was prevented from exerting control.[68] The demon could, however, attempt to corrupt the victim by obsessing him. This involved less total bodily control than in possession and, in particular, did not directly affect the ability of the sufferer to act, although it did affect perception.

Theologically, demonic obsession "consists in a series of unusually violent and persistent temptations," and might include visual, auditory, or even tactile hallucination.[69] There was good biblical precedent for obsession in Jesus' temptation by the devil. The devil appears in person, tempts Jesus with worldly power, and shows Him a vision of the world.[70] Following this precedent, many of the saints seem to have been obsessed at some time. Probably the best known example is that of St. Anthony whose temptations were later so vividly portrayed by the painter Hieronymus Bosch. Francis of Assisi saw a city surrounded and besieged by an army of devils, and on one occasion suffered a tactile hallucination in which he was severely beaten by devils.[71]

Occasionally, obsession seems to have developed into possession. One of the patients brought to St. Bartholomew's shrine was the daughter of a priest named Wymunde who sent her to live with a respectable matron. The daughter was chastely brought up and resisted the attentions of her suitors but in doing so aroused the devil's envy. The devil disguised himself as a handsome young man and tempted the virgin who resisted his subtle speeches. The young woman's nurse overheard her talking and arguing, apparently, with thin air. The devil came subsequently whenever the girl was alone, and one day became violent and threatened her. She then fell down and writhed on the floor foaming at the mouth. These fits continued two or three times every day until eventually she was taken to the shrine of St. Bartholomew where she was cured after a clergyman petitioned the saint for succor.[72]

An interesting aspect of medieval obsession is that the sufferers were not usually regarded as insane at all. No action was taken when the clergyman's daughter was overheard talking to the devil but only when she went into paroxysm. This was no isolated example: a recent study of 134 recorded medieval visionary experiences revealed that none of the visionaries was regarded as mentally ill by medieval observers even though the visions were not always accepted at face value. In fact only four of the visionaries, to judge by their other behavior, would have been regarded as mentally disordered by present-day standards. This is despite the fact that similar visions to those of the medieval visionaries are reported today by mentally disordered patients. These results suggest that hallucination may not be a culture-free measure of mental disorder at all, and certainly that we should not regard medieval reports of visions as necessarily indicating disorder in the visionary.[73]

An obvious question to ask about the activity of medieval demons in both possession and obsession is why they selected the victims they did. An equally obvious answer, and one which was occasionally used,[74] was that demons possessed or obsessed particularly sinful individuals. Yet this answer was rather rarely given: as a rule, possession and obsession were regarded as afflictions rather than as punishments, and the sufferers treated with sympathy rather than contempt.[75] Hence, for example, the usual medieval doctrine that the possessed could receive Holy Communion.[76] In *Malleus Maleficarum*, no less than five reasons are put forward as to why God permits possession to take place. A man can be possessed for his own later advantage, in punishment of a minor or grievous sin of his own, or in consequence of a minor or grievous sin committed by someone else. Such a multitude of possibilities effectively excluded the possibility of regarding the sufferer as necessarily being responsible for his own misfortune.[77]

A good practical reason why sin should not have been attributed as a necessary cause of demonic possession or obsession was the high frequency of obsession reported by the saints. Moreover, accounts of the possessed do not suggest that they led unusually sinful lives. The clergyman's daughter at St. Bartholomew's, for example, would seem to have had little chance to do so. Thus observation would have suggested that the simple punishment-for-sin theory was unlikely.

More frequently believed was that the demons took advantage of existing *physical* weakness—for example, a tendency toward melancholia—and, as the next section recounts, interactions of medical and demonic conditions received considerable medieval attention. However, many possessions were held to result from chance or strange coincidence. A particularly unlucky devil in the early Middle Ages entered into and possessed a nun by chance because he was sitting on a lettuce and was eaten by a nun along with the lettuce when she failed to cross herself before eating.[78] Less amusing was an idea that received growing support in the fourteenth and following centuries—that possession and obsession were induced by witchcraft.[79] In consequence, there was a growing tendency to seek out and prosecute possible witches when cases of possession occurred. The number of such prosecutions, however, remained small until the beginning of the early modern period.

Although sin was not regarded as a frequent cause of possession, it was implicated in other, nondemonic disorders. Acedia or accidie, which was named as a cardinal sin by Cassian, was a state in which the sufferer was lethargic, depressed, and frequently apathetic, and it was often encountered in monks who lost interest in their vocation and wished for a more secular life.[80] In the later Middle Ages the disorder seems to have "divided," being partly subsumed by the sin of sloth and partly by melancholy. Constantinus remarked that many ascetics and pious people became melancholic through fear of God or His wrath.[81]

INTEGRATION OF RELIGIOUS AND MEDICAL VIEWPOINTS

The tendency of most present-day historians of psychiatry and medical psychology has been to regard the religious and medical attitudes to mental disorder as opposed to each other. Thus, for example, Zilboorg contrasts "the restless surrender to demonology" with the "classical, reasonable, and extremely advanced" attitude of Bartholomaeus Anglicus.[82] Other writers more sympathetic to the Middle Ages have tended to stress the medical viewpoint while appearing to regard the religious and demonic traditions as rather embarrassing but essentially minor blemishes on the overall picture of medieval thought.[83] But, while the medical and religious traditions developed and were largely practiced separately from each other, there is little evidence that they were actively opposed in the Middle Ages. In general, the medical writers seem to have demonstrated little interest of any kind in the religious tradition. From this it could be argued either that they regarded demons as outside their range of competence or that they regarded the demonological tradition with a scepticism they were unwilling to voice. Perhaps also there were differing attitudes within the medical profession; John of Gaddesden, who thought it necessary to distinguish possession and epilepsy, might have been less sceptical than Bernard of Gordon. On the other hand, many of the religious writers seem to have been keenly aware of the medical tradition, as should already be clear from some of the examples given in this and the preceding chapter, particularly with respect to the physiological account of epilepsy. Moreover there was a good deal of interest in obtaining a synthesis of the demonic and physiological accounts of mental disorder.

It seems to have been admitted that often a demon or demons might take advantage of a preexisting physical defect. St. Hildegard, for example, suggested that when an imbalance of humors has affected the brain, demons rush to attack, because it is in their nature to drive people insane. Hildegard, however, is careful to distinguish this demonic activity from possession, because in this case the demon is not permitted to usurp the Holy Ghost and command the victim's voice.[84] In the *Book of Quinte Essence* it is noted that dark, melancholy men are more troubled with anxieties than others as they are born under the constellation of Saturn, the wicked planet. Devils often appear and minister to such men. These men, thus tormented with the passions of melancholy, commonly speak with the devil, striving and disputing when alone so that often other folk may hear it. Sometimes they fall into despair and kill themselves.[85] The possibility of such a synthesis is also taken up in *Malleus Maleficarum*. "Some material object can cause in the human body a disposition which makes it susceptible to the operations of the devil. For example, according to physicians, mania predisposes a man to dementia and consequently to demonic obsession."[86]

Much earlier, Augustine suggested that the operations of evil spirits in producing visions or clairvoyance might take place in the same way that visual images are produced and thus be similar to dreams.[87] The same idea is used, but in rather more sophistication and detail, in *Malleus Maleficarum*. Early in the book the workings of the inner senses are reviewed and it is stated that in sleep images are drawn from the faculty of the imagination. This same cognitive process is used by devils to cause hallucinations. They "excite the inner perceptions and humours, so that ideas retained in the repositories of their minds are drawn out and made apparent to the faculties of [cogitation] and imagination."[88] It is in this way that men are sometimes bewitched into seeing demons or believing they have lost their "virile members."[89] The authors go on to state that "it need not seem wonderful that devils can do this, when even a natural defect is able to effect the same result, as is shown in the case of frantic and melancholy men, and in maniacs and some drunkards, who are unable to discern truly."[90]

Thus Kramer and Sprenger use the accepted doctrine of the inner senses and the physiological account of imagery and hallucination to provide a mechanism for demonic activity. One might deplore the uses to which the authors' ingenuity is put—*Malleus Maleficarum* provided a theoretical rationale for centuries of witch-hunts involving the torture and execution of thousands of people—but it cannot be denied that a great effort was made to connect demonological with physiological levels of explanation.

Further evidence for the integration of the religious with the medical viewpoints comes from consideration of the remedies suggested for those troubled with demons. One would expect that, following the biblical example, exorcism or a more or less formal expulsion of the devil would be used in cases of demonic possession or obsession, and indeed such exorcisms were used in the Middle Ages. Francis of Assisi formally expelled several such demons, one example being given earlier in the chapter. *Malleus Maleficarum* recommends the use of exorcism, and suggests several forms of prayer that might be used in the process.[91] The formula suggested by John of Gaddesden and Constantinus Africanus for distinguishing possession from epilepsy is itself a form of exorcism.

Yet the use of exorcism to expel the demons was certainly not universally employed even by clergy in the Middle Ages. Bede's epileptic was cured not by exorcism but by attenuated contact with relics of the blessed Oswald. All of the St. Bartholomew's cases were cured simply by the prayers of the resident clergy,[92] as Aquilinus had been centuries before. While these methods of treatment resemble exorcism in their religious nature, they differ from it in that they were not used exclusively as a treatment of demoniacally based disorder. Saintly relics and prayer were used to treat any type of affliction not just those of demonic origin: the majority of the illnesses treated with prayer at St. Bartholomew's, for example, were ordinary physical disorders and were not ascribed to demonic causes at all.[93]

The obverse of using religious remedies for physically based ailments was the use of physical, and particularly herbal, remedies to treat demonic possession. For example, an Anglo-Saxon herbarium prescribes "for witlessness, that is, for devil sickness, or demoniacal possession, take from the body of this same wort mandrake, by weight of three pennies, administer to drink in warm water."[94] Similar remedies were recommended even toward the end of the Middle Ages. In *The Book of Quinte Essence* we are told that if a man is troubled with a fiend, he should drink a little quinte essence, together with gold and pearl and a herb called ypericonum (*Fuga demonum*).[95] In *Malleus Maleficarum* it is stated that "a man possessed by a devil can be indirectly relieved by the power of music, as was Saul by David's harp, or of a herb, or of any other bodily matter in which there lies some natural virtue."[96]

Taken as a whole the remedies for demonic possession were clearly a mixed bunch, and in their diversity and often seemingly *ad hoc* nature do not, with the exception of exorcism, seem to have derived from theoretical consideration of the nature of demons or the disorders they were held to cause. It is difficult, for example, to see why demons should have been agitated or displaced by particular herbs or by music. Thus many of the treatments recommended for demoniacally based disorders resemble those recommended for physiologically based disorders in lacking a truly scientific base. Furthermore, it is noticeable that many of the remedies suggested—music, mandrake, quinte essence, and saintly relic—were actually the same for both kinds of disorder.

One final feature common to the religious and legal medieval traditions (and to a certain extent the medical tradition as well) should be remarked: there is a common definition of insanity. In both cases, insanity can be defined as the inability of the mind, the rational soul, to control behavior. In practice, a rather strict interpretation of insanity resulted, as is suggested by the fact that hallucination was not in itself regarded as firm evidence of insanity. This common definition had its root in the widely held view of psychology in which the normal human soul was governed by the will, or intellectual appetite, operating in conjunction with reason. Furthermore, at least in England, it seems probable that the clerical approach to insanity, as expressed in canon law, influenced the English common law rather than vice versa. Thus the scholastic inquiry into the nature of the soul produced at least one element that was widespread in medieval society and not restricted to the scholars of Oxford or the Sorbonne.

CONCLUSIONS

It seems fairly certain that as knowledge of the physiologically based medical models of mental disorder became more widespread in the later Middle Ages so did the tendency to attribute a wide range of mental disorders to demonic possession decrease. On the other hand, although medieval observers might, and sometimes did, question whether a particular disorder had a demonic cause, there is no evidence of anyone disbelieving that demonic possessions actually occurred. This type of scepticism seems to have first become apparent in the early modern period following the Reformation. It is worthwhile perhaps to consider briefly the reasons why it did so.

In effect, scepticism arose because of the failure of the demons to pass tests of discernment of the sort that Francis of Assisi used; tests that were based on the demon's presumed clairvoyance, unusual strength, and ability to determine true sanctity. Often, in the early modern period, these tests were conducted fairly rigorously: one could test, for example, to see whether physically indistinguishable holy and ordinary water were as abhorrent to the demon, as was done by Phillip Melanchthon (1497–1560). Usually, of course, as Melanchthon found, the demon failed the test.[97]

The increased use of these tests can be seen as part of an awakening interest in experimentation in early modern Europe. However, this new experimental spirit was itself dependent on the emergence of new legal and religious considerations. Two factors, in particular, that were not important in the Middle Ages can be isolated as important for the new approach. First, the tendency to suspect witchcraft when cases of possession occurred led to asking the alleged demon to identify the witch responsible. The legal importance thus attached to the claims of the devils led to their close scrutiny and inevitably occasional demonstrations of factual error. Hence arose doubt as to whether a demon was really present in an apparent case of possession. Second, following the Reformation the successful expulsion of demons became an instrument of propaganda for both Catholics and Protestants. An obvious way for each party to discredit the expulsions performed by adherents of the rival religion was to deny that there had been any possession in the first place. As an extreme example of this tendency, John Darrell, an English puritan, was in 1598 convicted of training patients to simulate possession symptoms. Thus while it is fair to claim that the early modern period saw the application of experimentation to the study of possession, the motives for doing so seem to have been legal and religious rather than the disinterested pursuit of scientific or rational knowledge.[98]

It is easy for the modern observer to see the medieval belief in possession as a fundamentally incompatible and irrational addition to the rational, empirical, physiological model of mental disorder derived from the Greek and Roman medical writers. One can only maintain such a view, however, if one disregards several important factors.

First of these factors must be the realization that Oesterreich's possession syndrome, which was likely to have been present in many, although not all, of the medieval cases ascribed to demonic possession, looks like a real possession. It is not at all surprising that an observer confronted with someone who suddenly changes his voice, expression, and behavior and proclaims loudly that he actually is a demon should consider that there is a real possession taking place. When one adds to this the fact that many of the possessed appeared to display clairvoyance, predicted the future, and performed apparently superhuman feats of strength, it becomes less surprising still.

Second, while it may be objected that straightforward experimental investigation of cases of possession would have at least led to suspicion about the reality of diabolical possession, it should be noted that straightforward anatomical investigation would also have shown up the deficiencies in the medical model. Such investigation would have shown, for example, that the human brain does not contain a rete system for distilling animal spirits, and that the doctrine of the inner senses was not very well related to the actual placement of the cerebral ventricles. In short, neither the demonological nor the medical model of mental disorder would have stood up to experimental investigation.

Third, I suspect that one of the main reasons why the demonological account is regarded today as an irrational addition to the classical medical account is simply that to modern eyes it appears such a different type of account. Yet, in the Middle Ages the existence of demonic possession was not only compatible with the almost universally held theological beliefs of the time, but it could also be reconciled with existing psychological and even medical theory. In fact the reconciliation of the demonic and physiological traditions is a good example of the medieval taste, and indeed talent, for synthesizing different theoretical perspectives. To modern eyes this may seem merely an interesting exercise in armchair psychology, but it is worthwhile to ask whether some talent of this kind might not be useful, for example, in producing a detailed account of precisely how genetic and environmental factors can combine to influence behavior.

NOTES

1. Aquinas, *Summa Theologiae*, 3.80.9.

2. Edward Peters, ed., *Monks, Bishops, and Pagans: Christian Culture in Gaul and Italy, 500–700* (Philadelphia: University of Pennsylvania Press, 1975).

3. Felix, *Life of Saint Guthlac*, 42.

4. Marion A. Habig, ed., *St. Francis of Assisi: Writings and Early Biographies* (London: Society for Promoting Christian Knowledge, 1973), 287.

5. Some of the material in the chapter is taken from Simon Kemp, "Demonic Possession and Mental Disorder in Medieval and Early Modern Europe." *Psychological Medicine* 17 (1987): 21–29; and Simon Kemp, "Ravished of a Fiend: Demonology and Medieval Madness." In C. Ward ed., *Altered States of Consciousness and Mental Health: A Cross-Cultural Perspective* (London: Sage, 1989).

6. T. K. Oesterreich, *Possession: Demoniacal and Other*, trans. D. Ibberson (New York: University Books, 1966), 16.

7. Ibid., 21.

8. Ibid., 26–90.

9. See Morgan D. Enoch and William H. Trethowan, *Uncommon Psychiatric Syndromes*, 2nd ed. (Bristol: John Wright and Sons, 1979); and E. Mansell Pattison, "Possession States and Exorcism." In Claude T. H. Freedman and Robert A. Faguet, eds., *Extraordinary Disorders of Human Behavior* (New York: Plenum, 1982).

10. See American Psychiatric Association, *Diagnostic and Statistical Manual of Mental Disorders*, 3rd ed. (Washington, D.C.: APA, 1980).

11. F. S. Abuzzahab, "Gilles de la Tourette Syndrome or Multiple Tic Dis-

order." In T. H. Freedman and Robert A. Faguet, eds., *Extraordinary Disorders of Human Behavior* (New York: Plenum, 1982), 79–97; and Enoch and Trethowan, *Uncommon Psychiatric Syndromes*, 95–115.

12. Oesterreich, *Possession*, 91; Enoch and Trethowan, *Uncommon Psychiatric Syndromes*; and Erika Bourguignon, *Possession* (San Francisco: Chandler and Sharp, 1976).

13. Rodney W. Francis, *Counselling and Deliverance* (Christchurch, N.Z.: Outreach, 1981); and Hal Lindsey, *Satan Is Alive and Well on Planet Earth* (Grand Rapids, Mich.: Zondervan, 1972).

14. Lindsey, *Satan Is Alive and Well*, 160.

15. Erika Bourguignon, "Introduction: A Framework for the Comparative Study of Altered States of Consciousness." In E. Bourguignon, ed., *Religion, Altered States of Consciousness, and Social Change* (Columbus: Ohio State University Press, 1973).

16. See Linda Greenbaum, "Societal Correlates of Possession Trance in Sub-Saharan Africa." In E. Bourguignon, ed., *Religion, Altered States of Consciousness, and Social Change* (Columbus: Ohio State University Press, 1973); and I. M. Lewis, *Ecstatic Religion: An Anthropological Study of Spirit Possession and Shamanism* (Harmondsworth, UK: Penguin, 1971).

17. Felicity D. Goodman, Jeanette H. Henney, and Esther Pressel, *Trance, Healing and Hallucination: Three Field Studies in Religious Experience* (New York: Wiley, 1974).

18. Lewis, *Ecstatic Religion*, 29–36.

19. Ibid. See also Goodman, Henney, and Pressel, *Trance, Healing and Hallucination*; and Colleen Ward, "Spirit Possession and Mental Health: A Psycho-Anthropological Perspective." *Human Relations* 33 (1980): 149–163.

20. Colleen Ward and Michael H. Beaubrun, "Spirit Possession and Neuroticism in a West Indian Pentecostal Community." *British Journal of Clinical Psychology* 20 (1981): 295–296.

21. Lindsey, *Satan Is Alive and Well*, 142.

22. Goodman, Henney, and Pressel, *Trance, Healing and Hallucination*, 231–364.

23. See Carlos A. Leon, "El Duende and Other Incubi." *Archives of General Psychiatry* 32 (1975): 155–162.

24. Scott, *Hermetica*, 181.

25. Roccatagliata, *History of Ancient Psychiatry*, 70.

26. Plutarch, *De Iside et Osiride*, 157.

27. Plato, *Timaeus*, 51–56.

28. Mark 1.23–26; Mark 5.2–10; Mark 9.17–29; and Acts 19.13–17.

29. Mark 5.2–10.

30. Mark 9.17–18, 20–22, 25, 28–29.

31. See D. P. Walker, *Unclean Spirits* (London: Scolar, 1981), 12.

32. Habig, *St. Francis of Assisi*, 287.

33. For example, Luke 9.49–50; 10.17.

34. See also Acts 19.13–17.

35. A good example of this is in the records of the tomb of Henry VI at Windsor. See Clarke, *Mental Disorder*, 151–175.

36. Tertullian, *Apologeticus*, trans. T. R. Glover (London: Heinemann, 1931), 22.6.

37. Ibid., 23.4–14.

38. O. Chadwick, *John Cassian* (Cambridge, UK: Cambridge University Press, 1968), 96–99.

39. Augustine, *The Literal Meaning of Genesis*, 12.17. 34–38.

40. O. J. Reichel, *A Complete Manual of Canon Law Vol. I: The Sacraments* (London: John Hodges, 1896), 193, 194; and C. J. Hefele, *A History of the Christian Councils*, Vol. 2 (Edinburgh, UK: T and T Clark, 1872), 417.

41. Hefele, *Christian Councils*, Vol. 1, 148–149.

42. Ibid., Vol. 3, 162.

43. Reichel, *Canon Law*, 237.

44. Temkin, *The Falling Sickness*, 84.

45. *Herbarium of Apuleius*, 132.5. In Oswald Cockayne, ed., *Leechdoms, Wort-cunning, and Starcraft of Early England* (London: Longman, 1864), Vol. 1, 249.

46. Sharpe, *Isidore of Seville*, 58.

47. Bede, *An Ecclesiastical History of the English People* (London: Trubner, 1890), 23.11. The incident is also described by Alcuin in *The Bishops, Kings, and Saints of York*, ed. Peter Goodman (Oxford, UK: Clarendon, 1982), 37.

48. Charles M. Radding, *A World Made by Man: Cognition and Society, 400–1200* (Chapel Hill: University of North Carolina, 1985), 110–116.

49. Bartholomaeus Anglicus, *On the Properties of Things*, 84–89, 348–354.

50. Lennox, "Bernard of Gordon"; and Von Storch and Von Storch, "Arnold of Villanova."

51. Temkin, *The Falling Sickness*, 105.

52. Ibid., 106.

53. Lennox, "John of Gaddesden," 297.

54. H. J. Schroeder, *Disciplinary Decrees of the General Councils* (St. Louis: B. Herder, 1937), 201–202.

55. Hildegard, *Heilkunde*, 238.

56. Moore, *The Book of the Foundation of St. Bartholomew*, 47 (Case 2.11).

57. Habig, *St. Francis of Assisi*, 285.

58. Kramer and Sprenger, *Malleus Maleficarum*, 2.1.11.

59. Aquinas, *Summa Theologiae*, 3.68.12.

60. Moore, *The Book of the Foundation of St. Bartholomew*, Cases 2.9, 2.10, 2.12, 2.15, 2.19.

61. Ibid., 60, Case 2.19. The other cases are 2.9 and 2.12.

62. Ibid., 46, Case 2.10.

63. Clarke, *Mental Disorder*, 165.

64. G. G. Coulton, *Life in the Middle Ages*, Vol. 1 (Cambridge, UK: Cambridge University Press, 1928), 231–232.

65. Keith Thomas, *Religion and the Decline of Magic* (London: Weidenfeld and Nicolson, 1971), 492.

66. Baring-Gould, *The Lives of the Saints*, Vol. 4 (April), 197.

67. Rosen, *Madness in Society*, 145.

68. For example, Kramer and Sprenger, *Malleus Maleficarum*, 2.1.10.

69. This definition, although of medieval origin, is still used today by the Roman Catholic Church. Adolphe Tanquerey, *The Spiritual Life: A Treatise on*

Ascetical and Mystical Theology, 2nd ed., trans. H. Branderis (Tournai, Belgium: Society of St. John the Evangelist, 1923), 718.

70. Matthew 4.1–11.

71. Habig, *St. Francis of Assisi*, (1372), 461.

72. Moore, *The Book of the Foundation of St. Bartholomew*, 49, Case 2.12.

73. Jerome Kroll and Bernard Bachrach, "Visions and Psychopathology in the Middle Ages." *The Journal of Nervous and Mental Disease* 170 (1982): 41–49; and Jerome Kroll and Bernard Bachrach, "Medieval Visions and Contemporary Hallucinations." *Psychological Medicine* 12 (1982): 709–721.

74. For example, Kramer and Sprenger, *Malleus Maleficarum*, 2.1.7; 2.1.10.

75. For example, Jerome Kroll and Bernard Bachrach, "Sin and Mental Illness in the Middle Ages." *Psychological Medicine* 14 (1984): 507–514. These authors show that sin was more likely to be mentioned as a cause of mental disorder where the sufferer was a political opponent.

76. Chadwick, *John Cassian*, 97; Aquinas, *Summa Theologiae*, 3.80.9; and Kramer and Sprenger, *Malleus Maleficarum*, 2.2.5.

77. Kramer and Sprenger, *Malleus Maleficarum*, 2.1.10.

78. Bonser, *Medical Background*, 259.

79. As argued by Kramer and Sprenger, *Malleus Maleficarum*, 2.1.0ff.

80. Stanley W. Jackson, "Acedia the Sin and Its Relationship to Sorrow and Melancholia in Medieval Times." *Bulletin of the History of Medicine* 55 (1981): 172–185.

81. Constantine, *De Melancholia*, 103.

82. Zilboorg, *History of Medical Psychology*, 118, 138.

83. See Jackson, "Unusual Mental States."

84. Hildegarde, *Heilkunde*, 163.

85. Furnivall, *Book of Quinte Essence*, 17.

86. Kramer and Sprenger, *Malleus Maleficarum*, 2.2.5.

87. Augustine, *The Literal Meaning of Genesis*, 12.18.39.

88. Kramer and Sprenger, *Malleus Maleficarum*, 1.7. See also 2.1.7.

89. Ibid., 2.1.7.

90. Ibid.

91. Ibid., 2.2.5–7.

92. Moore, *Book of the Foundation of St. Bartholomew*.

93. Ibid.

94. *Herbarium of Apuleius*, 132.5. In Oswald Cockayne, ed., *Leechdoms, Wortcunning, and Starcraft of Early England* (London: Longman, 1864), Vol. 1, 249. Note that mandrake was recommended in antiquity for treating physically based mental disorder as well.

95. Furnivall, *Book of Quinte Essence*, 19.

96. Kramer and Sprenger, *Malleus Maleficarum*, 2.2.5.

97. Jean Bodin, *Colloquium of the Seven about Secrets of the Sublime*, trans. Marion Kuntz (Princeton, N.J.: University Press, 1975), 46.

98. See especially Walker, *Unclean Spirits*. Also interesting is Thomas, *Religion and the Decline of Magic*.

9

Other Areas of
Psychology

In the preceding chapters, medieval accounts of perception, cognition, emotion, individual differences, and mental disorder were outlined separately and briefly contrasted with modern views. At the same time, the areas of physiological psychology and neuropsychology—how, in short, the brain and its processes relate to behavior—were covered and compared. The choice of these particular areas is partly a personal one, as my knowledge of both modern and medieval psychology is of course incomplete. In general, though, I have tried to include the areas that appear to have been perceived as important by medieval scholars or physicians, and for which there seemed to be some equivalent in modern psychology. These areas are, however, exhaustive neither of medieval nor of modern psychology.

LEARNING AND ANIMAL BEHAVIOR

One obvious omission is the area of learning, which has generally been regarded as important in modern psychology. However, there appears to have been only moderate medieval interest shown in the subject. Some interest was shown by Aquinas, and his account of dispositions, which was examined briefly in Chapter 6, considers a few of the issues raised by modern accounts of learning. Psychological dispositions, such as the tendency to behave courageously or the ability to speak and understand a foreign language, are, according to Aquinas, acquired by acts of will.[1] Like modern behavioral repertoires they are generally acquired gradually and strengthened by repeated action as the passive potentialities are acted on by active elements, and may be lost or extinguished through lack of use.[2] Aquinas, however, would part company with most modern psychologists of learning with his denial that animals possessed dispositions at all.[3] Moreover, Aquinas does not consider the mechanisms, for example, repeated association or reward for successful performance, by which learning might take place.

The psychological accounts of the Middle Ages, in contrast to their modern successors, make little reference to animal behavior, the main exception occurring when, as outlined in Chapter 4, the inner senses were under discussion. Moreover even these animal references show little evidence of real interest in animal behavior: the same examples, of the lamb fleeing the wolf or the spider spinning its web, occur repeatedly in the medieval accounts. An exception to these repetitious examples occurs in the writings of Augustine who stated that fish had memory, and cited his own observation that the fish in a fountain at Bulla Regia had learned to swim beside people walking near the fountain in the hope (or expectation) of being fed.[4]

In some respects the limited reference to animal behavior in scholastic writing was perhaps fortunate, as much of what was believed about animals was quite inaccurate. In Bartholomaeus Anglicus' encyclopedia, the reader learned that the basilisk, the king of serpents, could kill with his breath or even by looking at another animal.[5] Information about the more common animals is generally more accurate but even here there are errors: it is perilous to leave lambs alone because they can be killed by loud thunder owing to the feebleness of their heads.[6]

The lack of interest shown by the medieval schoolmen in animals is perhaps unsurprising given their overriding concern with human psychological functioning and their overall view of the soul, which indicated major qualitative differences between human beings and animals. On a more practical level, however, animal behavior certainly could not have been ignored in the Middle Ages. Teams of oxen or horses had to be trained to plow and war-horses taught to charge and obey the commands of the knights who rode them.

Most of this knowledge was probably passed on orally and not written down, but some insight into this practical side of animal psychology is given by the work of the Holy Roman Emperor Frederick II (1194–1250) on falconry.[7] In his book the training and care of falcons is discussed in detail, from the point of view of someone who had considerable experience with the birds: hawking was a popular aristocratic pastime in the Middle Ages. Both experience and a capacity for acute observation are evident throughout the book. It is correctly stated, for example, that many species of fledgling defecate easily disposable pellets and that vultures detect carrion by sight and not by smell.[8] Indeed, one of Frederick's stated motives for writing the book is the inaccuracy of Aristotle's remarks on birds.[9] In the training of falcons, Frederick emphasized the use of a controlled environment, in which the bird was deprived of the use of its senses and then gradually allowed to taste, touch, hear, and see by the falconer. In common with modern operant training techniques the falcon was trained by slow stages with the aid of frequent rewards of food. Thus Frederick's approach was essentially practical, "a technology of animal behavior" as it has been recently described.[10]

SOCIAL PSYCHOLOGY AND BEHAVIOR

There does not appear to have been a systematic study of social psychology in the Middle Ages, although isolated phenomena were fairly frequently remarked. For example, Aquinas discussed the nature of love and friendship in some detail at different places.[11] However, in general, love and friendship provided themes for medieval literature rather than psychology, as of course they still do today. Again, given the importance of the individual in medieval psychology and the importance of individual salvation in medieval theology, it is perhaps not surprising that social psychology was not pursued by medieval scholars,[12] but, as in the case of animal psychology, one would suspect that at least some aspects of social psychology must have been studied from a practical point of view in the Middle Ages. For example, contrary to the general belief that knights fought as individuals, it is now clear that they fought as units.[13] Clearly the training of groups of knights to act together in a disciplined way must have involved some practical applied social psychology.

Some indication of how people behaved in social situations, or at least of how they were supposed to behave in them, is given by medieval books of instruction and advice. Such books make it clear, for example, that politeness and courtesy and even table manners were highly valued. William Caxton in his *Book of Curtesye*, written in the later fifteenth century, states that "manners make man" and discusses in detail how one should behave at the table, refraining from picking at one's teeth with a knife, for example, or eating with one's mouth open.[14] The value of courtesy and gentle manners at home is also stressed by Peter Idley in his mid-fifteenth century *Instructions to His Son*. If, he warns, you speak roughly to your wife and are hard to please, you will lose her love.[15]

Much of the advice given in these books of instruction was on moral and religious issues, indicating that Christian values were important in social behavior. Thus most of Peter Idley's instructions are on the themes of the Ten Commandments or the Seven Deadly Sins. These are also major themes of John Mirk's *Instructions for Parish Priests*, written in the mid-twelfth century. Mixed with the moral exhortation, however, is some practical advice: pride may be cured by frequently gazing on the bones of the dead; to avoid lechery, children should not be left to sleep together after they have reached the age of seven.[16]

One of the most interesting of these works is *The Book of the Knight of La Tour-Landry*, written by Geoffroy de La Tour-Landry in the late fourteenth century as instruction to his daughters. The instructions, like those of Mirk and Idley, are an elaborate interleaving of exhortation and example, with most of the examples showing either virtue rewarded or, more frequently, sin punished. Thus a woman should not make herself late for church by spending too long getting dressed. One woman who did so was greatly shocked to find a devil taking her own place in the mirror.[17] Several examples, taken from a sermon, are given of women suffering in hell for their vanity. One particular unfortunate had to endure burning needles thrust into her head because she had plucked her brows and forehead to make herself more attractive.[18]

In general Geoffroy's advice appears to a modern reader to be rather reactionary—at one point he remarks how much better off England and France would be if the death penalty was introduced for adultery.[19] Certainly the book indicates the subservient role played by women in medieval society: women should be quiet and humble, fast regularly, and not try to seek vengeance for wrongs done them. She should keep the secrets of her husband, and generally honor and serve him even if he is old, and by inference unattractive. Some of his advice, however, has a more liberal flavor. He advocates educating both boys and girls, and a frequent theme is the need for charity toward less fortunate members of society.

DEVELOPMENTAL PSYCHOLOGY

A more puzzling omission of medieval academic psychology, to my mind, than that of social psychology is the failure to develop a systematic account of developmental psychology. Numerous passages in medieval writing testify that children, and particularly young children, were thought of as being psychologically different from adults. In particular they were not generally thought to be rational in the same way that adults were. Aquinas, for example, felt that for this reason religious vows could not be taken before puberty and Bracton stated that children resembled madmen in being unable to intend the committing of a crime.[20]

Both Aquinas and Albertus Magnus held that the child was born with a rational soul, although they disagreed about whether the fetus was

successively inhabited by a succession of vegetative, sensitive, and finally, rational souls as Aquinas maintained, or whether the soul gradually acquired new powers.[21] The question of why the neonate is then
not itself immediately rational was addressed briefly. Aquinas held that
the capacity for intellectual thought in infants was hindered by the excessive moistness of its brain—a common medieval belief. Also, the use
of reason was impaired simply because of lack of knowledge.[22] Aquinas'
account, however, falls short of a detailed description of how adult
rationality is acquired.

Although children were perceived to be different from adults, they
were certainly not regarded as subhuman or frequently subjected to
abuse. Rather, they seem to have been generally cherished by their
parents. Some indication of this is given in the fifteenth-century English
poem "Pearl," which describes a father's dream dialogue with his much-
loved and now-dead daughter.[23] There are, moreover, numerous in-
stances in medieval writing of parents going to great lengths to try to
help children who were dying or ill: the preceding two chapters in fact
include examples of parents seeking treatment for their mentally disordered children. In addition, many European countries had laws re-
cognizing the vulnerable status of children and offering protection for
them, and the Church encouraged the provision of homes for orphaned
or abandoned children.[24]

If there was no systematic medieval theory of how children develop,
there was no shortage of advice on how children ought to be reared.[25]
Bartholomaeus Anglicus was one of many who recommended that mothers should suckle their own children instead of sending them to wet
nurses as was common in upper- and middle-class society. He also
recommended that children sleep in their own cradles.[26] The latter recommendation was partly based on the consideration that the rocking
motion was good for the child, but it also followed the official policy of
the Church. Robert Grosseteste as Bishop of Lincoln from 1235 to 1253
ordered that "mothers and nurses are not to keep little babies beside
them in bed, lest by chance they carelessly smother them, as often
happens, and as a consequence what is thought to be giving affection
to a tender life is the occasion of death."[27]

It seems to have been generally accepted that even very young children
benefited from affection and social interaction. Bartholomaeus Anglicus
recommended singing lullabies and cradle songs to please the wits.
Moreover, his recommendation that mothers breast-feed their own children is partly based on the consideration that true mothers will be more
affectionate than a wet-nurse.[28] A striking example of the belief in the
importance of affection is given by a remark of Salimbene (ca. 1221–
1290) when discussing the "follies" of the Emperor Frederick II. The
emperor, in an attempt to establish which was the "natural" language

for children to speak, arranged for a number of children to be brought up by foster mothers and nurses who suckled and washed the babies, but were forbidden to speak to them. However, the experiment failed as all the children died before speaking, because they "could not live without the petting and the joyful faces and loving words of their foster mothers. [Also, without cradle songs] a child sleeps badly and has no rest."[29]

It was generally reckoned in the Middle Ages that children knew right from wrong at about age seven and were hence educable. Quite how the education should be accomplished, however, was a matter of debate. Boys, in particular, were thought difficult to teach, because, as Bartholomaeus Anglicus explained, they lead carefree lives and fear nothing except being beaten. This is because the hot humors make them lithe but unstable. They have bad manners and think only of the present and like playing games. They want everything they see and are only still when they sleep. You cannot keep them clean, they do not like to wash, and they want to eat and drink all the time.[30]

The early Christians believed parents would be held responsible for the sins of their children and that they should therefore educate them properly, beating them when necessary.[31] John Chrysostom (ca. 347–407), whose tract on bringing up children is untrammeled by any consideration for the feelings of the child, offered the following advice:

If good precepts are impressed on the soul while it is yet tender, no man will be able to destroy them when they have set firm, even as does a waxen seal. The child is still trembling and fearful and afraid in look and speech and in all else. Make use of the beginning of his life.[32]

Children who behave badly should be sometimes punished with a look or spoken to sharply. At other times they should be treated gently. They should not be constantly beaten because then the punishment will lose its effect and the child will no longer fear the blows.[33] Chrysostom also gives quite specific advice as to how stories can be used to make particular points and he recommends children not be told of hell when they are young lest it dismay them.[34] They should be discouraged from striking slaves and taught to maintain a philosophical attitude to the loss of possessions.[35]

Corporal punishment seems to have been often regarded as a useful educational aid in the Middle Ages, and many tutors beat their charges when they did not learn. Guibert of Nogent writes that he "was pelted almost every day while he [the tutor] was forcing me to learn what he could not teach."[36] Occasionally beating seems to have been administered with the simple object of making an event more memorable. In

Anglo-Saxon England, for example, this sometimes occurred when important ceremonies were witnessed by children.[37]

Not all medieval education was carried out under Chrysostom's regime or by frequent beating. An abbot of Croyland is supposed to have used positive reinforcement and handed out fruit when his pupils showed progress.[38] Anselm (1033–1109), who later became archbishop of Canterbury, was one who gave special attention to teaching the young. One day he was approached by an abbot who remarked that he found it difficult to keep discipline in the monastery even though the boys were beaten day and night. Anselm suggested that the boys should be given more freedom and beaten less. Because, he said, they sense

no love or pity, good-will or tenderness in your attitude towards them, they have in future no faith in your goodness but believe that all your actions proceed from hatred and malice against them. . . . But . . . why [are you] so incensed against them? Are they not human? Would you like to have been treated as you treat them?[39]

Anselm's warnings against the dangers of too rigid and brutal a system of education were echoed both by his contemporaries and by later medieval teachers. Guibert, for example, remarked that some leisure is necessary and that a master should try to moderate his teaching methods.[40] One spur to the reform of educational methods may in fact have been the increased number of young oblates to monasteries in the later Middle Ages, and the reconsideration of teaching methods that their presence caused. Generally it seems that education became more sympathetic in the later Middle Ages and that clerics were often among the most active reformers.[41]

CONCLUSIONS

That modern psychology undertakes a more systematic study of some areas than its medieval counterpart does not necessarily argue that medieval psychology was the narrower and more restricted discipline. A medieval scholar would probably question why theological, moral and ethical issues play so small a part in modern psychology. In summarizing Aquinas' account of the will in Chapter 5, for example, the—to my mind—purely moral and ethical issues that are discussed alongside the psychological ones have been discarded. Aquinas might well consider my summary of questionable value for this reason. Similarly, much of the medieval discussion of cognition and the intellect bears little reference to modern psychology, but instead similar issues are discussed by modern philosophers. In short the subject matter of the medieval study of the soul was not quite the same as that of present-day psychology.

NOTES

1. Aquinas, *Summa Theologiae*, 1.2. 54.4; 1.2. 51.4.
2. Ibid., 1.2. 50–53.
3. Ibid., 1.2. 50.3.
4. Augustine, *The Literal Meaning of Genesis*, 3.8.12.
5. Bartholomaeus Anglicus, *On the Properties of Things*, 1153.
6. Ibid., 1116.
7. Frederick II of Hohenstaufen, *The Art of Falconry*, trans. C. A. Wood and F. Marjorie Fyfe (Boston, Mass.: Charles Brandford, 1955).
8. Ibid., 55, 22.
9. Ibid., 3–4.
10. Paul T. Mountjoy, James H. Bos, Michael O. Duncan, and Robert B. Verplank, "Falconry: Neglected Aspect of the History of Psychology." *Journal of the History of the Behavioral Sciences* 5 (1969): 66.
11. For example, Aquinas, *Summa Theologiae*, 1.2.4.8; 1.20.1.
12. Radding, in *A World Made by Men*, argues that the idea of people relating to one another as equals was almost unknown in the early Middle Ages.
13. For example, J. F. Verbruggen, *The Art of Warfare in Western Europe during the Middle Ages*, trans. S. Willard and S.C.M. Southern (Amsterdam, The Netherlands: North Holland, 1977), 65–97.
14. William Caxton, *Book of Curtesye*, ed. Frederick J. Furnivall (London: Early English Text Society, Early Series 3, 1868), 23–25.
15. Peter Idley, *Instructions to His Son*, ed. Charlotte d'Evelyn (Boston: Heath, 1935), 101.
16. John Mirk, *Instructions for Parish Priests*, ed. Edward Peacock (London: Early English Text Society, Old Series 31, 1868), 51, 7.
17. Geoffroy de La Tour-Landry, *The Book of the Knight of La Tour-Landry*, trans. Anon., ed. Thomas Wright (London: Early English Text Society, Old Series 33, 1868), 45.
18. Ibid., 67.
19. Ibid., 162.
20. Aquinas, *Summa Theologiae*, 2.2.88.9; Bracton, *Laws and Customs*, 324, 384, 423.
21. Aquinas, *Summa Theologiae*, 1.76.3; 1.118.2; and Katherine Park, "Albert's Influence on Late Medieval Psychology." In James A. Weisheipl, ed., *Albertus Magnus and the Sciences: Commemorative Essays, 1980.* (Toronto: Pontifical Institute of Medieval Studies, 1980).
22. Aquinas, *Summa Theologiae*, 1.101.1–2.
23. "Pearl," ed. I. Gollancz (New York: Cooper Square, 1966).
24. Jerome Kroll, "The Concept of Childhood in the Middle Ages." *Journal of the History of the Behavioral Sciences* 13 (1977): 384–393; and Jerome Kroll and Bernard Bachrach, "Child Care and Child Abuse in Early Medieval Europe." *Journal of the American Academy of Child Psychiatry* 25 (1986): 562–568.
25. For an overall view of child rearing in the Middle Ages, see Lloyd De Mause, ed., *The History of Childhood* (New York: Psychohistory Press, 1974), especially chapts. 1–6.

26. Bartholomaeus Anglicus, *On the Properties of Things*, 299, 303.

27. Marshall W. Baldwin, ed., *Christianity Through the Thirteenth Century* (New York: Harper & Row, 1970), 326.

28. Bartholomaeus Anglicus, *On the Properties of Things*, 299, 303.

29. James Bruce Ross and Mary Martin McLaughlin, eds., *The Portable Medieval Reader* (Harmondsworth, UK: Penguin, 1949), 366–367.

30. Bartholomaeus Anglicus, *On the Properties of Things*, 300–301.

31. M.L.W. Laistner, *Christianity and Pagan Culture in the Later Roman Empire* (Ithaca, N.Y.: Cornell University, 1967), 30–31.

32. Ibid., 95.

33. Ibid., 99–100.

34. Ibid., 105–109.

35. Ibid., 114–117.

36. Guibert of Nogent, *Self and Society*, 47.

37. John Thrupp, *The Anglo-Saxon Home: A History of the Domestic Institutions and Customs of England from the Fifth to the Eleventh Century* (London: Longman, Green, Longman, and Roberts, 1862), 100.

38. Ibid., 101.

39. Eadmer, *The Life of St. Anselm*, trans. R. W. Southern (London: Nelson, 1962), 38.

40. Guibert of Nogent, *Self and Society*, 47–48.

41. Mary Martin McLaughlin, "Survivors and Representatives: Children and Parents from the Ninth to the Thirteenth Century." In Lloyd De Mause, ed., *The History of Childhood* (New York: Psychohistory Press, 1974).

10

Conclusions

Any conclusions that one may draw about the state of psychology in medieval Europe must be tempered by the realization that the Middle Ages lasted a thousand years and saw many changes. In particular, it must be remembered that by almost any account intellectual life before, say, 1100 A.D. was much more rudimentary than in the later Middle Ages. There was very little academic psychology, and very few scholars to pursue it, in the earlier period. Moreover, the approach to mental disorder then, at least so far as we can tell from the limited number of written accounts, seems to have been rather more influenced by religious than medical tradition, probably because religious writings survived better the collapse of Roman power in the west. In sum, it seems scarcely possible to talk about the study of any aspect of psychology prior to 1100 A.D. In contrast, psychological issues, like many others, were vigorously discussed and debated in the later Middle Ages, and especially in the thirteenth century. The conclusions that are drawn to the remainder of this chapter relate solely to the later psychology.

A broad comparison of modern and medieval psychology reveals both similarities and differences. Clearly many of the areas and issues addressed in the Middle Ages were the same as those addressed today, although, as we have just seen, there were also some differences. On a broader scale, comparing similarities and differences in more than one area, a number of features stand out.

First, medieval psychology resembled its modern counterpart in attempting detailed consideration of the physiology underlying psychological processes. In fact, the use of the doctrine of the humors to explain
both individual differences and mental disorder, and reference to the
cerebral ventricles in medieval accounts of the inner senses display a
readiness to employ physiological facts in psychological explanation that
has no modern equivalent. Paradoxically this somewhat greater readiness to resort to physiology occurred even though in the Middle Ages
some psychological processes, those performed by the mind alone, were
not usually believed to have a physiological substratum at all. In contrast,
most modern psychologists would accept that all psychological processes
are carried out by the brain.

Second, there is a very great difference between medieval and modern
methods of investigation. The bulk of published work in present-day
psychology consists of empirical, usually quantitative, investigations of
rather specific questions. Many of these investigations are experimental.
That is, they feature the manipulation of one or more hypothesized
causal factors or independent variables, whose effect on one or more
dependent variables is then assessed. No experimental investigations of
this kind seem to have been performed at all in the area of psychology
in the Middle Ages, and indeed there appears to have been very little
empirical investigation of any kind.

On occasion the unwillingness to investigate, or to attempt to confirm
the investigations of others, led to the perpetuation of error. The pages
of *Malleus Maleficarum* are littered with improbable anecdotes that were
often, although not always, accepted by the authors at face value. Gal-
en's identification of a rete system in the human brain responsible for
the production of animal spirits passed unchallenged through the Middle
Ages, and was a key element in the anatomical base on which much of
medieval psychology was constructed. The oversimplified version of the
arrangement of the cerebral ventricles was another erroneous element
with psychological consequences, although in this case one might argue
that the physiological error permitted the development of an interesting
psychological theory. Errors of more purely psychological fact also occurred but these, perhaps because they could be more readily checked
by simple observation, were much rarer. One fairly common one was
the belief that drunken men could sometimes see a reflection of themselves in the air just as if they were looking into a mirror.[1]

A reasonable question to ask at this point is: Why was there so little
empirical investigation in the Middle Ages? One suggestion has been
that the Church discouraged experimentation; for example, it has been
suggested that it prohibited the dissection of human cadavers.[2] Such a
prohibition would of course have inhibited the discovery of the true
placement of the cerebral ventricles and perpetuated the myth of the

human rete system. In fact, however, the evidence for the Church discouraging experimentation is nowhere very compelling and can be decisively refuted in the case of dissection. It is true that the Church regulated the treatment of the dead, but this did not prevent dissection. Public dissections were performed for teaching purposes in the medical faculty of the University of Bologna from the late thirteenth century.[3] From 1340 the chancellor of Montpellier was required to ensure that a public dissection was performed every two years, and from 1376 Duke Louis of Anjou permitted the release of cadavers of executed prisoners for the purpose. Objections to the dissections appear to have come from the students or even the masters themselves rather than from the Church authorities.[4]

If dissection was performed, why was the real arrangement of the system of cerebral ventricles not discovered sooner? One possible answer is that the dissections were probably not performed often enough to enable the anatomist to do much more than confirm Galen's more obvious hypotheses. The regulations of Bologna University stated that no student was to witness more than one female and two male dissections during the course of his training. Moreover dissection was clearly intended as a teaching aid and not as an opportunity for research.[5]

If clerical attitudes were not responsible for the failure to undertake anatomical investigation in the Middle Ages, they were also unlikely to have inhibited purely psychological investigation. Indeed, as the tolerance of many astrological ideas and the abandonment of the demonological explanation of epilepsy in favor of a physiological one shows, the medieval Church was generally quite open to new ideas. But if the Church did not discourage empirical investigation of psychological questions in the Middle Ages, why did it then not occur? No definite answer to this question can be made, but two discouraging factors might be identified as playing some possible role.

First, there was no precedent. Medieval psychology leaned heavily, as we have seen, on the writings of Greek, and to a lesser extent Roman and Arabic, thinkers. None of these, however, had shown much interest in empirical psychological research, or, for that matter, in empirical investigation in most other areas of knowledge. Galen's anatomical research, the detail of which was in any case largely unknown in the Middle Ages, appears to have been rather unusual in this respect.[6] Thus the medieval scholars simply continued the tradition of "armchair psychology," a tradition, it is worth remembering, that dominated until the middle of the nineteenth century.[7]

Second, the medieval idea of the soul, in which free will played such an important part, made the idea of conducting psychological experimentation an exercise of dubious value. A psychological experiment assesses the effect on behavior of manipulating some variable that is controlled by the experimenter. However, if the manipulation has an effect on behavior then the behavior may be said to be at least partly determined by the manipulated independent variable. Such research makes sense if the experimenter believes behavior to be determined by external, environmental factors, and, of course, many modern psychologists do believe this. The research also makes sense if it is believed that behavior is partly determined by external factors and partly by free choice, and if the investigator also possesses some kind of statistical method that will allow an averaging out of the individual free choices. In the Middle Ages, however, such a statistical method was not available, although, as is clear from Aquinas' remarks on prudence and astrology (see chapters 2 and 6),[8] at least one medieval scholar understood the psychological implications of it. In the absence of such a method, and given the general belief that behavior was determined largely by free will, that is by internal factors outside the control of the experimenter, little was to be expected from experimentation.

Perhaps related to the reluctance of medieval scholars and physicians to test questions of fact is a certain lack of originality in their psychological writings. Unoriginality is not evident so much in medieval psychological theory, where, as we have seen, although basic theoretical elements were taken from ancient writers, they were often combined together in new and sometimes surprising ways. It would be difficult, for example, to argue that Aquinas' psychology, although owing so much to Aristotle and other earlier writers, was not a creative and original synthesis of apparently irreconcilable elements. Where the lack of originality is most evident is again with respect to questions of fact, and it is demonstrated most clearly in the empirical examples given of phenomena. For example, Galen's story of the glass vases, which was held to demonstrate how reason but not imagination might be disordered, was repeated in many subsequent accounts, but rarely supplemented by new examples. Similarly the same examples were used repeatedly to demonstrate the cognitive powers of animals: the sheep fleeing the wolf it has never seen; the spider building its web. It is difficult not to see this apparent reluctance to introduce or look for new examples from their own observations as not having some inhibiting effect on the ability of medieval scholars to produce original psychology.

If medieval psychology appears to a twentieth-century psychologist such as myself to be empirically weak in comparison to modern psychology, it should also be admitted that it was correspondingly stronger with respect to coherence. Modern psychology, like many other twentieth-century disciplines, is rather fragmented, in large part, of course, because of the sheer volume of new empirical work published every year. Because no one can possibly keep up with all of this new material, the tendency has been for psychologists to specialize in particular subfields; for example, the psychology of hearing or of memory, or the study of schizophrenia. In consequence psychological theory is characteristically rather limited in scope and usually seeks to explain only a limited range of phenomena within a particular subfield. In the Middle Ages, however, theories were very much broader and, for example, the presumed workings of the humors or the cerebral ventricles were invoked to explain a wide range of psychological phenomena.

The coherence of medieval psychology, however, went beyond possessing physiologically based theories such as those of the humors and the inner senses that had a broad range of application. In the Middle Ages there was also an explicitly stated and more or less commonly agreed account of psychology as a whole. The immortal soul, following the synthesis of Christian and Aristotelian thinking, was ruled by the incorporeal mind, comprising reason and will, and contained a number of other powers, for example, those of sensation or emotion, that made use of or were housed in parts of the body. This view of what people were, which was developed largely in the academic writings of the schoolmen, was not restricted to them but was held throughout educated medieval society. A socially useful implication of this common view seems to have been at least some area of agreement on the nature of mental disorder between medieval physicians, churchmen, and jurists. By contrast, no common view is explicitly shared by modern psychologists, and it is not easy to see what common agreement unites, say, modern economists, jurists, and medical practitioners. In this respect modern psychology might have something to learn from, or at least something to envy in, its medieval predecessor.

NOTES

1. For example, Bacon, *Opus Majus*, 558.
2. See Andrew Dickson White, *A History of the Warfare of Science with Theology in Christendom*, Vol. 2 (New York: Dover, 1896), 31–32.
3. Vern L. Bullough, "Medieval Bologna and the Development of Medical Education." *Bulletin of the History of Medicine* 32 (1958): 201–215.
4. Luke Demaitre, "Theory and Practice in Medical Education at the University of Montpellier in the Thirteenth and Fourteenth Centuries." *Journal of the History of Medicine and Allied Sciences* 30 (1975): 103–123.
5. Bullough, "Medieval Bologna."
6. Probably Galen's clearest account of his experiments into cerebral anatomy is given in *On the Doctrines of Hippocrates and Plato*, but this was not translated until the sixteenth century, although his results were described in other places.
7. See Boring, *History of Experimental Psychology*.
8. Aquinas, *Summa Theologiae*, 2.2.49.1; 1.115.4 ad 3.

Selected Bibliography

These suggestions for further reading consist of only some of the more important works available in English. Some medieval works, particularly those anonymously written, are listed in the ancient and medieval works section under the name of their modern editor.

ANCIENT AND MEDIEVAL WORKS

Aristotle. *The Works of Aristotle*, ed. W. D. Ross. Oxford, U.K.: Clarendon, 1931.

Aquinas, Thomas. *Summa Theologiae*. London: Blackfriars, 1964.

Augustine. *Confessions*. In A. C. Outler, ed., *The Library of Christian Classics*, Vol. 7, *Augustine: Confessions and Enchiridion*. London: SCM Press, 1955.

————. *On the Trinity*, trans. A. W. Hadden. In P. Schaff, ed., *A Select Library of the Nicene and Post-Nicene Fathers of the Christian Church*, Ser. 1, Vol. 3. Grand Rapids, Mich.: Eerdmans, 1956.

————. *The Greatness of the Soul*, trans. Joseph M. Colleran. Westminster, Md.: Newman, 1964.

————. *The Literal Meaning of Genesis*, trans. John H. Taylor. New York: Newman, 1982.

Averroes. *Epitome of Parva Naturalia*, trans. Harry Blumberg. Cambridge, Mass.: Medieval Academy of America, 1961.

Avicenna. *Avicenna's Psychology: An English Translation of Kitab Al-Najat, Bk. II, Ch. VI with Historico-Philosophical Notes and Textual Improvements on the Cairo Edition*, trans. F. Rahman. London: Oxford University Press, 1952.

Bacon, Roger. *The Opus Majus*, trans. Robert D. Burke. New York: Russell & Russell, 1962.

Bartholomaeus Anglicus. *On the Properties of Things*, trans. John Trevisa (1398–1399), ed. M. C. Seymour. Oxford, U.K.: Clarendon, 1975.

Bracton, Henry. *On the Laws and Customs of England, Vol. 2*, trans. Samuel E. Thorne. Cambridge, Mass.: Bellknap, 1968.

Caelus Aurelianus. *On Acute Diseases and On Chronic Diseases*, trans. I. E. Drabkin. Chicago: University of Chicago Press, 1950.

Chaucer, Geoffrey. *The Tales of Canterbury*, ed. Robert A. Pratt. Boston: Houghton Mifflin, 1966.

Cockayne, Oswald, ed., *Leechdoms, Wortcunning, and Starcraft of Early England*. London: Longman, 1864.

de La Tour-Landry, Geoffroy. *The Book of the Knight of La Tour-Landry*, trans. Anon., ed. Thomas Wright. London: Early English Text Society, Old Series No. 33, 1868.

Eadmer. *The Life of St. Anselm*, trans. R. W. Southern. London: Nelson, 1962.

Firmicus Maternus, Julius. *Ancient Astrology: Theory and Practice*, trans. J. H. Bram. Park Ridge, NJ: Noyes, 1975.

Frederick II of Hohenstaufen. *The Art of Falconry*, trans. C. A. Wood and F. Marjorie Fyfe. Boston, Mass.: Charles Brandford, 1955.

Furnivall, Frederick J., ed. *The Book of Quinte Essence or the Fifth Being*. London: Early English Text Society, Old Series No. 16, 1866.

Galen. *On the Affected Parts*, trans. Rudolph E. Siegel. Basel: Karger, 1976.

———. *On the Doctrines of Hippocrates and Plato*, trans. P. De Lacy. Berlin: Akademie-Verlag, 1980.

———. *On the Passions and Errors of the Soul*, trans. P. W. Harkins. Columbus: Ohio State University Press, 1963.

Guibert of Nogent. *Self and Society in Medieval France: The Memoirs of Abbot Guibert of Nogent*, trans. John F. Benton. New York: Harper & Row, 1970.

Habig, Marion A., ed., *St. Francis of Assisi: Writings and Early Biographies*. London: Society for Promoting Christian Knowledge, 1973.

Hippocrates. *Medical Works*, trans. J. Chadwick and W. N. Mann. Springfield, Ill.: Charles C. Thomas, 1950.

Kramer, Heinrich, and James Sprenger. *Malleus Maleficarum*, trans. Montague Summers. London: Arrow, 1971.

Lennox, W. G. "Bernard of Gordon on Epilepsy." *Annals of Medical History* Third Series, 3 (1941): 372–83.

———. "John of Gaddesden on Epilepsy." *Annals of Medical History* Third Series, 1 (1939): 283–307.

Maimon, Moses ben (Maimonides). *The Eight Chapters of Maimonides on Ethics*, trans. Joseph I. Gorfinkle. New York: Columbia University Press, 1912.

Moore, Sir Norman, ed., *The Book of the Foundation of St. Bartholomew's Church in London*. London: Early English Text Society, Old Series No. 163, 1923.

Nemesius. *A Treatise on the Nature of Man*. In W. Telfer, ed., *The Library of Christian Classics, Vol. 4, Cyril of Jerusalem and Nemesius Of Emesa*. London: SCM Press, 1955.

Plato. *Timaeus*, trans. H.D.P. Lee. Harmondsworth, U.K.: Penguin, 1965.

Plotinus. *Enneads*, trans. A. H. Armstrong. London: Heinemann, 1966–1984.

Ptolemy, Claudius. *Tetrabiblos*, trans. F. E. Robbins. London: Heinemann, 1938.

Sharpe, W. D. "Isidore of Seville: The Medical Writings." *Transactions of the American Philosophical Society* 54 (1964): 3–75.

RECENT WORKS

Baring-Gould, S. *The Lives of the Saints*. Edinburgh, U.K.: John Grant, 1914.

Bourguignon, Erika, ed., *Religion, Altered States of Consciousness, and Social Change*. Columbus: Ohio State University Press, 1973.

Clarke, Basil. *Mental Disorder in Earlier Britain*. Cardiff, U.K.: University of Wales, 1975.

De Mause, Lloyd, ed., *The History of Childhood*. New York: Psychohistory Press, 1974.

Harvey, E. Ruth. *The Inward Wits: Psychological Theory in the Middle Ages and the Renaissance*. London: Warburg Institute, 1975.

Jackson, Stanley W. *Melancholia and Depression: From Hippocratic Times to Modern Times*. New Haven, Conn.: Yale University Press, 1986.

Kieckhefer, Richard. *European Witch Trials: Their Foundations in Popular and Learned Culture, 1300–1500*. Berkeley, Cal.: University of California Press, 1976.

Klibansky, Raymond, Erwin Panofsky, and Fritz Saxl. *Saturn and Melancholy*. London: Nelson, 1964.

Lindberg, David C. *Theories of Vision from Al-Kindi to Kepler*. London: University of Chicago Press, 1976.

Moody, Ernest A. *Studies in Medieval Philosophy, Science, and Logic*. Berkeley, Cal.: University of California Press, 1975.

Oesterreich, T. K. *Possession: Demoniacal and Other*, trans. D. Ibberson. New York: University Books, 1966.

Peters, Edward, ed., *Monks, Bishops, and Pagans: Christian Culture in Gaul and Italy, 500–700*. Philadelphia: University of Pennsylvania Press, 1975.

Sorabji, R. *Aristotle on Memory*. London: Duckworth, 1972.

Talbot, C. H. *Medicine in Medieval England*. London: Oldbourne, 1967.

Thorndike, Lynn. *A History of Magic and Experimental Science during the First Thirteen Centuries of Our Era*. London: Macmillan, 1923.

————. *A History of Magic and Experimental Science, Vols. 3 and 4. Fourteenth and Fifteenth Centuries*. New York: Columbia University Press, 1934.

————. *University Records and Life in the Middle Ages*. New York: Columbia University Press, 1944.

Ward, Colleen, ed., *Altered States of Consciousness and Mental Health: A Cross-Cultural Perspective*. London: Sage, 1989.

Wedel, Theodore. *The Medieval Attitude toward Astrology, Particularly in England*. Hamden, Conn.: Archon, 1968.

Weisheipl, James A., ed., *Albertus Magnus and the Sciences: Commemorative Essays, 1980*. Toronto: Pontifical Institute of Medieval Studies, 1980.

Index

About the Author

SIMON KEMP is Senior Lecturer in the Department of Psychology at the University of Canterbury, Christchurch, New Zealand. His current areas of interest are in perception, cognition, and the history of psychology.